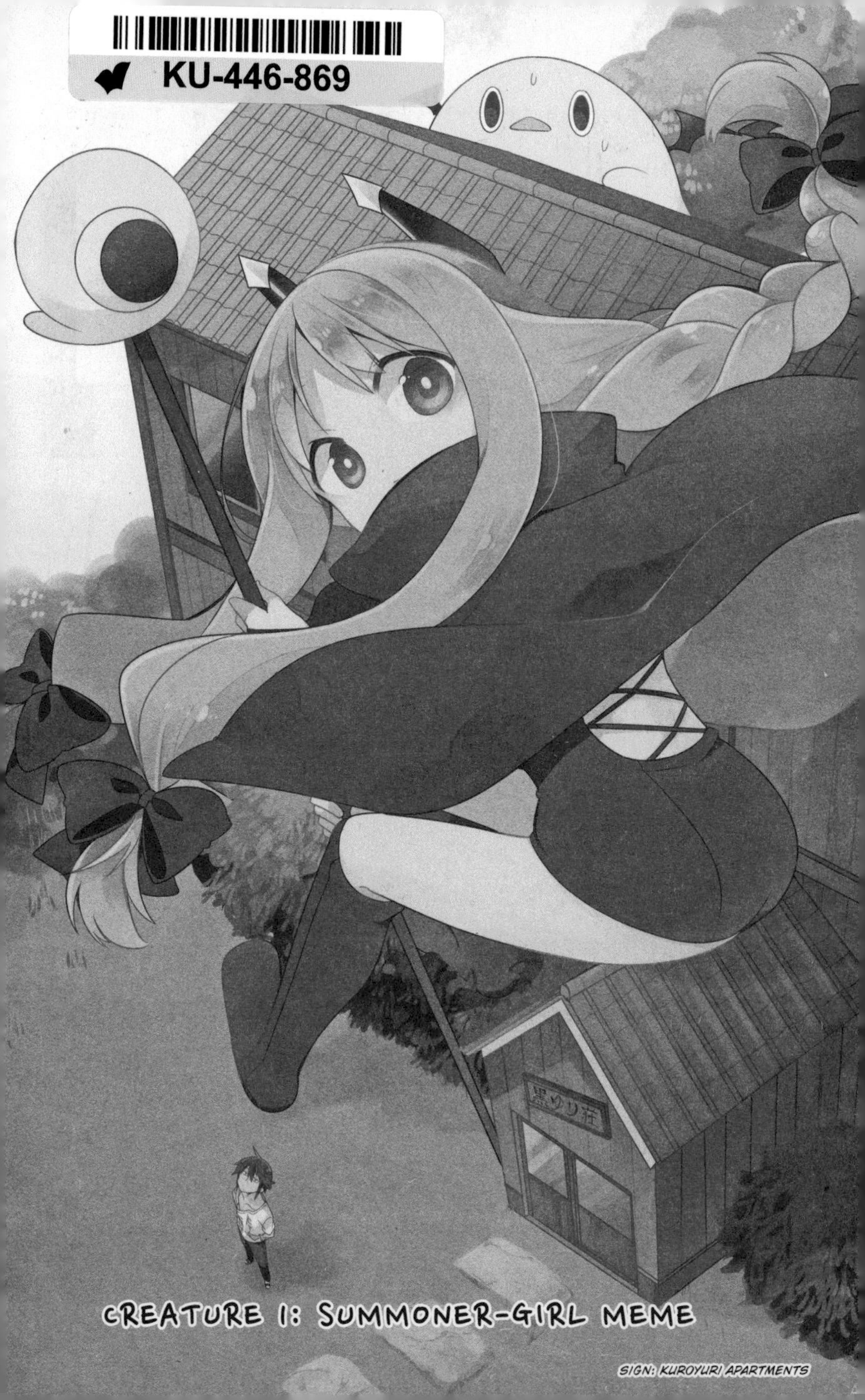
黒ゆり荘
SIGN: KUROYURI APARTMENTS

CREATURE 1: SUMMONER-GIRL MEME

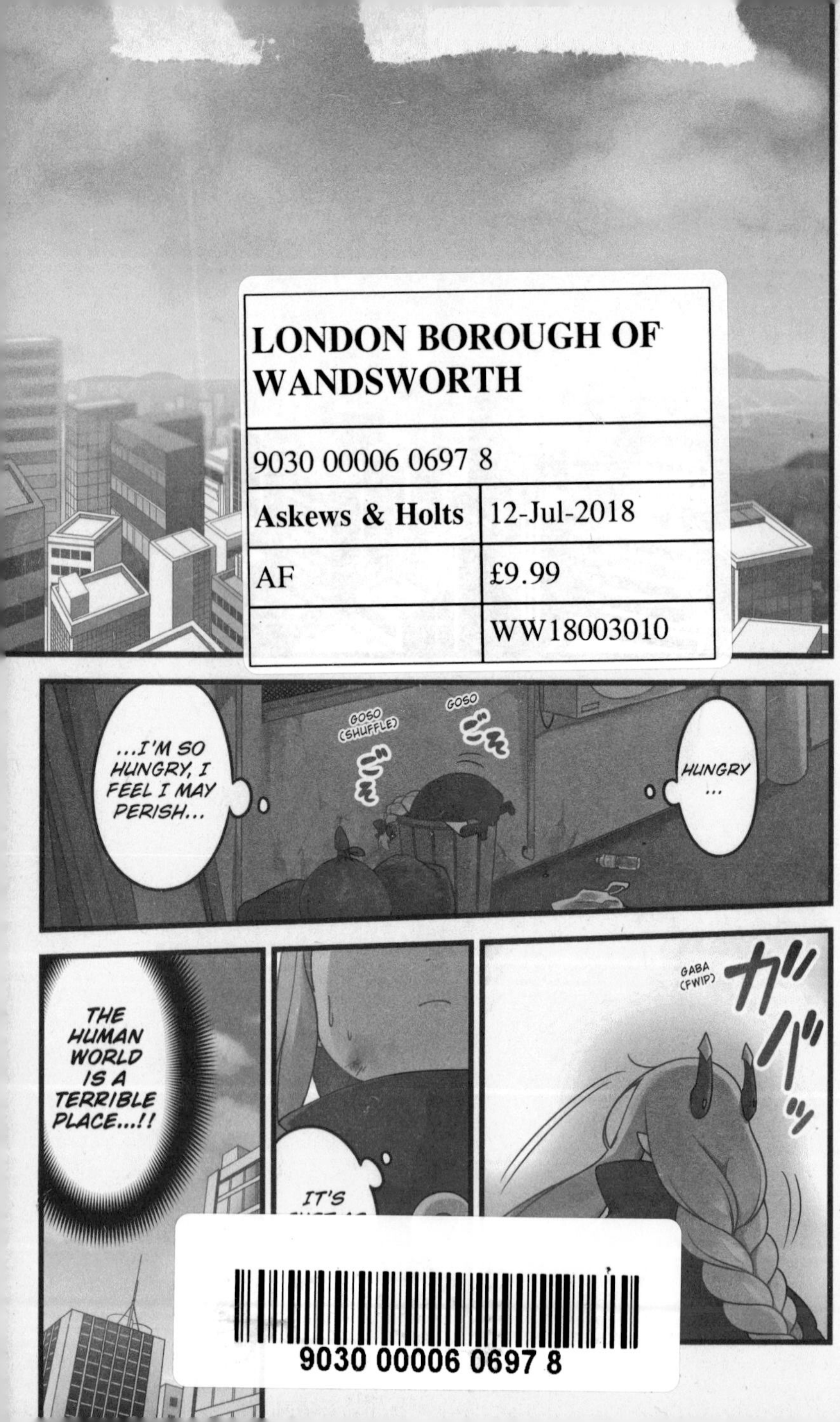
HUNGRY ...
GOSO
GOSO (SHUFFLE)
...I'M SO HUNGRY, I FEEL I MAY PERISH...
GABA (FWIP)
IT'S
THE HUMAN WORLD IS A TERRIBLE PLACE...!!

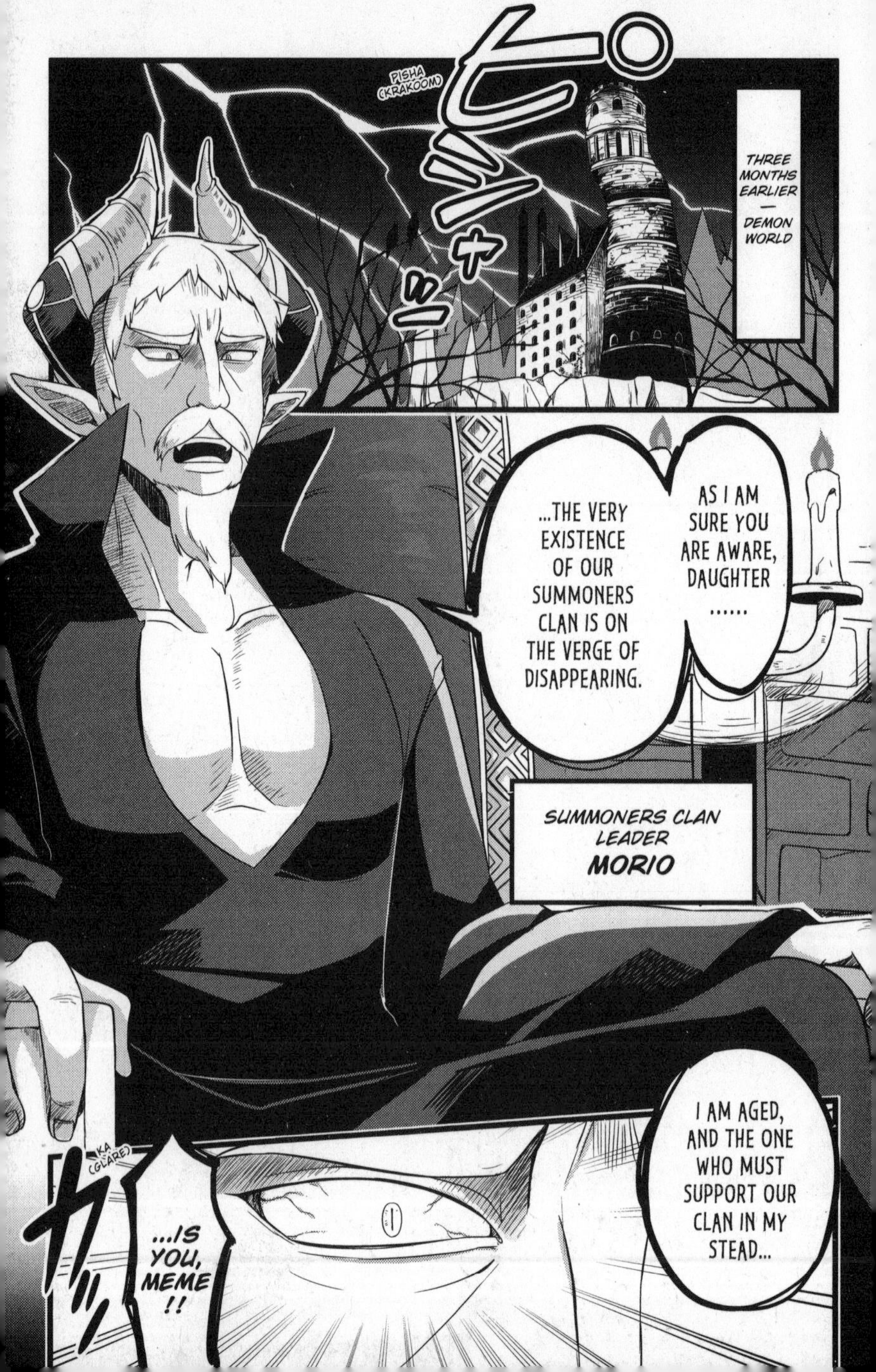
THREE MONTHS EARLIER — DEMON WORLD
PISHA (KRAKOOM)
AS I AM SURE YOU ARE AWARE, DAUGHTER ......
...THE VERY EXISTENCE OF OUR SUMMONERS CLAN IS ON THE VERGE OF DISAPPEARING.
SUMMONERS CLAN LEADER MORIO
I AM AGED, AND THE ONE WHO MUST SUPPORT OUR CLAN IN MY STEAD...
KA (GLARE)
...IS YOU, MEME!!

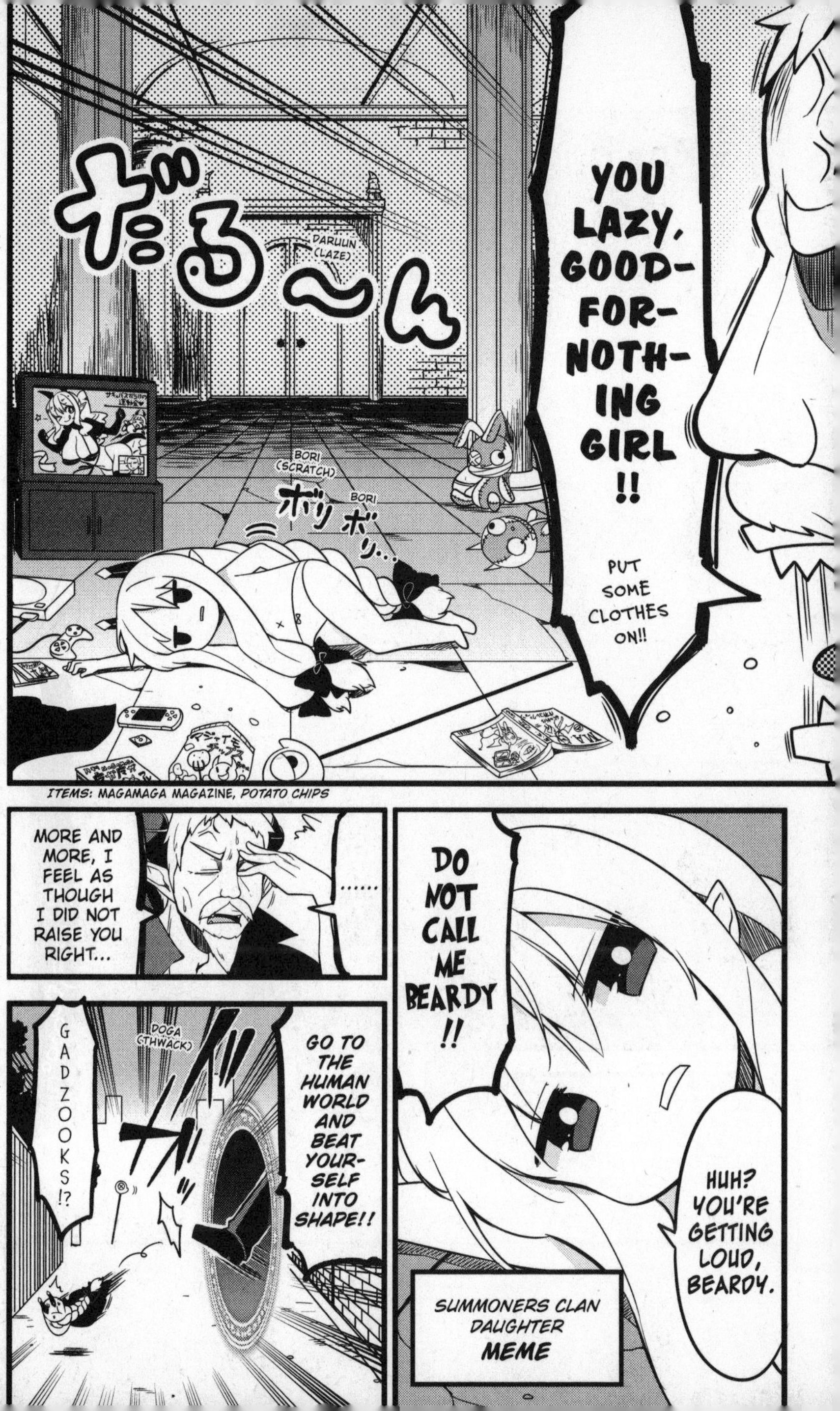
YOU LAZY, GOOD-FOR-NOTHING GIRL!!
PUT SOME CLOTHES ON!!
DARUUN (LAZE)
BORI (SCRATCH) BORI
ITEMS: MAGAMAGA MAGAZINE, POTATO CHIPS
HUH? YOU'RE GETTING LOUD, BEARDY.
SUMMONERS CLAN DAUGHTER MEME
DO NOT CALL ME BEARDY!!
......
MORE AND MORE, I FEEL AS THOUGH I DID NOT RAISE YOU RIGHT...
GO TO THE HUMAN WORLD AND BEAT YOURSELF INTO SHAPE!!
DOGA (THWACK)
GADZOOKS!?

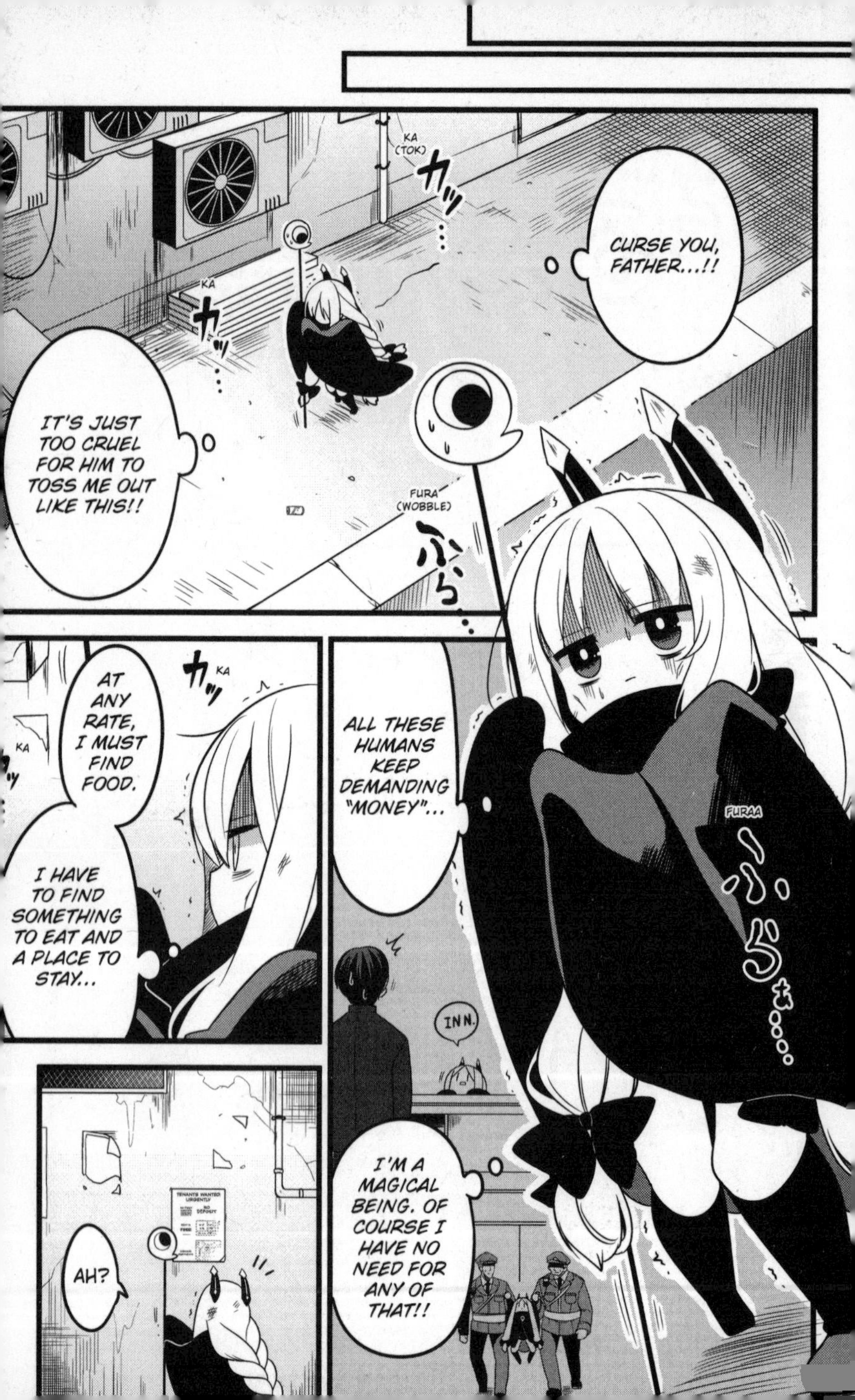
CURSE YOU, FATHER...!!
KA (TOK)
KA
IT'S JUST TOO CRUEL FOR HIM TO TOSS ME OUT LIKE THIS!!
FURA (WOBBLE)
FURAA
ALL THESE HUMANS KEEP DEMANDING "MONEY"...
INN.
I'M A MAGICAL BEING. OF COURSE I HAVE NO NEED FOR ANY OF THAT!!
KA
KA
AT ANY RATE, I MUST FIND FOOD.
I HAVE TO FIND SOMETHING TO EAT AND A PLACE TO STAY...
TENANTS WANTED! URGENTLY
NO DEPOSIT
AH?

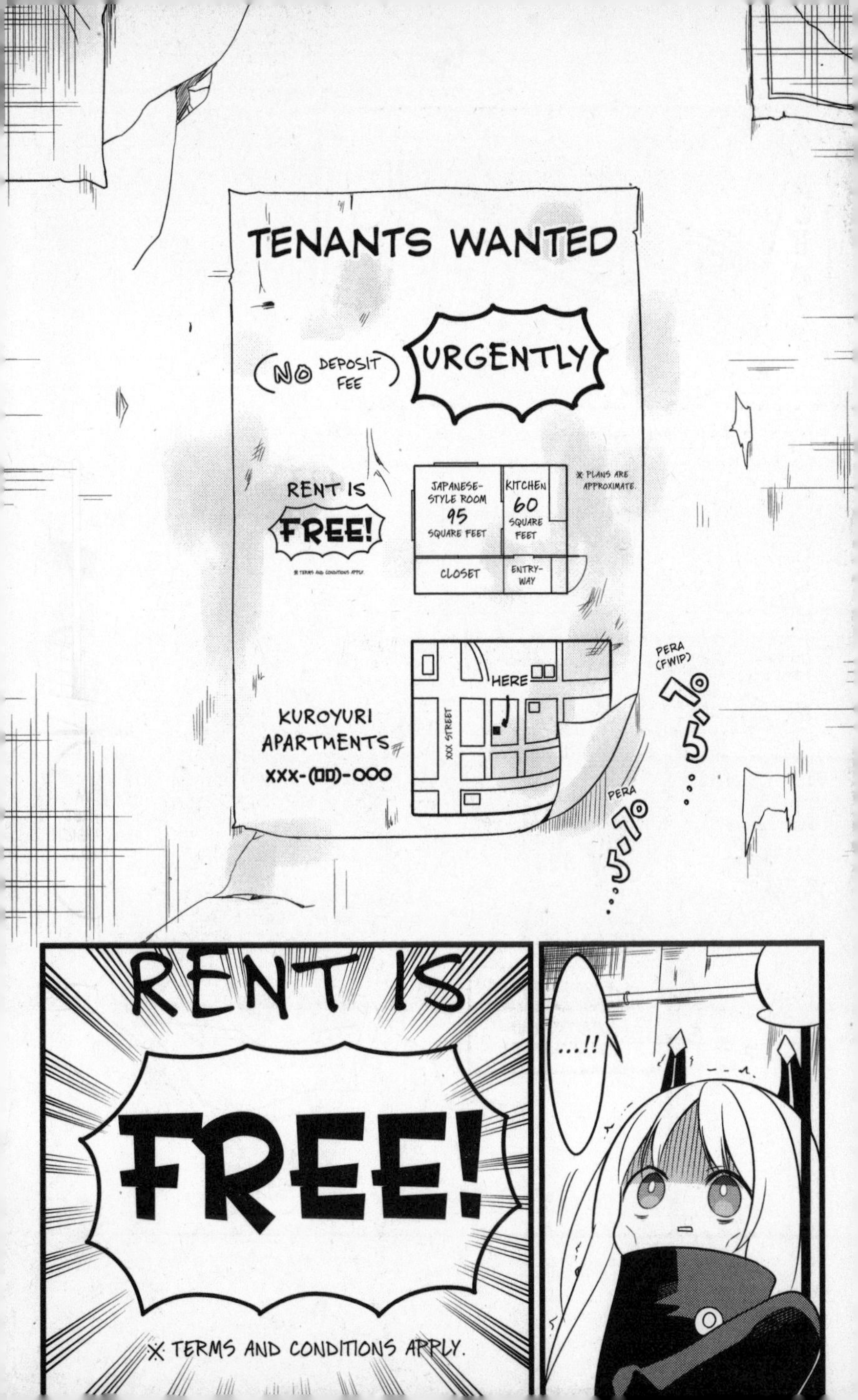
TENANTS WANTED
URGENTLY
(NO DEPOSIT FEE)
RENT IS FREE!
※ TERMS AND CONDITIONS APPLY.
JAPANESE-STYLE ROOM 95 SQUARE FEET
KITCHEN 60 SQUARE FEET
CLOSET
ENTRY-WAY
※ PLANS ARE APPROXIMATE.
HERE
XXX STREET
KUROYURI APARTMENTS
XXX-(□□)-OOO
PERA (FWIP)
PERA
...!!
RENT IS FREE!
※ TERMS AND CONDITIONS APPLY.

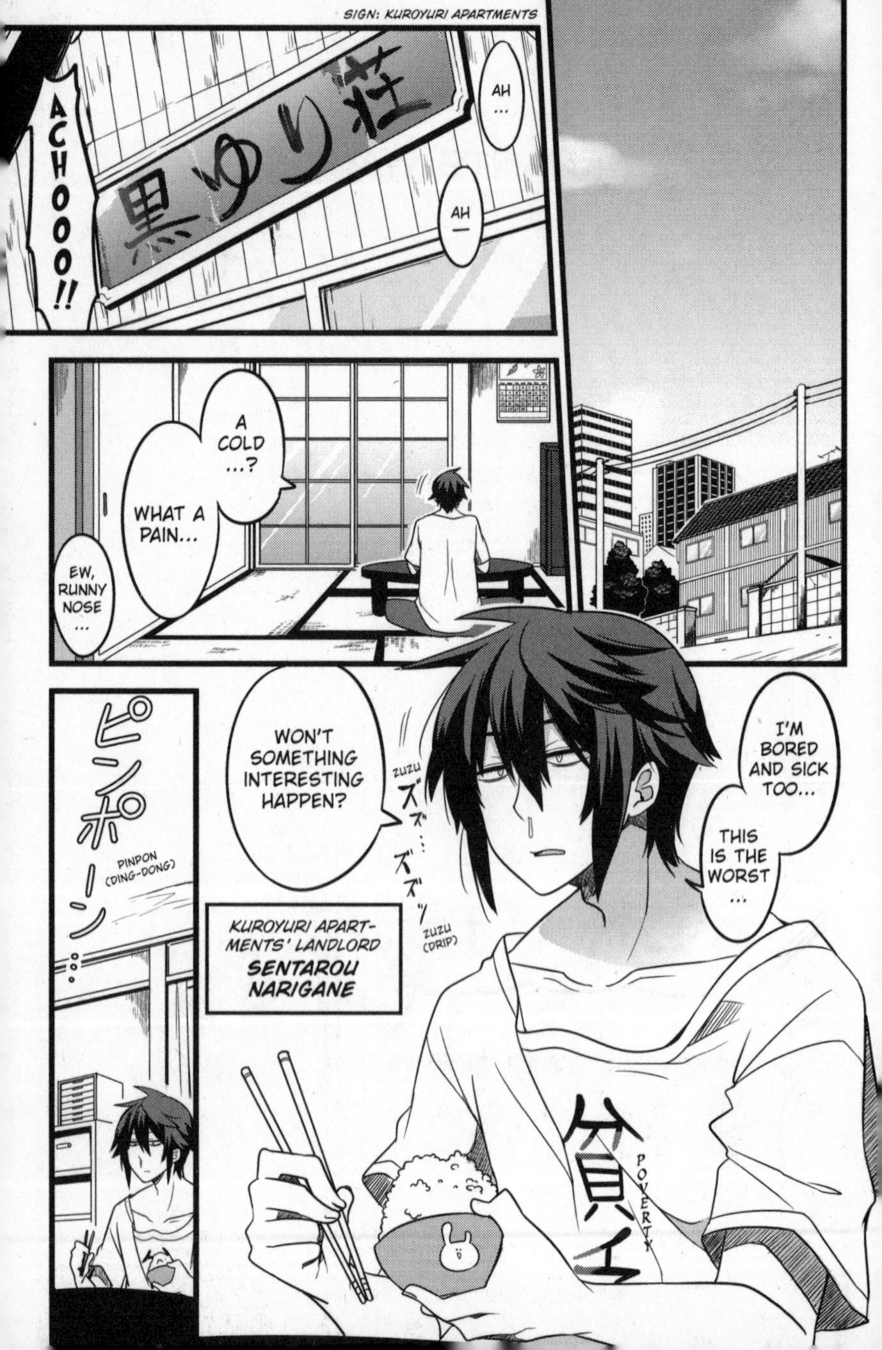
SIGN: KUROYURI APARTMENTS
AH ...
AH —
ACHOOO!!
A COLD ...?
WHAT A PAIN...
EW, RUNNY NOSE ...
I'M BORED AND SICK TOO...
THIS IS THE WORST ...
ZUZU (DRIP)
WON'T SOMETHING INTERESTING HAPPEN?
KUROYURI APARTMENTS' LANDLORD SENTAROU NARIGANE
POVERTY
PINPON (DING-DONG)

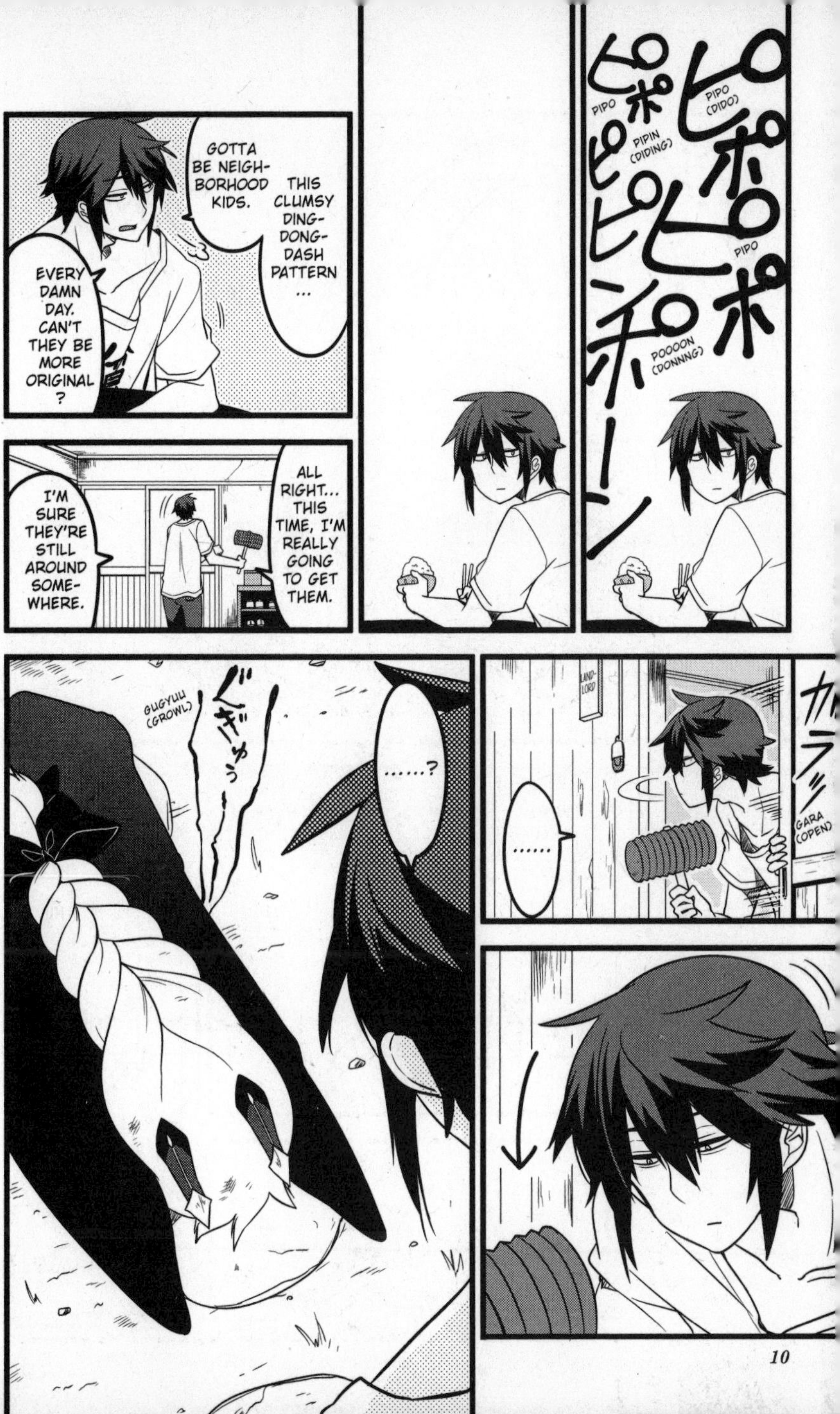
PIPO (DIDO)
PIPO
PIPO
PIPIN (DIDING)
POOOON (DONNNG)
GOTTA BE NEIGH-BORHOOD KIDS.
THIS CLUMSY DING-DONG-DASH PATTERN...
EVERY DAMN DAY. CAN'T THEY BE MORE ORIGINAL?
ALL RIGHT... THIS TIME, I'M REALLY GOING TO GET THEM.
I'M SURE THEY'RE STILL AROUND SOME-WHERE.
GARA (OPEN)
LAND-LORD
......
......?
GUGYUU (GROWL)
10

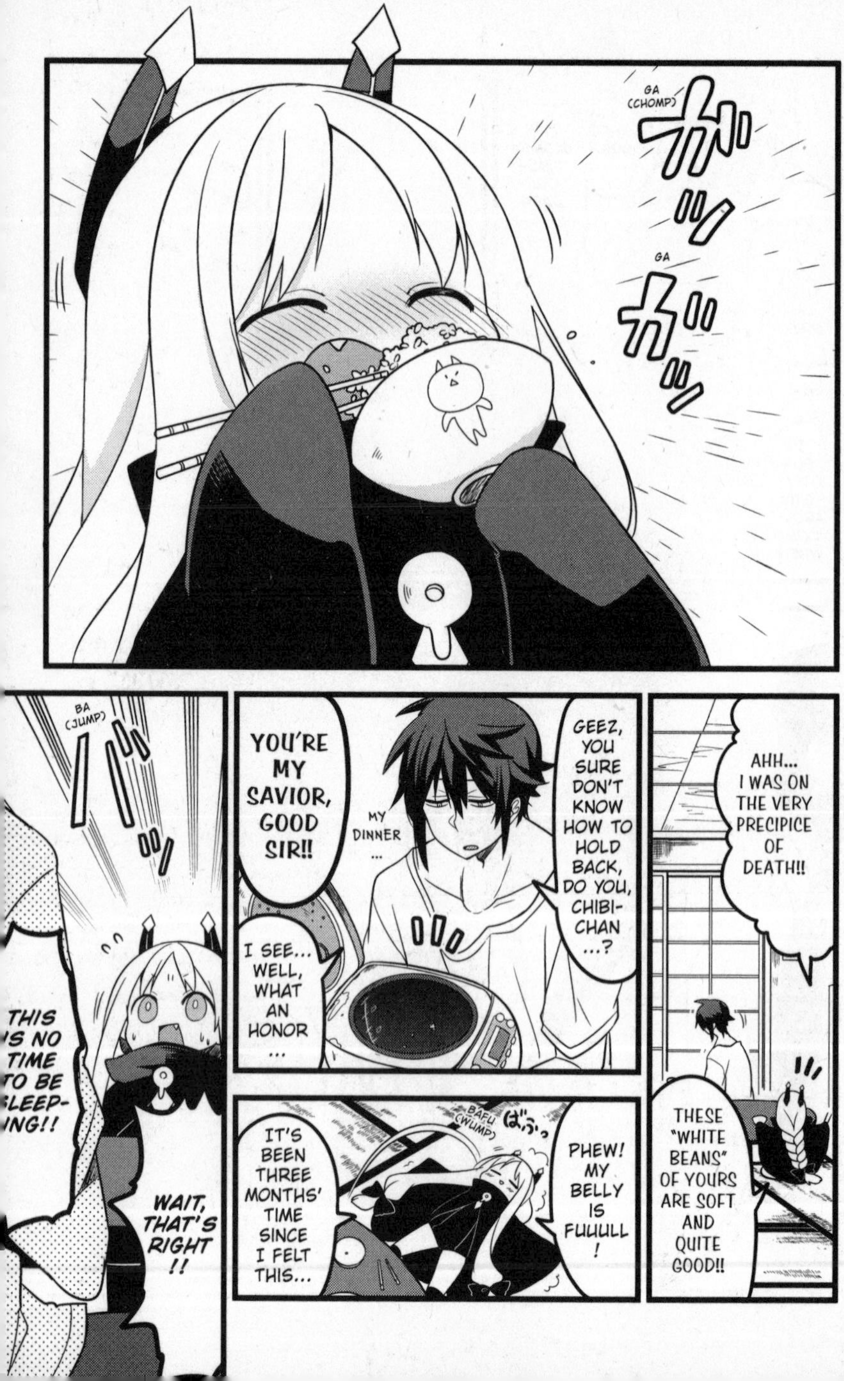
GA (CHOMP)
GA
AHH... I WAS ON THE VERY PRECIPICE OF DEATH!!
THESE "WHITE BEANS" OF YOURS ARE SOFT AND QUITE GOOD!!
GEEZ, YOU SURE DON'T KNOW HOW TO HOLD BACK, DO YOU, CHIBI-CHAN...?
YOU'RE MY SAVIOR, GOOD SIR!!
MY DINNER...
I SEE... WELL, WHAT AN HONOR...
BAFU (WUMP)
PHEW! MY BELLY IS FUUUULL!
IT'S BEEN THREE MONTHS' TIME SINCE I FELT THIS...
BA (JUMP)
THIS 'S NO TIME 'O BE LEEP-ING!!
WAIT, THAT'S RIGHT!!

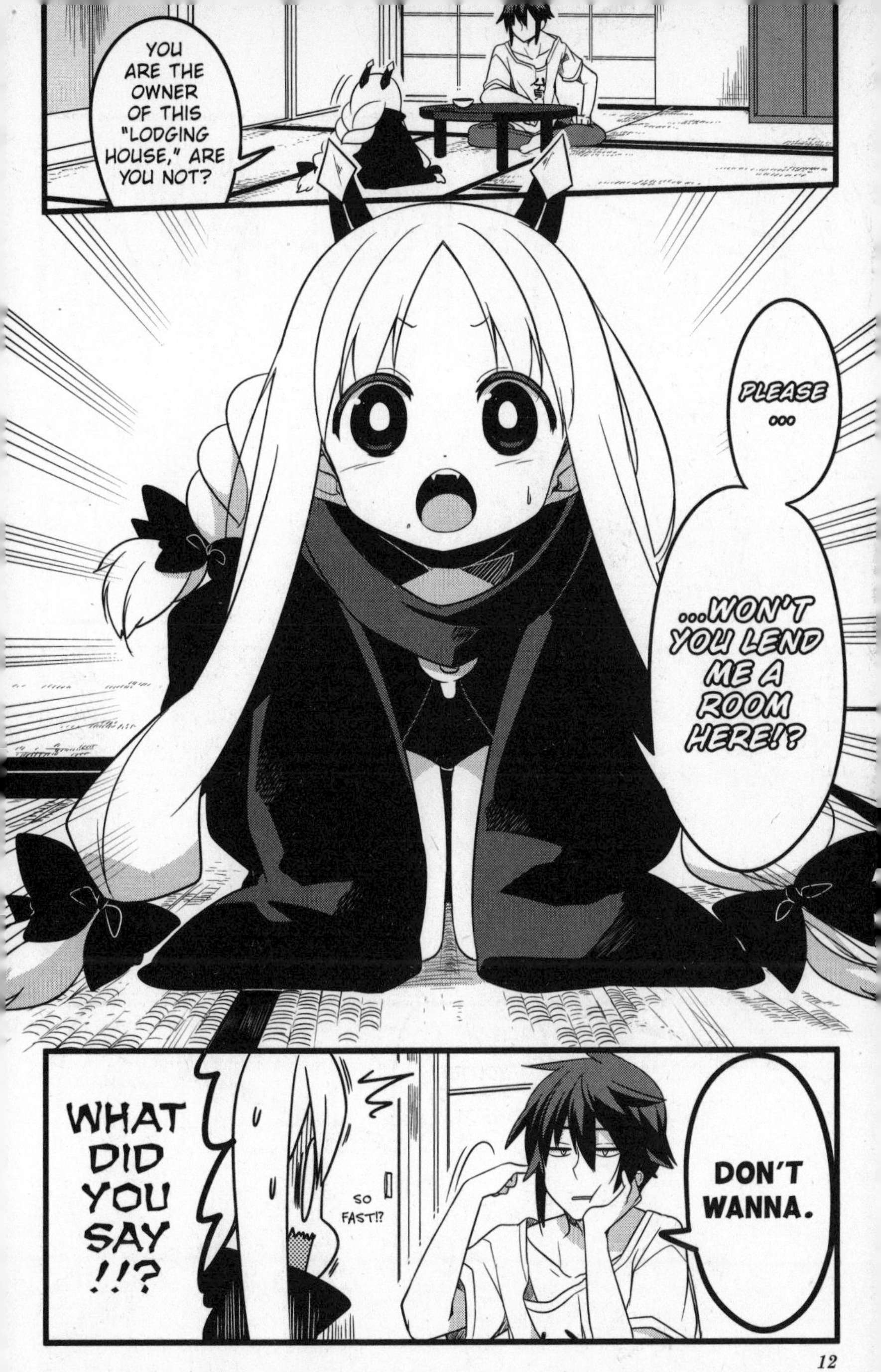
YOU ARE THE OWNER OF THIS "LODGING HOUSE," ARE YOU NOT?
PLEASE ...
...WON'T YOU LEND ME A ROOM HERE!?
DON'T WANNA.
SO FAST!?
WHAT DID YOU SAY!!?

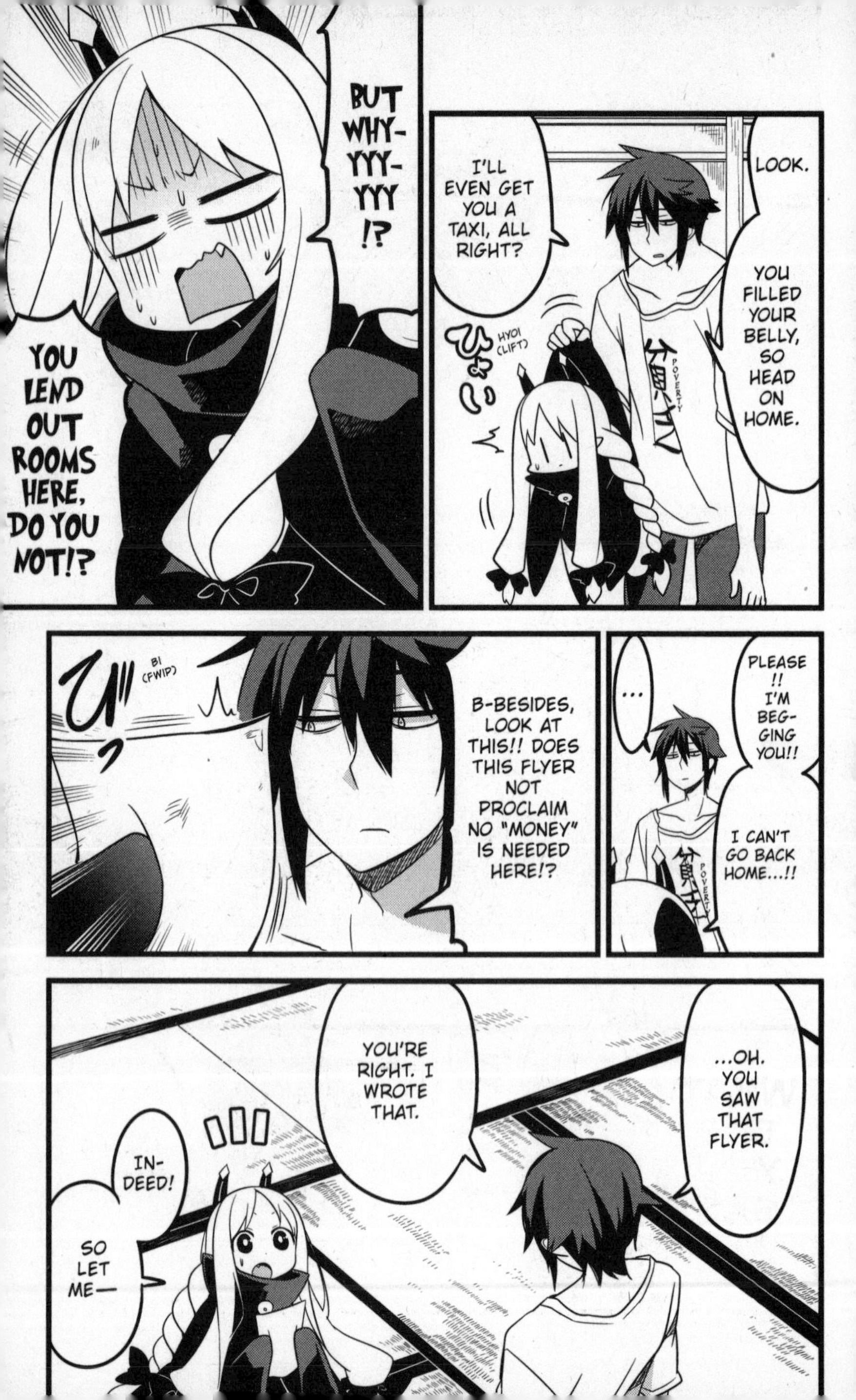
LOOK.
YOU FILLED YOUR BELLY, SO HEAD ON HOME.
I'LL EVEN GET YOU A TAXI, ALL RIGHT?
HYOI (LIFT)
POVERTY
BUT WHY-YYY-YYY!?
YOU LEND OUT ROOMS HERE, DO YOU NOT!?
...
PLEASE!! I'M BEG-GING YOU!!
I CAN'T GO BACK HOME...!!
POVERTY
BI (FWIP)
B-BESIDES, LOOK AT THIS!! DOES THIS FLYER NOT PROCLAIM NO "MONEY" IS NEEDED HERE!?
...OH. YOU SAW THAT FLYER.
YOU'RE RIGHT. I WROTE THAT.
!!!
IN-DEED!
SO LET ME—

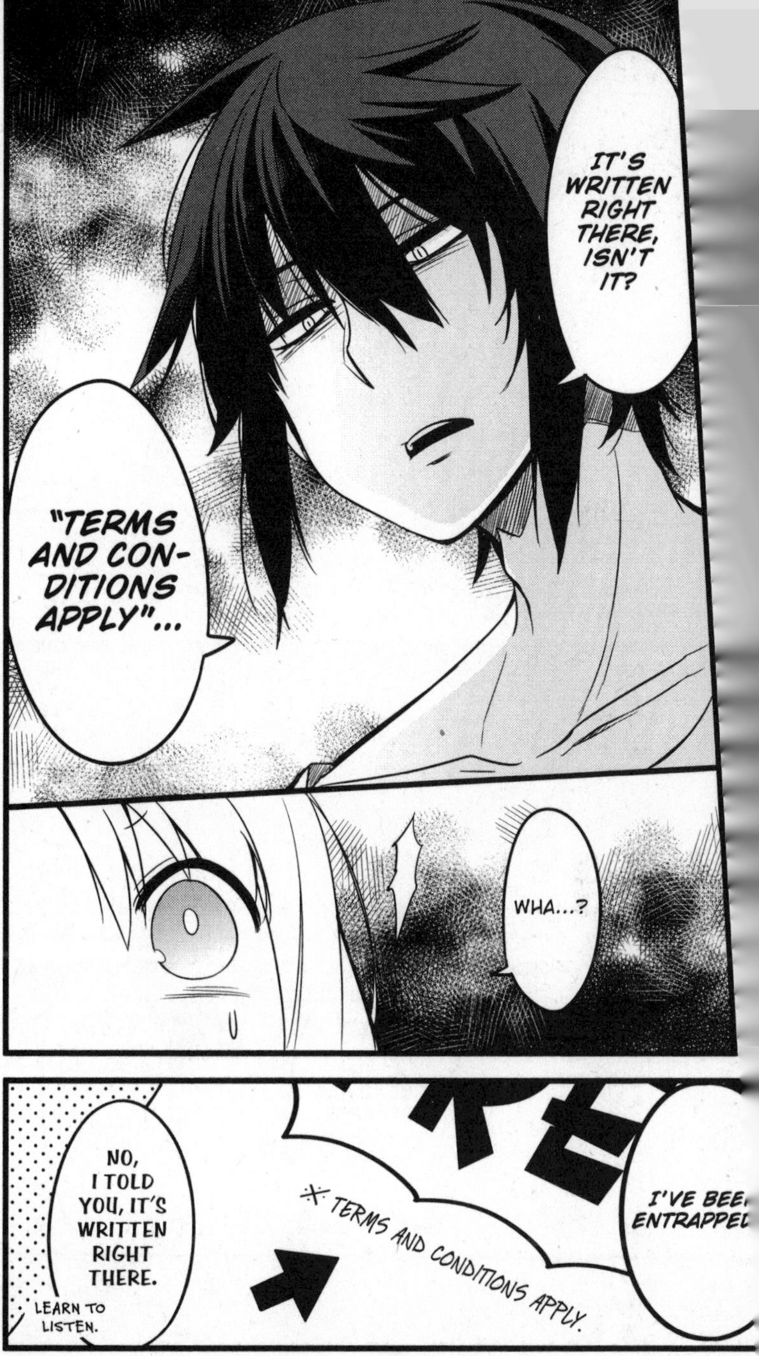
IT'S WRITTEN RIGHT THERE, ISN'T IT?
"TERMS AND CON-DITIONS APPLY"...
WHA...?
I'VE BEE ENTRAPPE
※ TERMS AND CONDITIONS APPLY.
NO, I TOLD YOU, IT'S WRITTEN RIGHT THERE.
LEARN TO LISTEN.

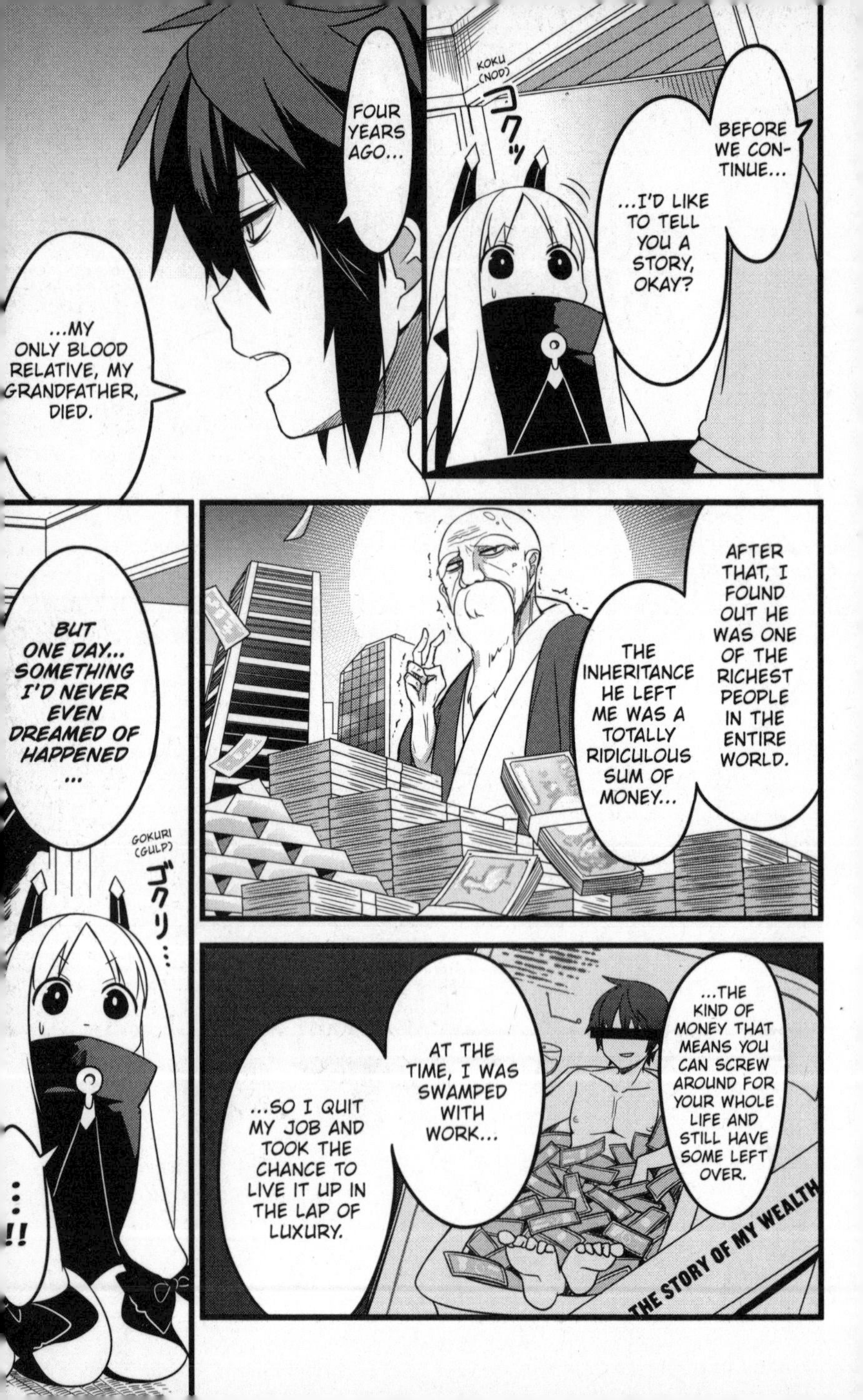
KOKU (NOD)
コクッ
BEFORE WE CONTINUE...
...I'D LIKE TO TELL YOU A STORY, OKAY?
FOUR YEARS AGO...
...MY ONLY BLOOD RELATIVE, MY GRANDFATHER, DIED.
AFTER THAT, I FOUND OUT HE WAS ONE OF THE RICHEST PEOPLE IN THE ENTIRE WORLD.
THE INHERITANCE HE LEFT ME WAS A TOTALLY RIDICULOUS SUM OF MONEY...
...THE KIND OF MONEY THAT MEANS YOU CAN SCREW AROUND FOR YOUR WHOLE LIFE AND STILL HAVE SOME LEFT OVER.
AT THE TIME, I WAS SWAMPED WITH WORK...
...SO I QUIT MY JOB AND TOOK THE CHANCE TO LIVE IT UP IN THE LAP OF LUXURY.
THE STORY OF MY WEALTH
BUT ONE DAY... SOMETHING I'D NEVER EVEN DREAMED OF HAPPENED...
GOKURI (GULP)
ゴクリ…
...!!

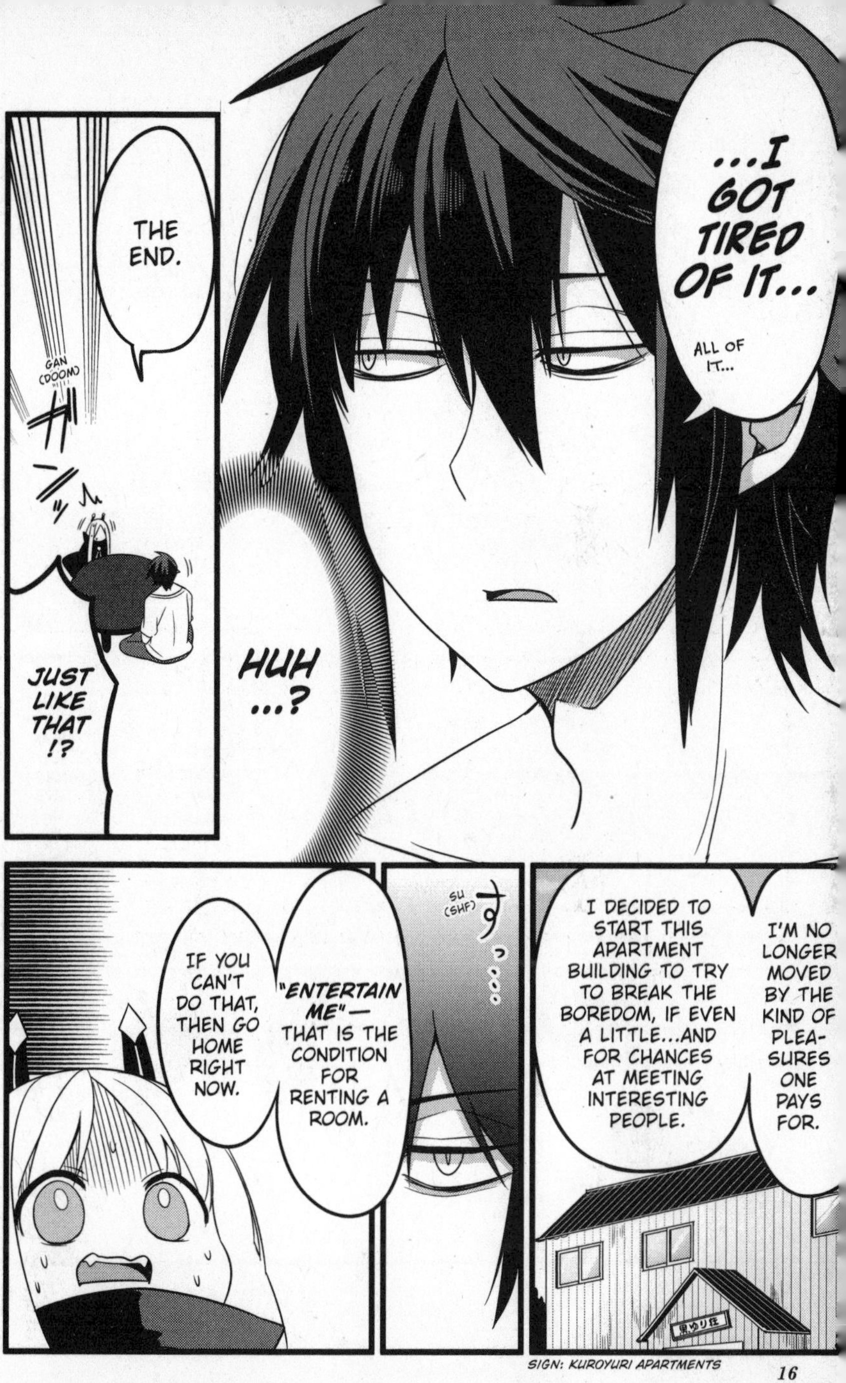
...I GOT TIRED OF IT...
ALL OF IT...
HUH ...?
THE END.
GAN (DOOM)
JUST LIKE THAT !?
I'M NO LONGER MOVED BY THE KIND OF PLEA-SURES ONE PAYS FOR.
I DECIDED TO START THIS APARTMENT BUILDING TO TRY TO BREAK THE BOREDOM, IF EVEN A LITTLE...AND FOR CHANCES AT MEETING INTERESTING PEOPLE.
SU (SHF)
す っ...
"ENTERTAIN ME"— THAT IS THE CONDITION FOR RENTING A ROOM.
IF YOU CAN'T DO THAT, THEN GO HOME RIGHT NOW.
SIGN: KUROYURI APARTMENTS

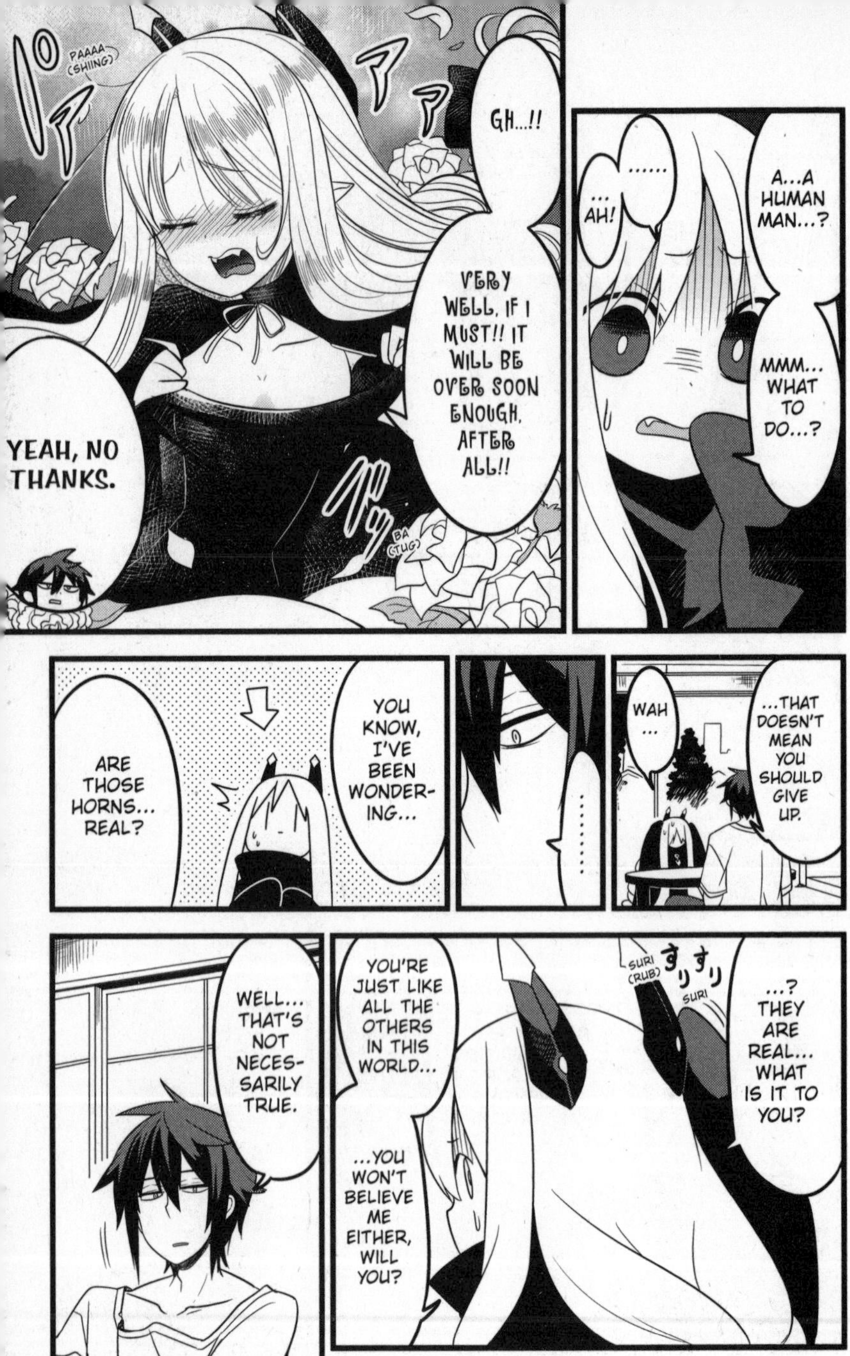
A...A HUMAN MAN...?
......
...AH!
MMM... WHAT TO DO...?
GH...!!
PAAAA (SHIING)
VERY WELL, IF I MUST!! IT WILL BE OVER SOON ENOUGH, AFTER ALL!!
BA (TUG)
YEAH, NO THANKS.
...THAT DOESN'T MEAN YOU SHOULD GIVE UP.
WAH...
......
YOU KNOW, I'VE BEEN WONDER-ING...
ARE THOSE HORNS... REAL?
...? THEY ARE REAL... WHAT IS IT TO YOU?
SURI (RUB) SURI
YOU'RE JUST LIKE ALL THE OTHERS IN THIS WORLD...
...YOU WON'T BELIEVE ME EITHER, WILL YOU?
WELL... THAT'S NOT NECES-SARILY TRUE.

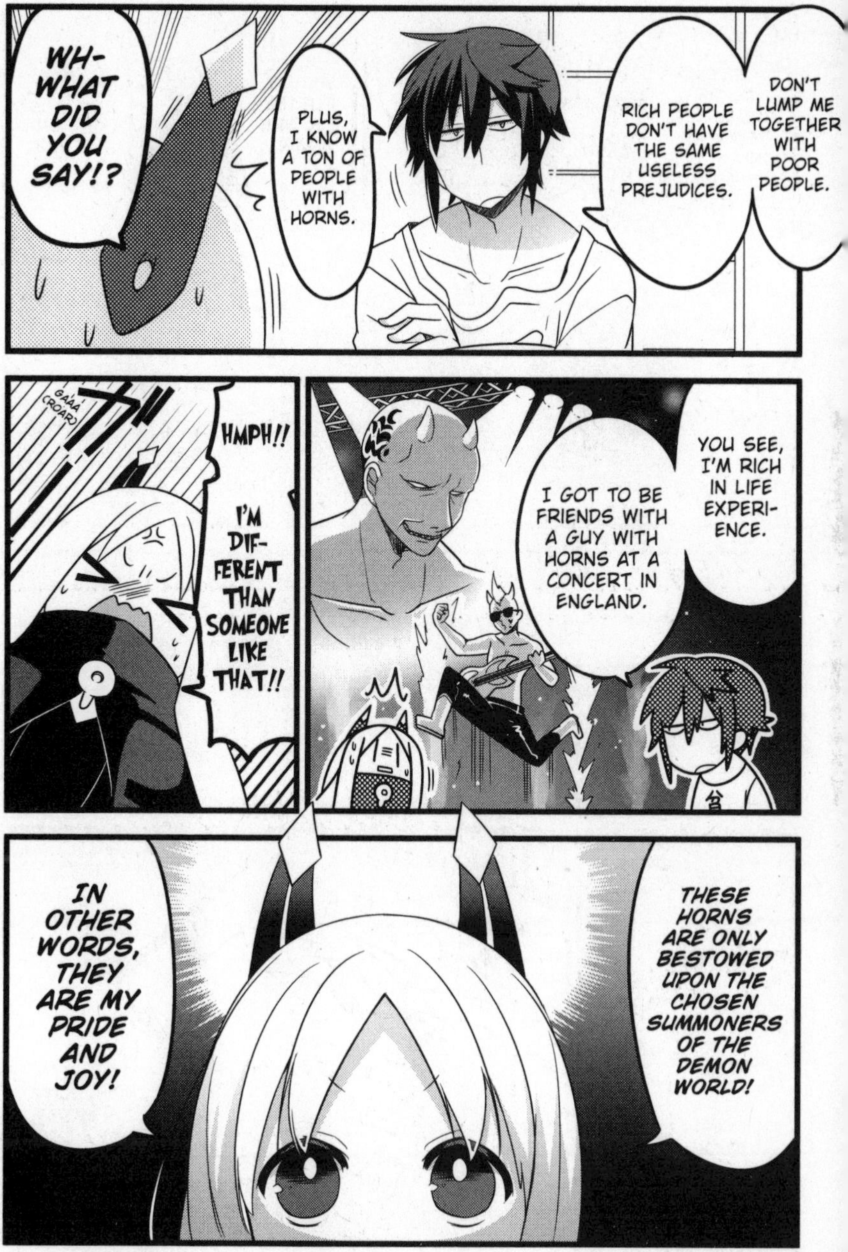
DON'T LUMP ME TOGETHER WITH POOR PEOPLE.
RICH PEOPLE DON'T HAVE THE SAME USELESS PREJUDICES.
PLUS, I KNOW A TON OF PEOPLE WITH HORNS.
WH-WHAT DID YOU SAY!?
YOU SEE, I'M RICH IN LIFE EXPERIENCE.
I GOT TO BE FRIENDS WITH A GUY WITH HORNS AT A CONCERT IN ENGLAND.
HMPH!!
I'M DIFFERENT THAN SOMEONE LIKE THAT!!
GAAA (ROAR)
THESE HORNS ARE ONLY BESTOWED UPON THE CHOSEN SUMMONERS OF THE DEMON WORLD!
IN OTHER WORDS, THEY ARE MY PRIDE AND JOY!

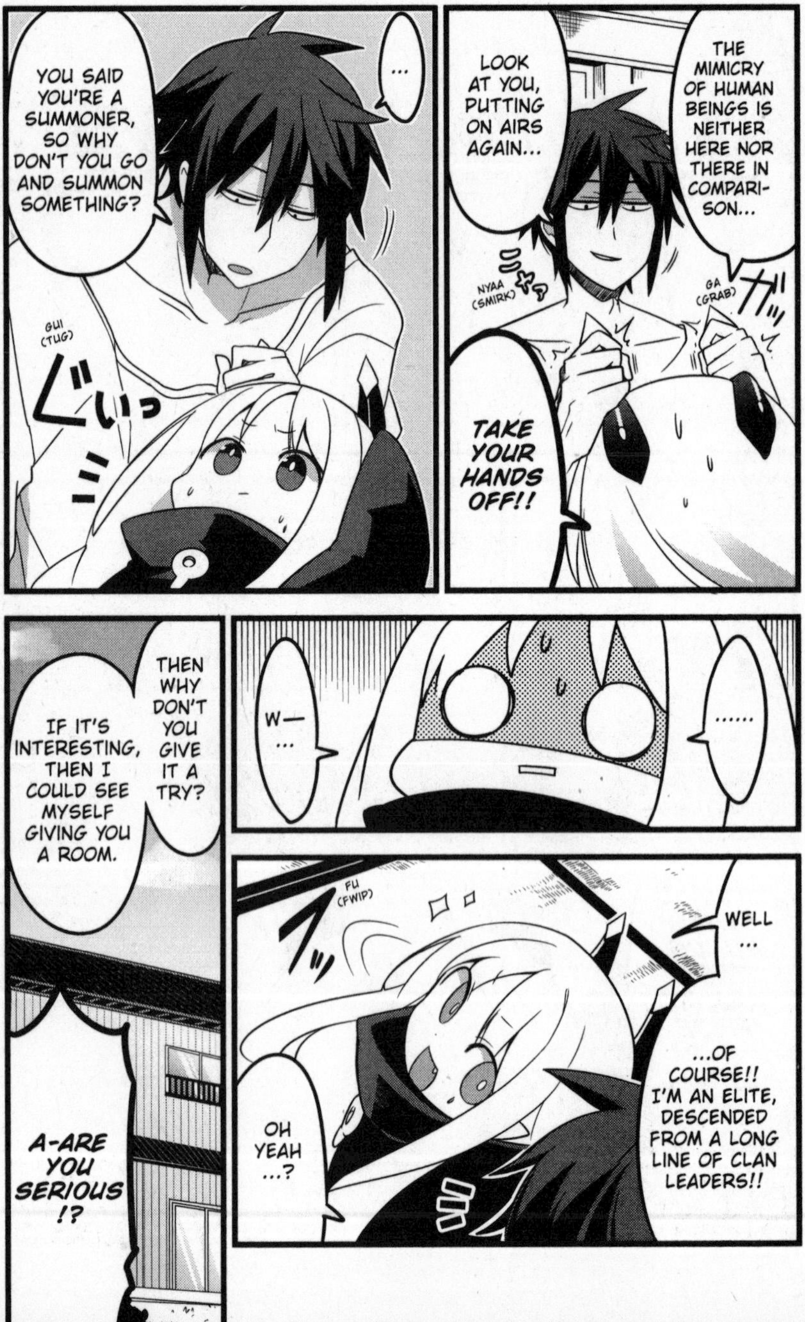
THE MIMICRY OF HUMAN BEINGS IS NEITHER HERE NOR THERE IN COMPARISON...
LOOK AT YOU, PUTTING ON AIRS AGAIN...
GA (GRAB)
NYAA (SMIRK)
TAKE YOUR HANDS OFF!!
...
YOU SAID YOU'RE A SUMMONER, SO WHY DON'T YOU GO AND SUMMON SOMETHING?
GUI (TUG)
......
W— ...
WELL ...
...OF COURSE!! I'M AN ELITE, DESCENDED FROM A LONG LINE OF CLAN LEADERS!!
FU (FWIP)
OH YEAH ...?
THEN WHY DON'T YOU GIVE IT A TRY?
IF IT'S INTERESTING, THEN I COULD SEE MYSELF GIVING YOU A ROOM.
A-ARE YOU SERIOUS!?

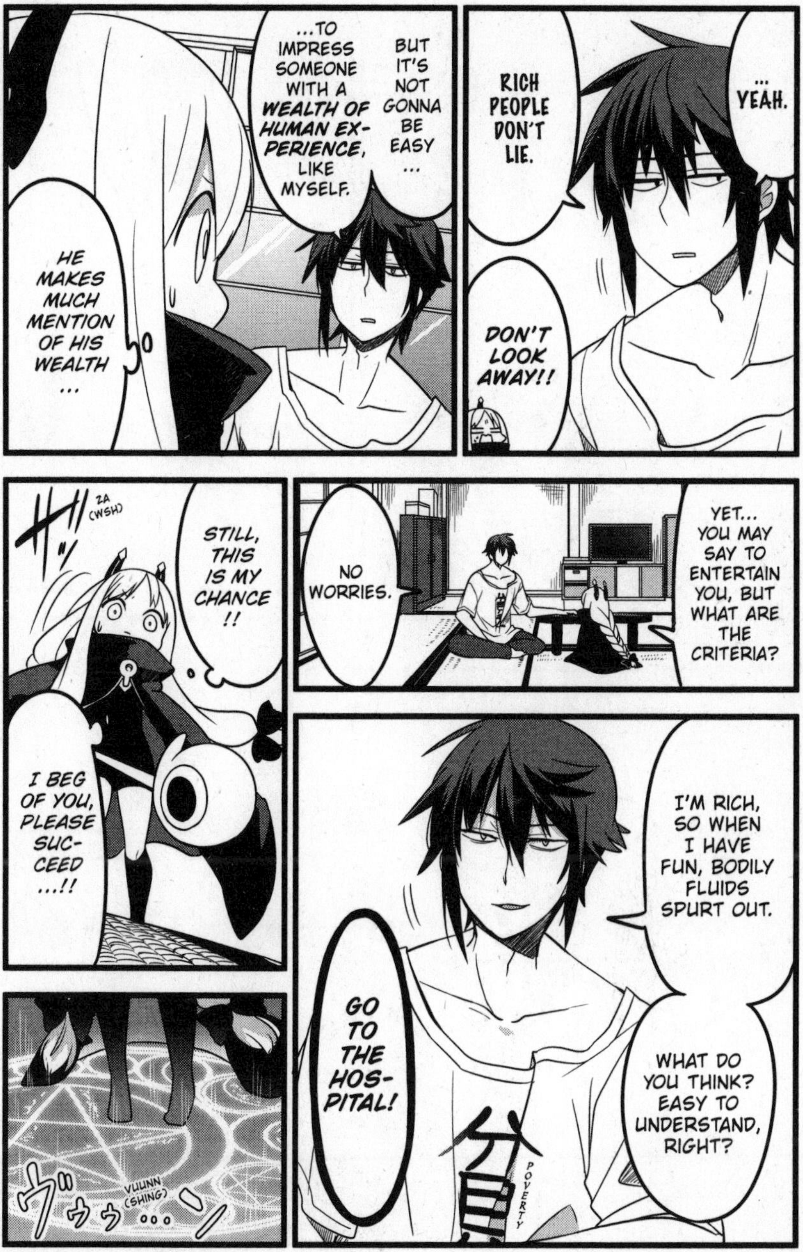
...YEAH.
RICH PEOPLE DON'T LIE.
DON'T LOOK AWAY!!
BUT IT'S NOT GONNA BE EASY...
...TO IMPRESS SOMEONE WITH A *WEALTH OF HUMAN EXPERIENCE*, LIKE MYSELF.
HE MAKES MUCH MENTION OF HIS WEALTH...
YET... YOU MAY SAY TO ENTERTAIN YOU, BUT WHAT ARE THE CRITERIA?
NO WORRIES.
I'M RICH, SO WHEN I HAVE FUN, BODILY FLUIDS SPURT OUT.
WHAT DO YOU THINK? EASY TO UNDERSTAND, RIGHT?
POVERTY
GO TO THE HOS-PITAL!
ZA (WSH)
STILL, THIS IS MY CHANCE!!
I BEG OF YOU, PLEASE SUC-CEED...!!
VUUNN (SHING)

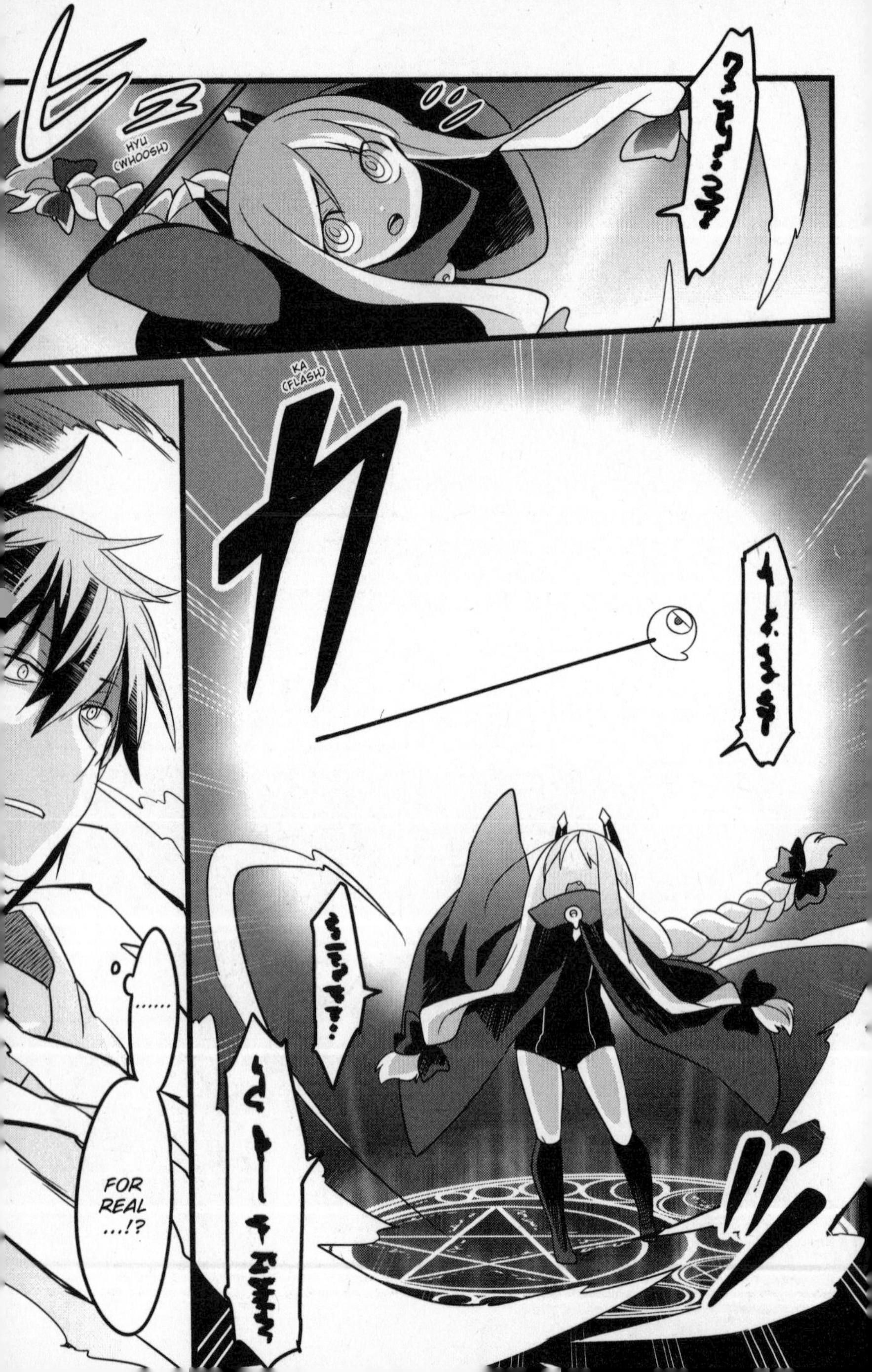
HYU
(WHOOSH)
KA
(FLASH)
......
FOR REAL ...!?

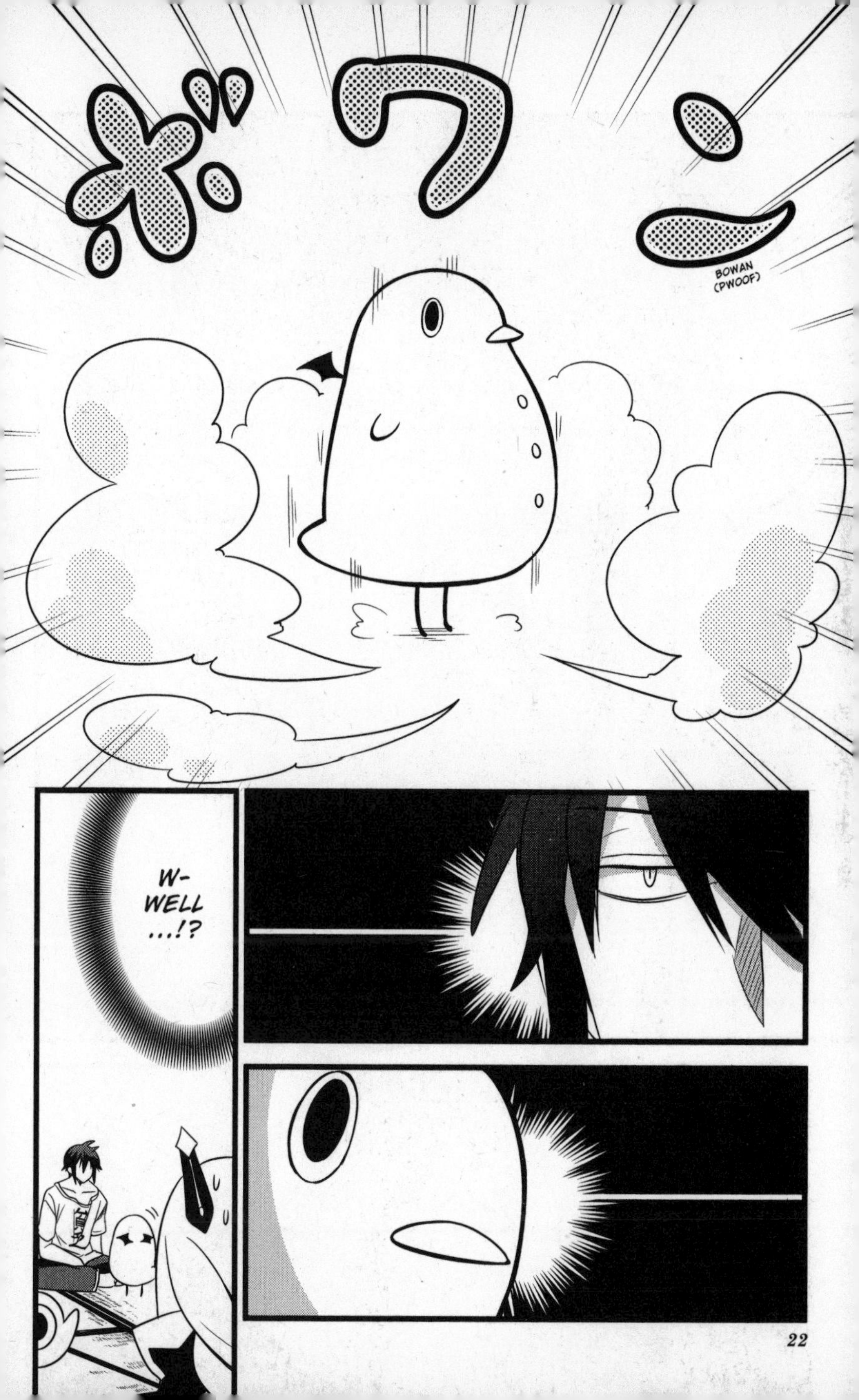
BOWAN (PWOOF)
W-WELL ...!?

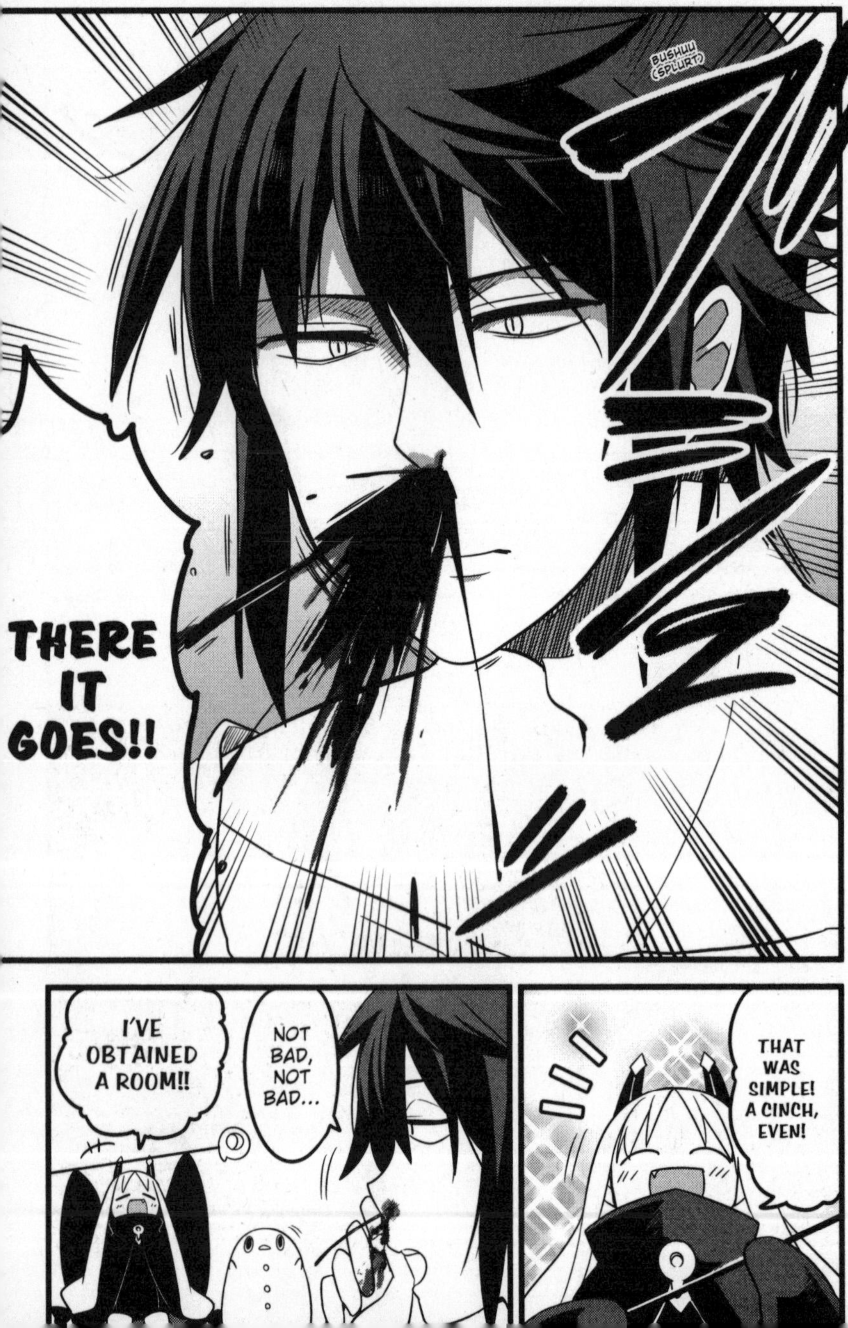
BUSHUU (SPLURT)
THERE IT GOES!!
THAT WAS SIMPLE! A CINCH, EVEN!
NOT BAD, NOT BAD...
I'VE OBTAINED A ROOM!!

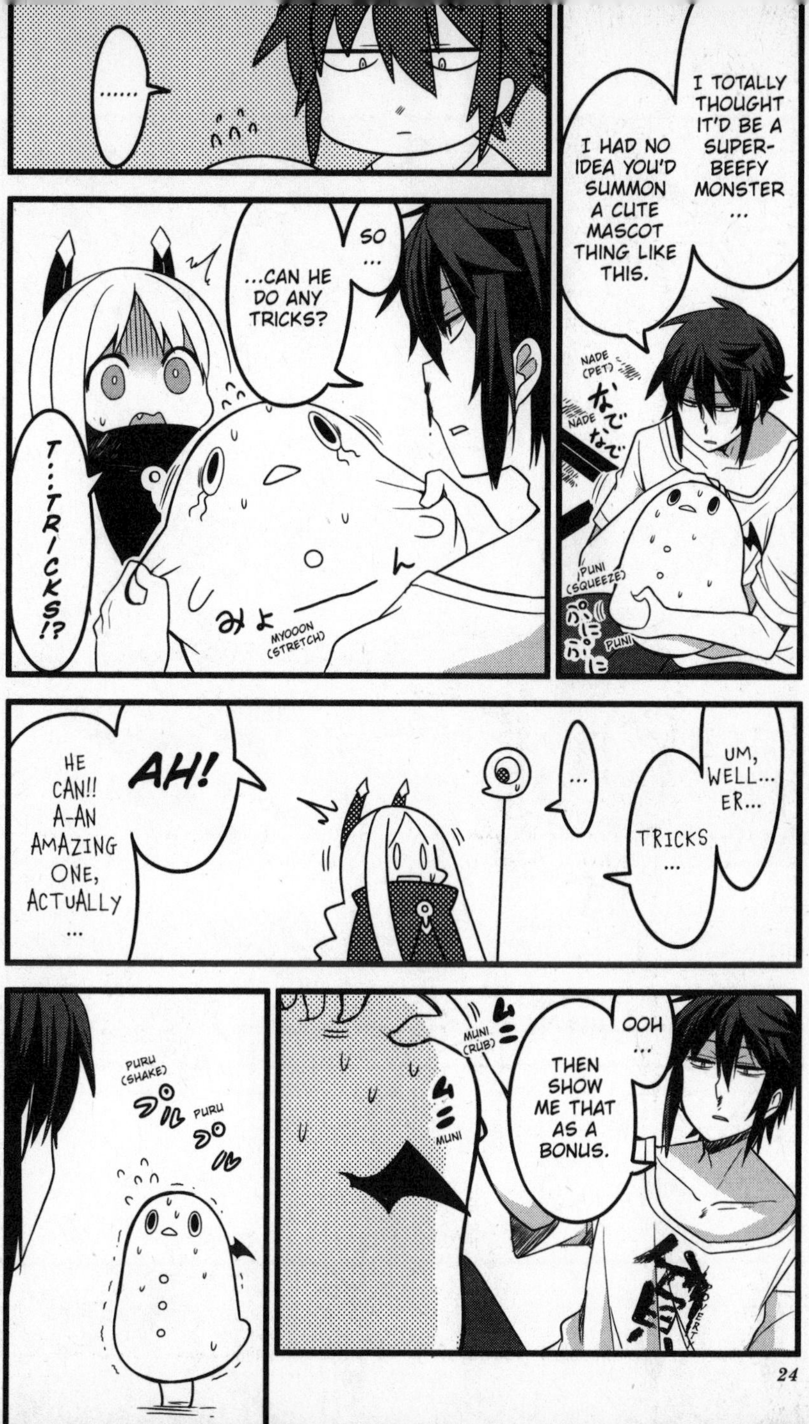

I TOTALLY THOUGHT IT'D BE A SUPER-BEEFY MONSTER...
I HAD NO IDEA YOU'D SUMMON A CUTE MASCOT THING LIKE THIS.
NADE (PET)
なでなで
NADE
PUNI (SQUEEZE)
ぷにぷに
PUNI
......
SO...
...CAN HE DO ANY TRICKS?
T...TRICKS!?
みょ――ん
MYOOON (STRETCH)
UM, WELL... ER...
TRICKS...
...
AH!
HE CAN!! A-AN AMAZING ONE, ACTUALLY...
OOH...
THEN SHOW ME THAT AS A BONUS.
MUNI (RUB)
むにむに
MUNI
PURU (SHAKE)
ぷるぷる
PURU

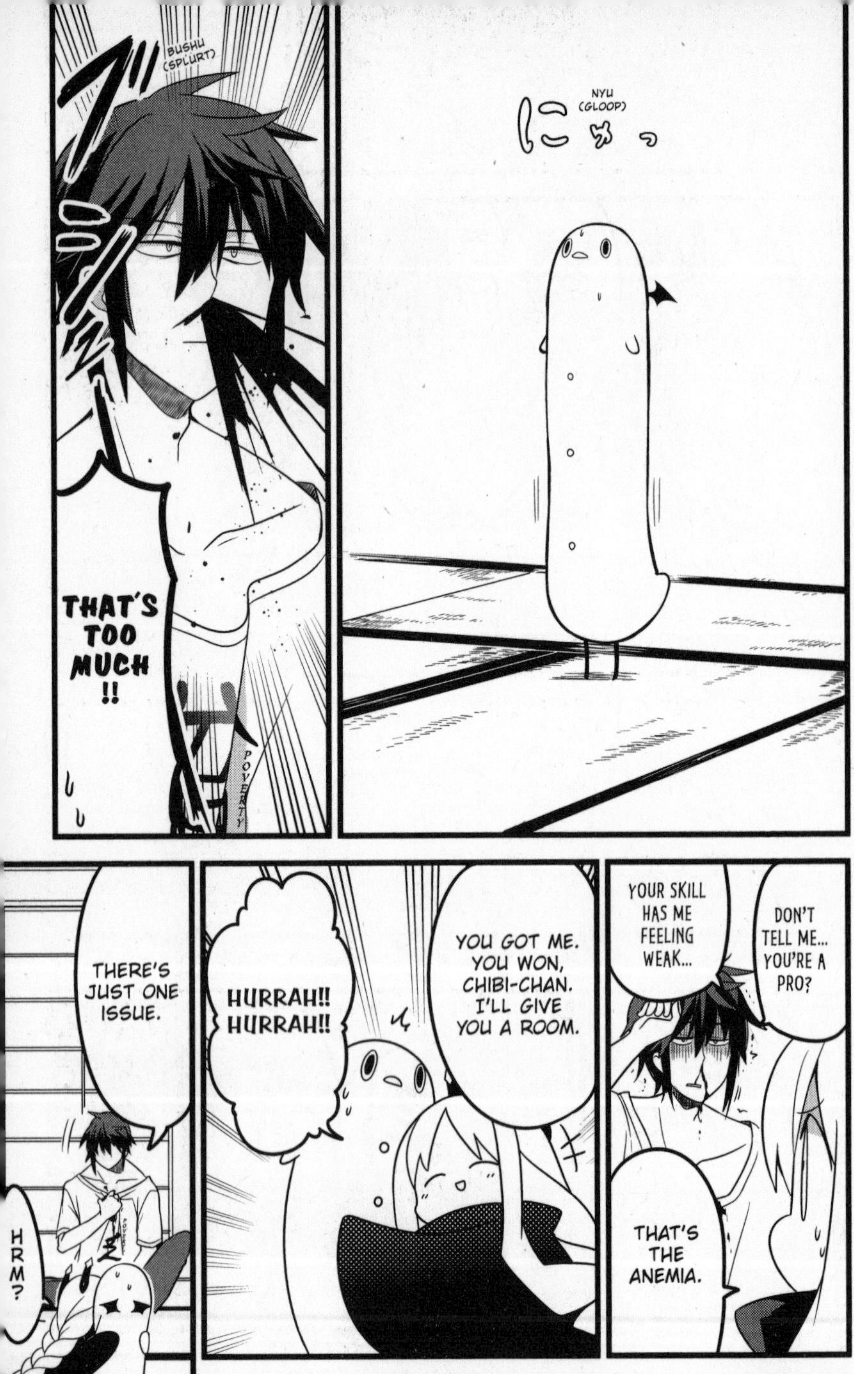
NYU (GLOOP)
にゅっ
BUSHU (SPLURT)
THAT'S TOO MUCH!!
POVERTY
DON'T TELL ME... YOU'RE A PRO?
YOUR SKILL HAS ME FEELING WEAK...
THAT'S THE ANEMIA.
YOU GOT ME. YOU WON, CHIBI-CHAN. I'LL GIVE YOU A ROOM.
HURRAH!! HURRAH!!
THERE'S JUST ONE ISSUE.
HRM?

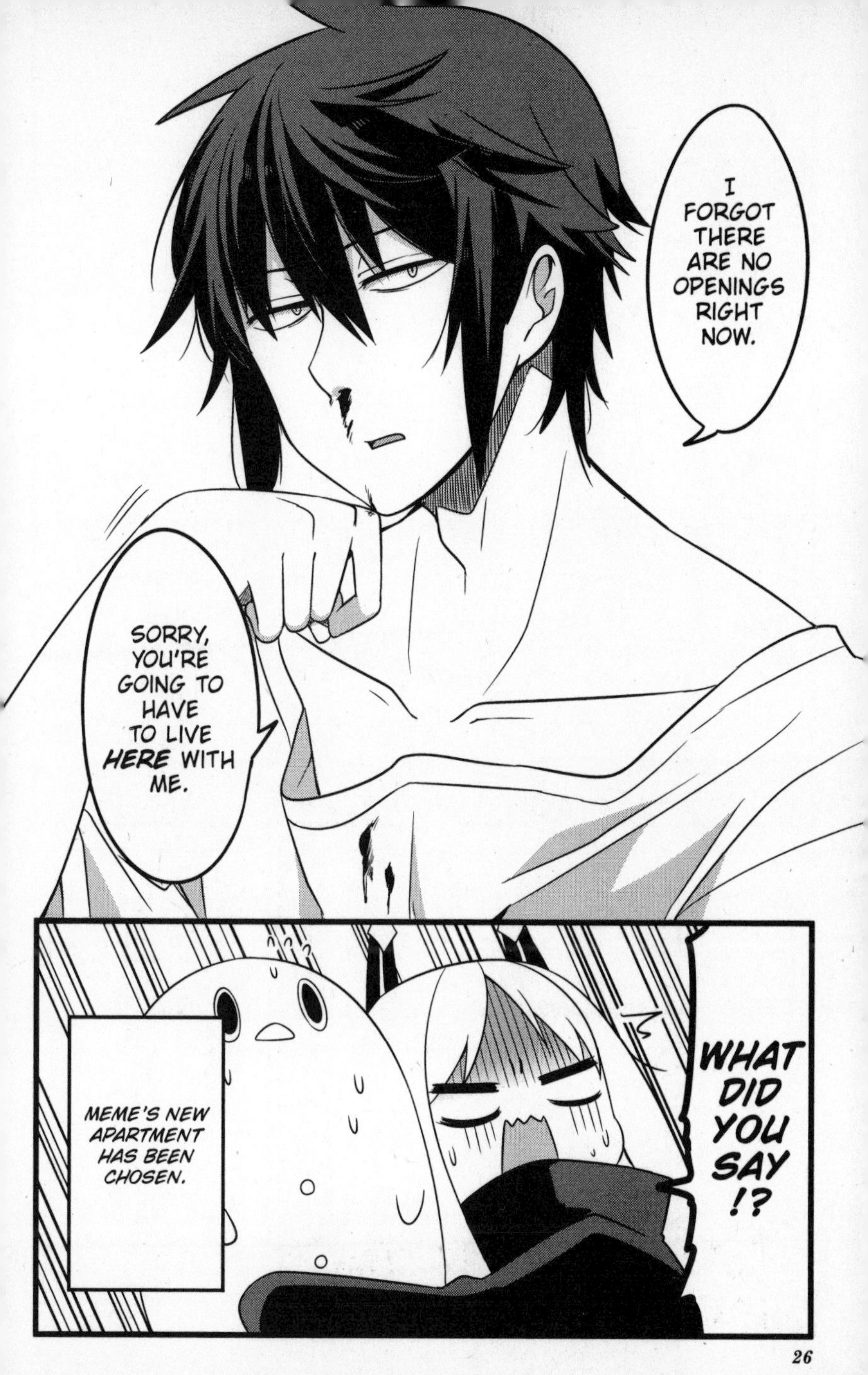
I FORGOT THERE ARE NO OPENINGS RIGHT NOW.
SORRY, YOU'RE GOING TO HAVE TO LIVE *HERE* WITH ME.
WHAT DID YOU SAY !?
MEME'S NEW APARTMENT HAS BEEN CHOSEN.

The Strange Creature at Kuroyuri Apartments

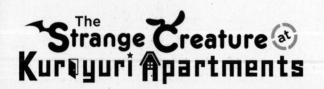

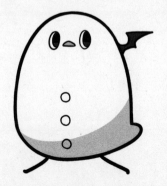

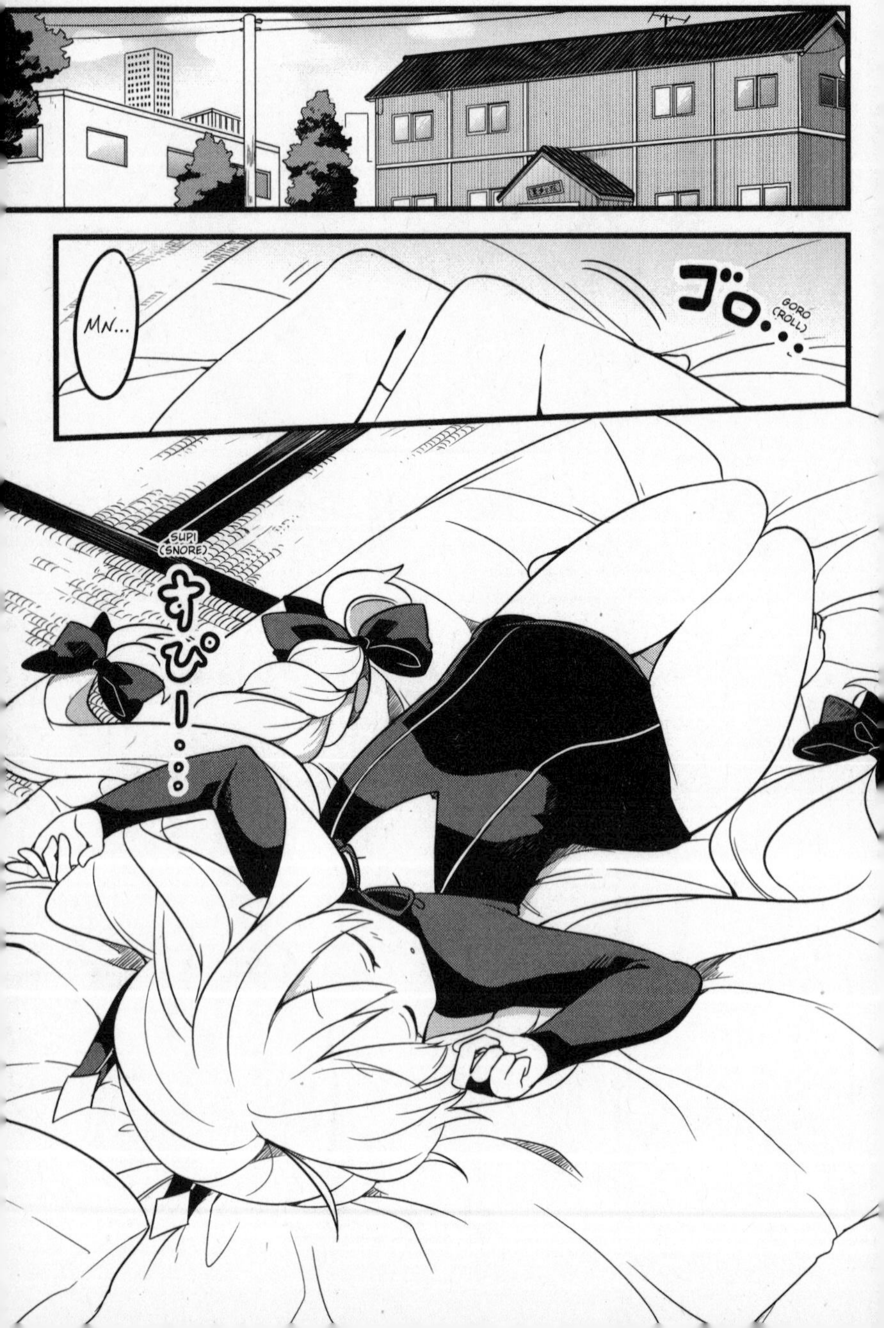
ゴロ...
GORO (ROLL)
MN...
すぴー。。。
SUPI (SNORE)

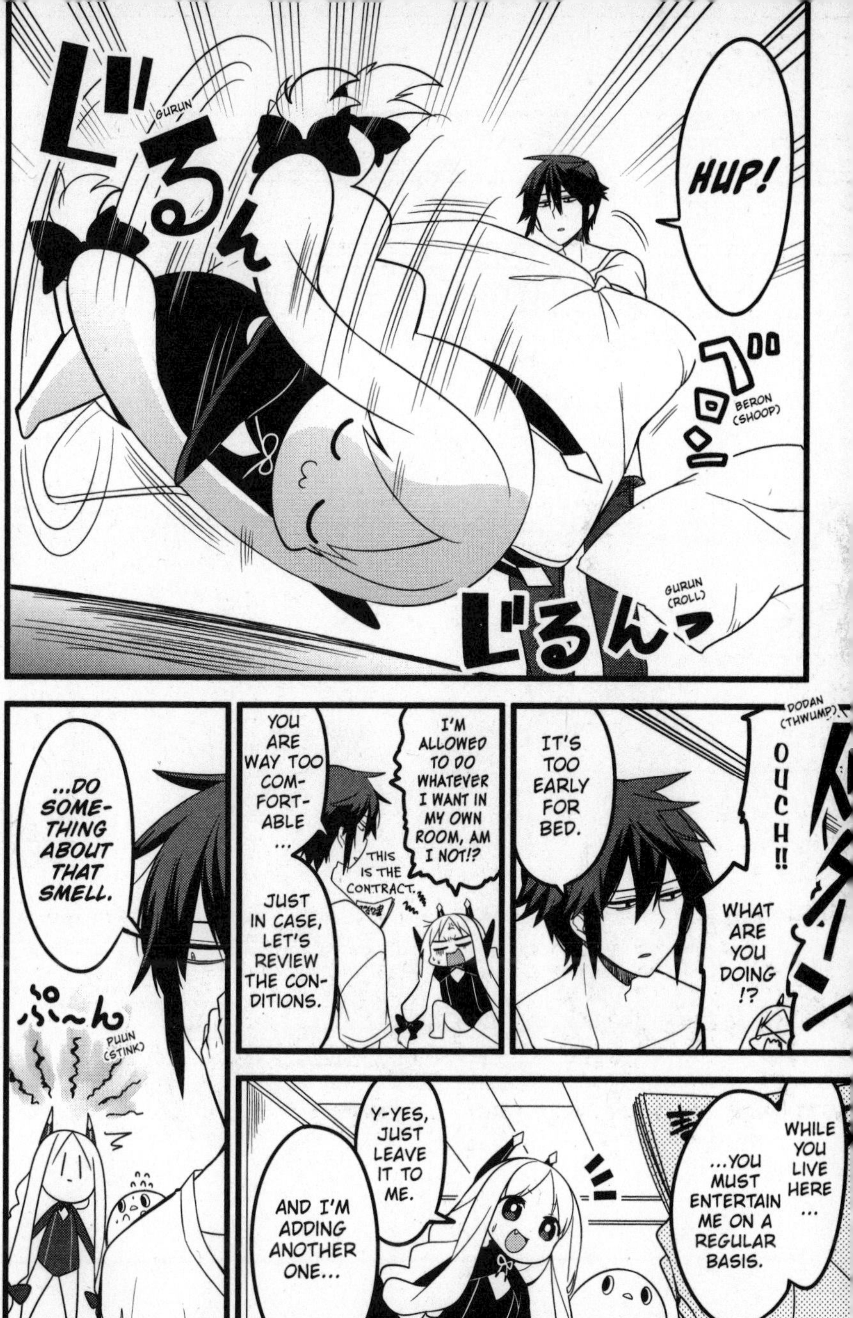
HUP!
BERON (SHOOP)
ぐるん
GURUN
ぐるんっ
GURUN (ROLL)
DODAN (THWUMP)
OUCH!!
WHAT ARE YOU DOING!?
IT'S TOO EARLY FOR BED.
I'M ALLOWED TO DO WHATEVER I WANT IN MY OWN ROOM, AM I NOT!?
YOU ARE WAY TOO COM-FORT-ABLE...
THIS IS THE CONTRACT.
JUST IN CASE, LET'S REVIEW THE CON-DITIONS.
WHILE YOU LIVE HERE...
...YOU MUST ENTERTAIN ME ON A REGULAR BASIS.
Y-YES, JUST LEAVE IT TO ME.
AND I'M ADDING ANOTHER ONE...
...DO SOME-THING ABOUT THAT SMELL.
ぷ~ん
PUUN (STINK)

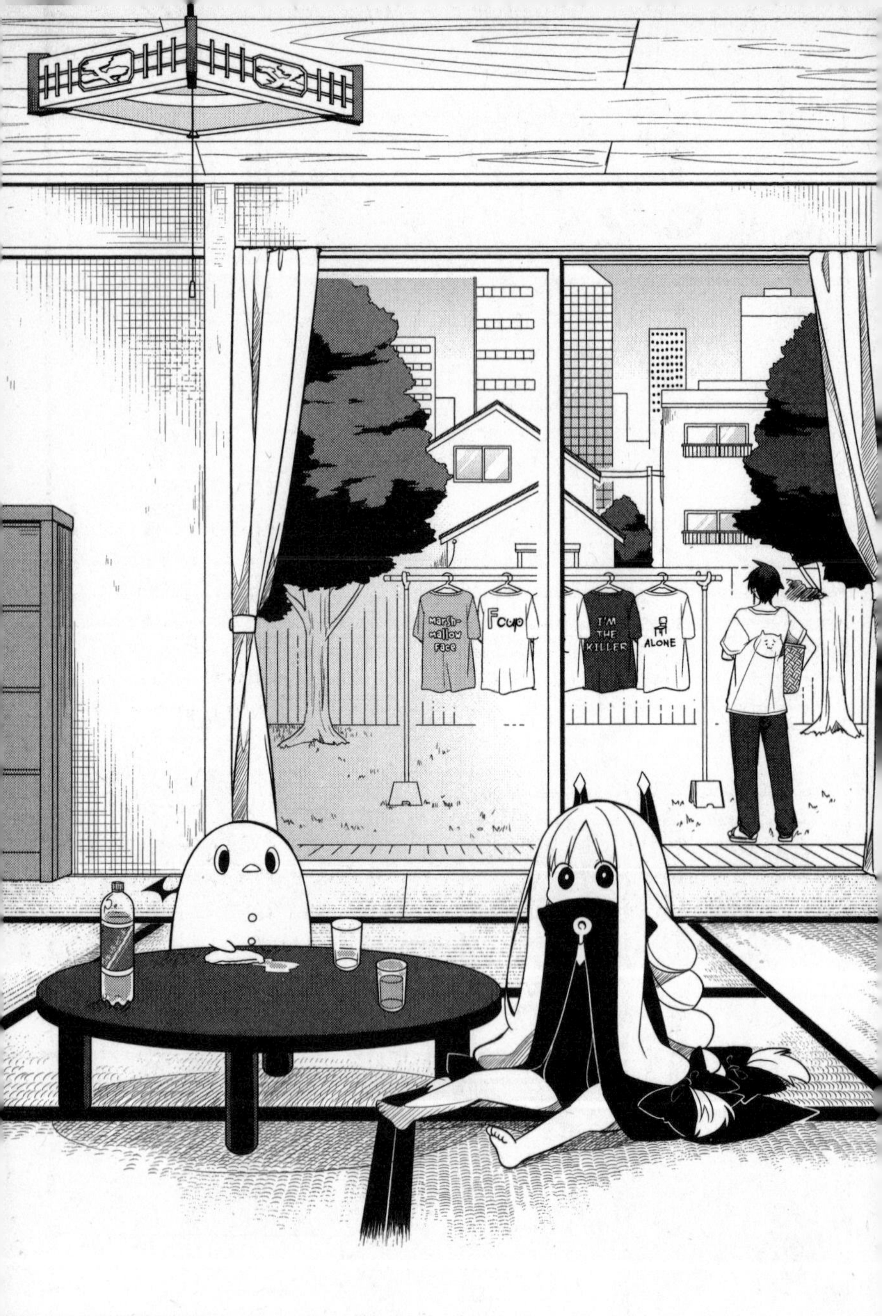
Marsh-
mallow
face
Fcup
I'M
THE
KILLER
ALONE

CREATURE 2: BATH ☆ PANIC!

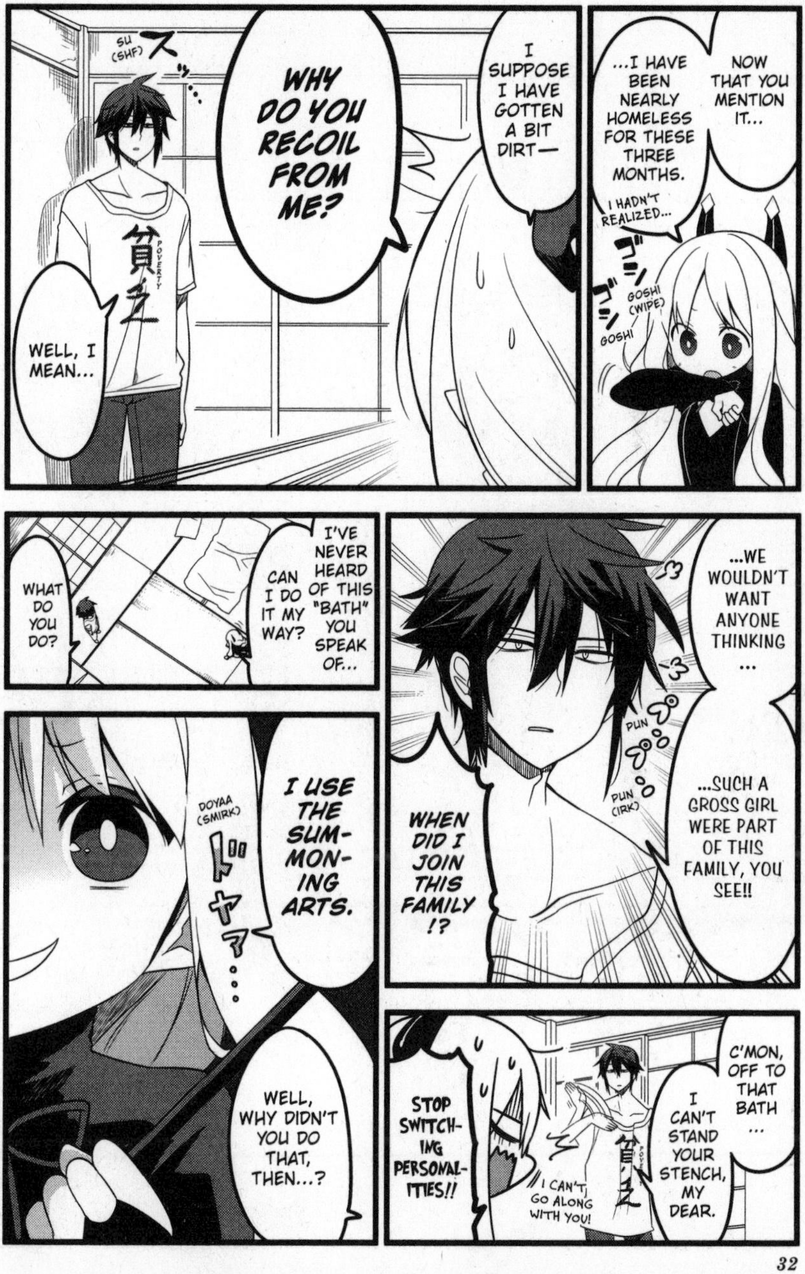
NOW THAT YOU MENTION IT...
...I HAVE BEEN NEARLY HOMELESS FOR THESE THREE MONTHS.
I HADN'T REALIZED...
ゴシ ゴシ
GOSHI (WIPE) GOSHI
I SUPPOSE I HAVE GOTTEN A BIT DIRT—
WHY DO YOU RECOIL FROM ME?
ス ッ...
SU (SHF)
POVERTY
WELL, I MEAN...
...WE WOULDN'T WANT ANYONE THINKING...
...SUCH A GROSS GIRL WERE PART OF THIS FAMILY, YOU SEE!!
PUN PUN (IRK)
WHEN DID I JOIN THIS FAMILY!?
I'VE NEVER HEARD OF THIS "BATH" YOU SPEAK OF...
CAN I DO IT MY WAY?
WHAT DO YOU DO?
I USE THE SUM-MON-ING ARTS.
DOYAA (SMIRK)
ドヤァ...
WELL, WHY DIDN'T YOU DO THAT, THEN...?
C'MON, OFF TO THAT BATH...
I CAN'T STAND YOUR STENCH, MY DEAR.
STOP SWITCH-ING PERSONAL-ITIES!!
I CAN'T GO ALONG WITH YOU!

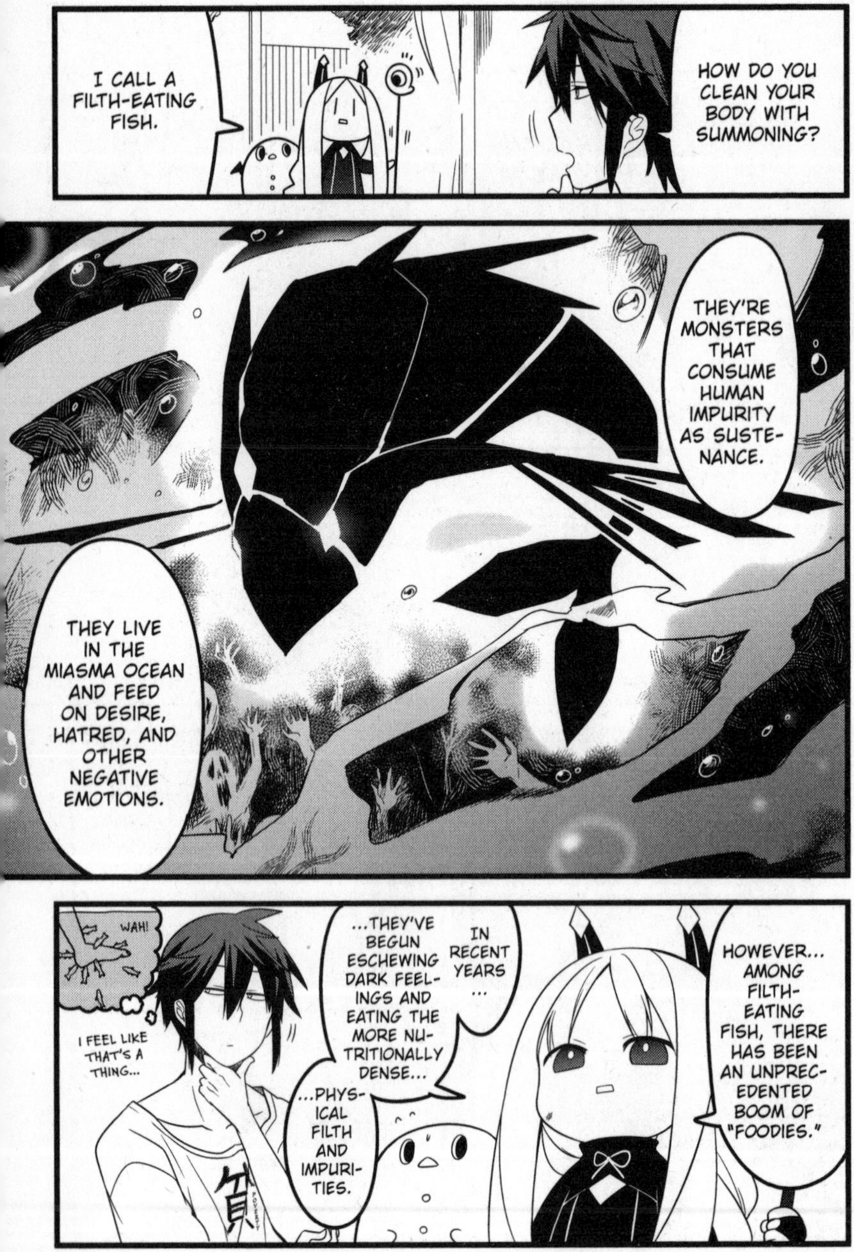
HOW DO YOU CLEAN YOUR BODY WITH SUMMONING?
I CALL A FILTH-EATING FISH.
THEY'RE MONSTERS THAT CONSUME HUMAN IMPURITY AS SUSTE-NANCE.
THEY LIVE IN THE MIASMA OCEAN AND FEED ON DESIRE, HATRED, AND OTHER NEGATIVE EMOTIONS.
HOWEVER... AMONG FILTH-EATING FISH, THERE HAS BEEN AN UNPREC-EDENTED BOOM OF "FOODIES."
IN RECENT YEARS ...
...THEY'VE BEGUN ESCHEWING DARK FEEL-INGS AND EATING THE MORE NU-TRITIONALLY DENSE...
...PHYS-ICAL FILTH AND IMPURI-TIES.
WAH!
I FEEL LIKE THAT'S A THING...

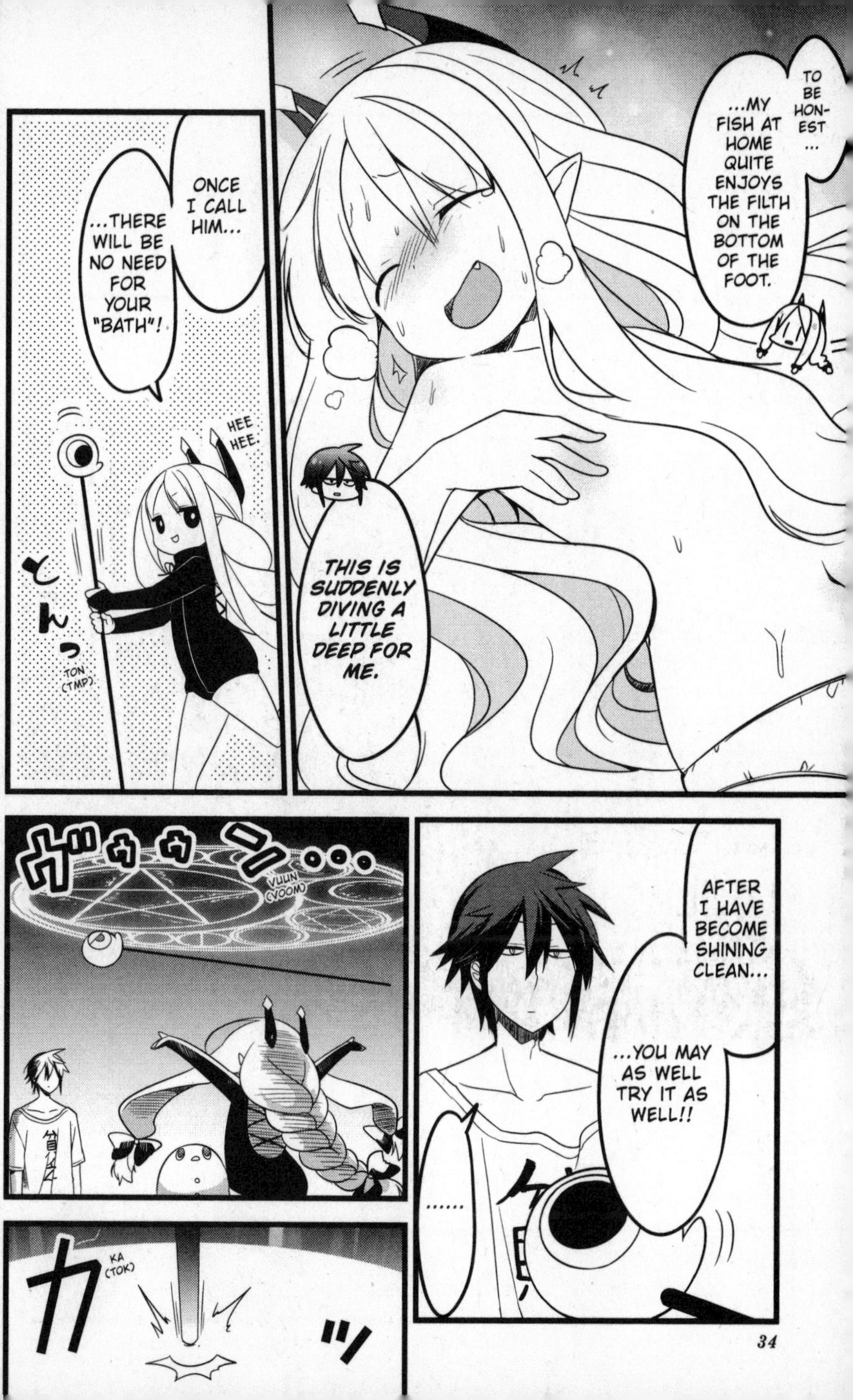
TO BE HON- EST...
...MY FISH AT HOME QUITE ENJOYS THE FILTH ON THE BOTTOM OF THE FOOT.
THIS IS SUDDENLY DIVING A LITTLE DEEP FOR ME.
ONCE I CALL HIM...
...THERE WILL BE NO NEED FOR YOUR "BATH"!
HEE HEE.
とんっ
TON (TMP)
AFTER I HAVE BECOME SHINING CLEAN...
...YOU MAY AS WELL TRY IT AS WELL!!
......
ヴゥゥゥン...
VUUN (VOOM)
カッ
KA (TOK)

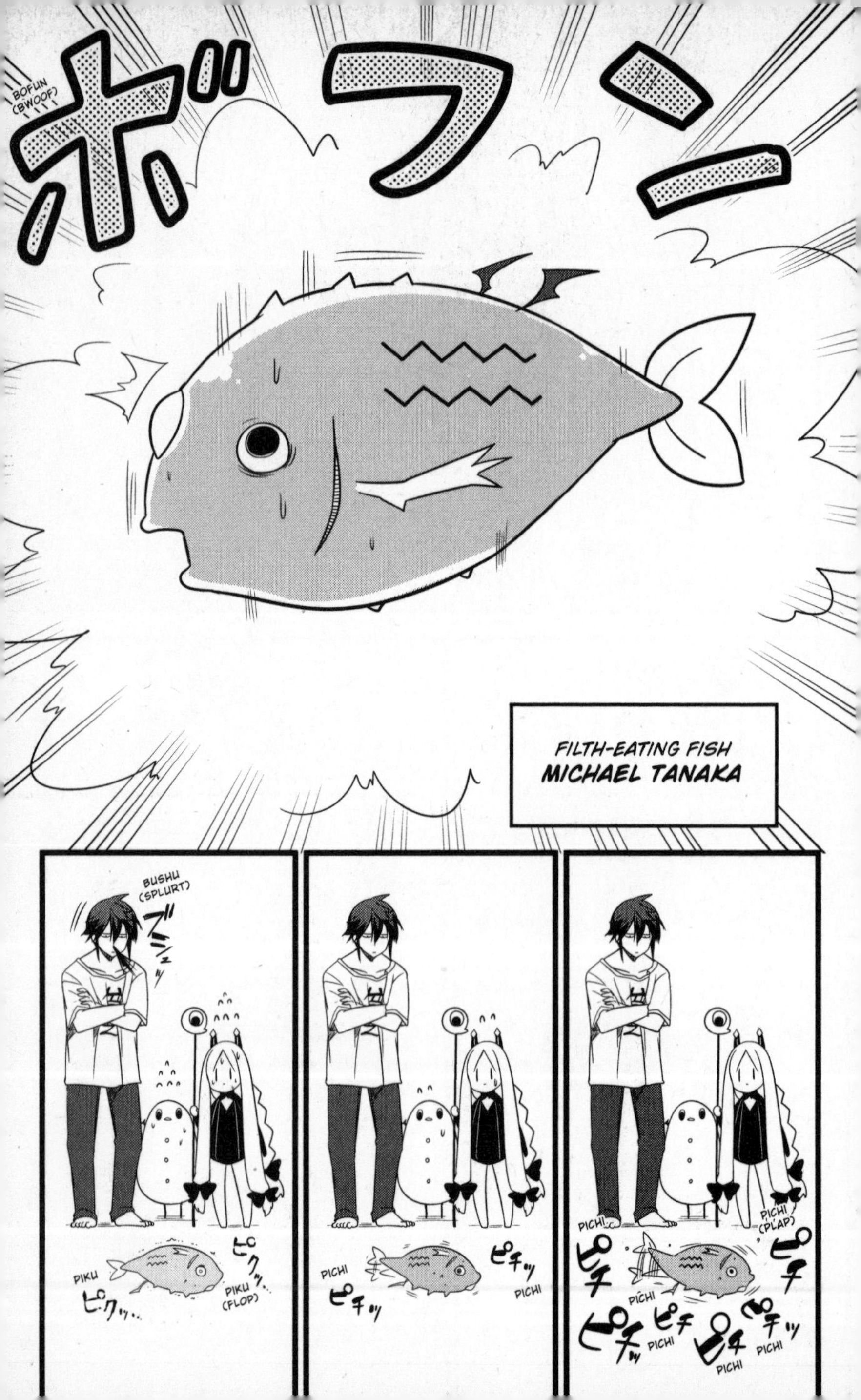
BOFUN (BWOOF)
ボフン
FILTH-EATING FISH
MICHAEL TANAKA
PICHI (PLAP)
ピチ
PICHI
ピチ
PICHI
ピチ
PICHI
ピチ
PICHI
ピチッ
PICHI
ピチッ
PICHI
ピチッ
PICHI
ピチッ
BUSHU (SPLURT)
ブシュ
PIKU (FLOP)
ピクッ…
PIKU
ピクッ…

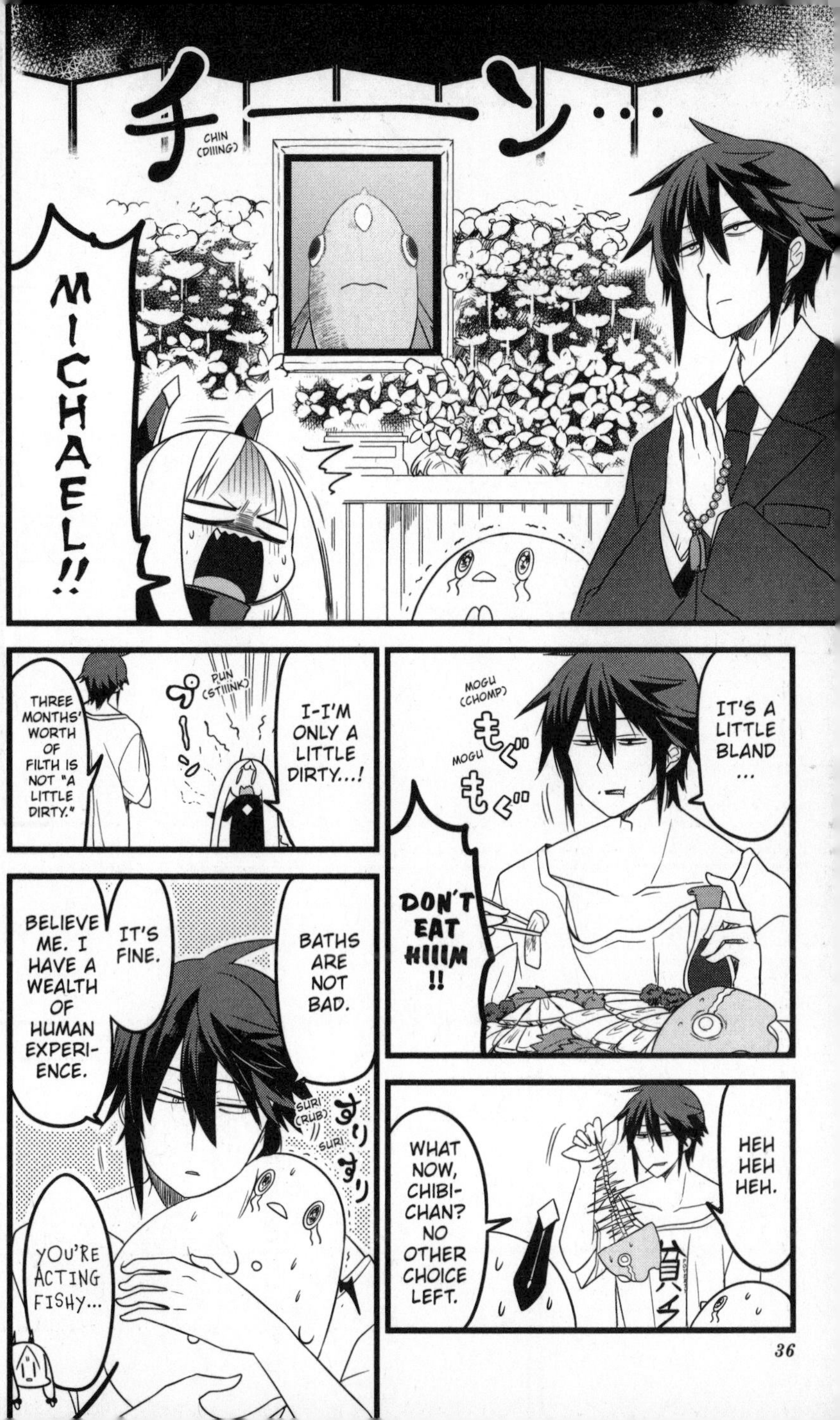

チーン…
CHIN (DIIING)
MICHAEL!!
IT'S A LITTLE BLAND...
MOGU (CHOMP) もぐ
MOGU もぐ
DON'T EAT HIIIM!!
I-I'M ONLY A LITTLE DIRTY...!
PUN (STIIINK)
THREE MONTHS' WORTH OF FILTH IS NOT "A LITTLE DIRTY."
HEH HEH HEH.
WHAT NOW, CHIBI-CHAN? NO OTHER CHOICE LEFT.
BATHS ARE NOT BAD.
IT'S FINE.
BELIEVE ME. I HAVE A WEALTH OF HUMAN EXPERI-ENCE.
SURI (RUB) すり
SURI すり
YOU'RE ACTING FISHY...

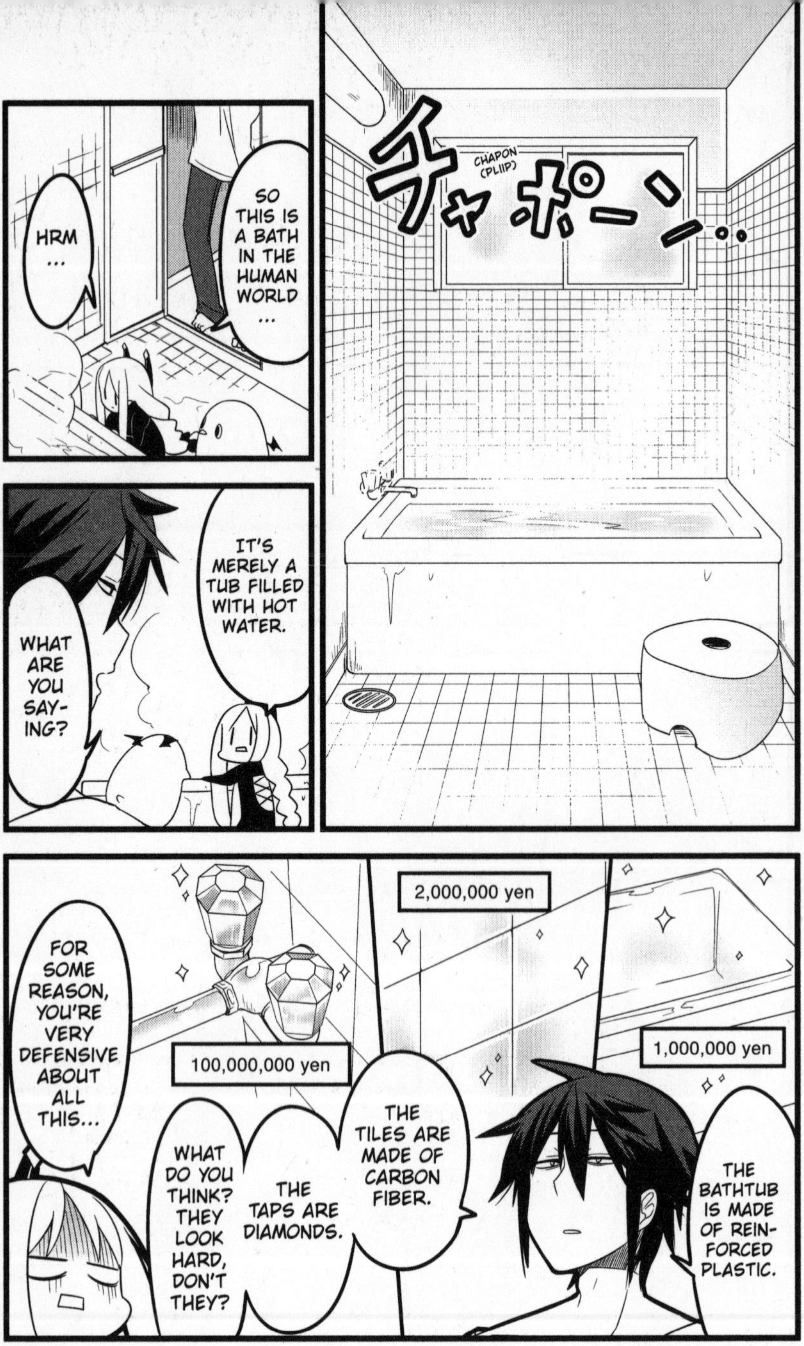
チャポーン。。
CHAPON (PLIIP)
SO THIS IS A BATH IN THE HUMAN WORLD...
HRM...
IT'S MERELY A TUB FILLED WITH HOT WATER.
WHAT ARE YOU SAYING?
1,000,000 yen
THE BATHTUB IS MADE OF REINFORCED PLASTIC.
2,000,000 yen
THE TILES ARE MADE OF CARBON FIBER.
100,000,000 yen
THE TAPS ARE DIAMONDS.
WHAT DO YOU THINK? THEY LOOK HARD, DON'T THEY?
FOR SOME REASON, YOU'RE VERY DEFENSIVE ABOUT ALL THIS...

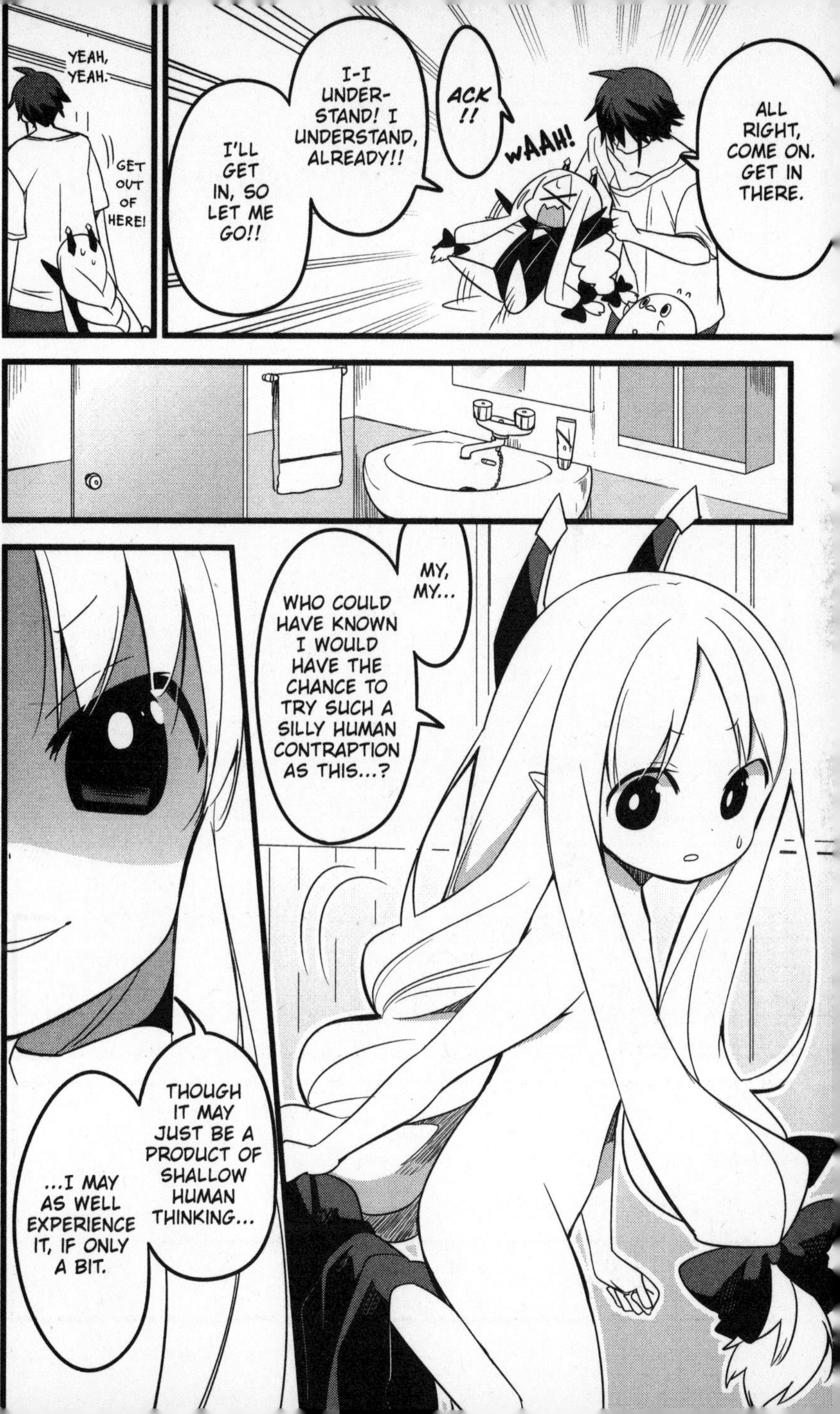
ALL RIGHT, COME ON. GET IN THERE.
wAAH!
ACK!!
I-I UNDERSTAND! I UNDERSTAND, ALREADY!!
I'LL GET IN, SO LET ME GO!!
YEAH, YEAH.
GET OUT OF HERE!
MY, MY...
WHO COULD HAVE KNOWN I WOULD HAVE THE CHANCE TO TRY SUCH A SILLY HUMAN CONTRAPTION AS THIS...?
THOUGH IT MAY JUST BE A PRODUCT OF SHALLOW HUMAN THINKING...
...I MAY AS WELL EXPERIENCE IT, IF ONLY A BIT.

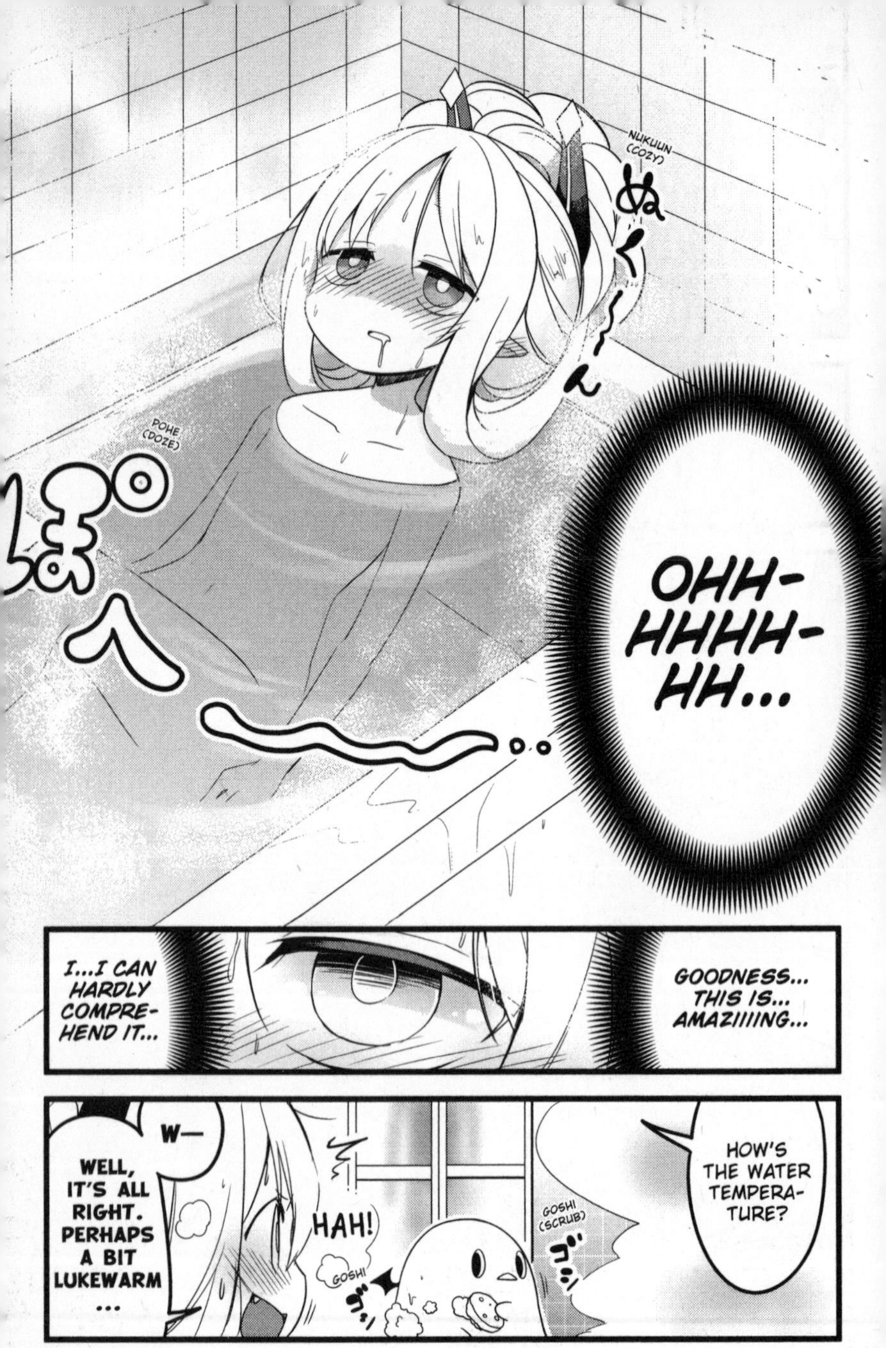
NUKUUN (COZY)
ぬく~~ん
OHH-HHHH-HH...
POHE (DOZE)
ぽへ~..
GOODNESS... THIS IS... AMAZIIIING...
I...I CAN HARDLY COMPRE-HEND IT...
HOW'S THE WATER TEMPERA-TURE?
GOSHI (SCRUB)
ゴシ
GOSHI
ゴシ
HAH!
W—
WELL, IT'S ALL RIGHT. PERHAPS A BIT LUKEWARM ...

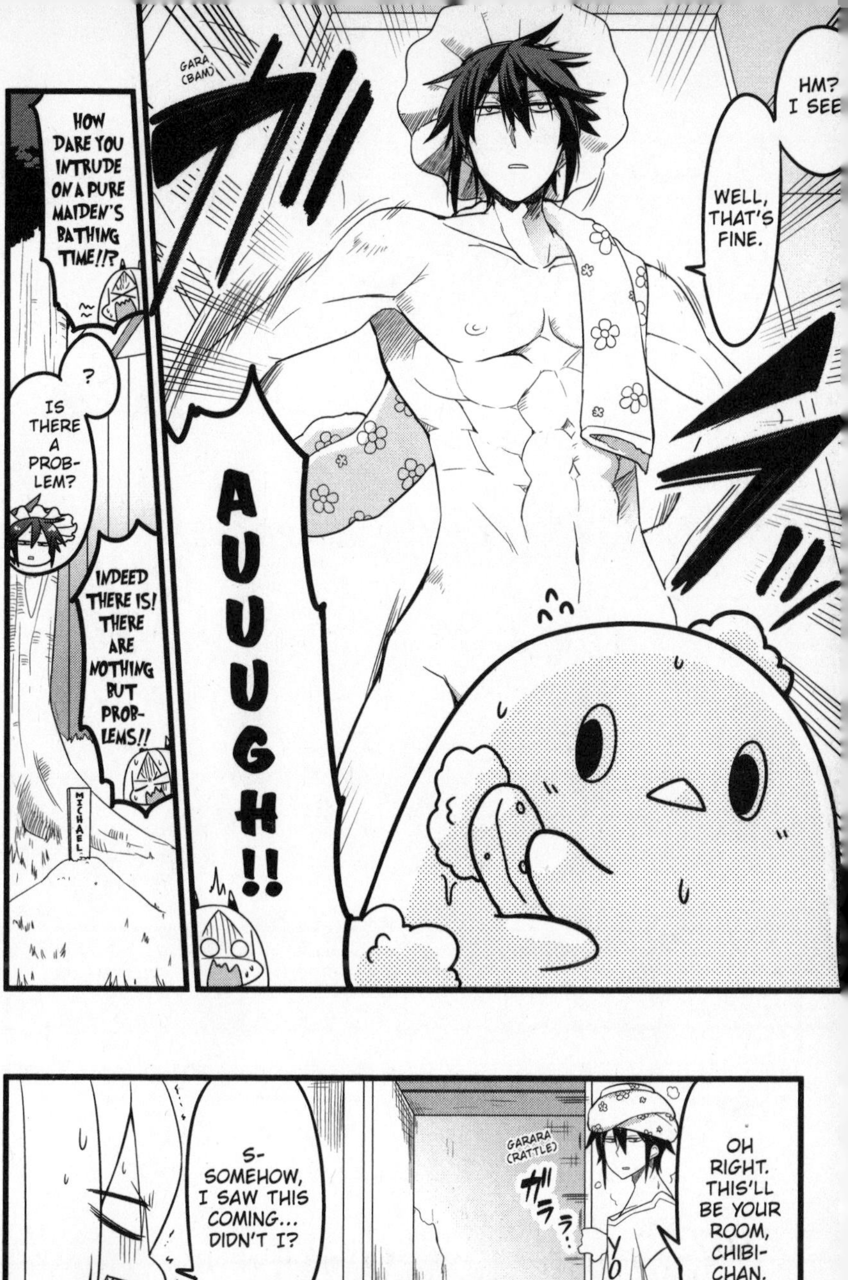
HM? I SEE
WELL, THAT'S FINE.
GARA (BAM)
AUUUGH!!
HOW DARE YOU INTRUDE ON A PURE MAIDEN'S BATHING TIME!!?
? IS THERE A PROB-LEM?
INDEED THERE IS! THERE ARE NOTHING BUT PROB-LEMS!!
MICHAEL
OH RIGHT. THIS'LL BE YOUR ROOM, CHIBI-CHAN.
YOSHI
GARARA (RATTLE)
S-SOMEHOW, I SAW THIS COMING... DIDN'T I?

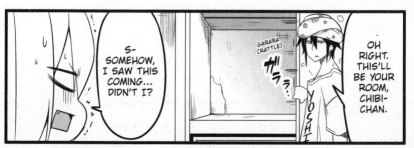

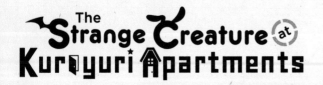
The Strange Creature at Kuroyuri Apartments

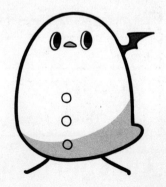

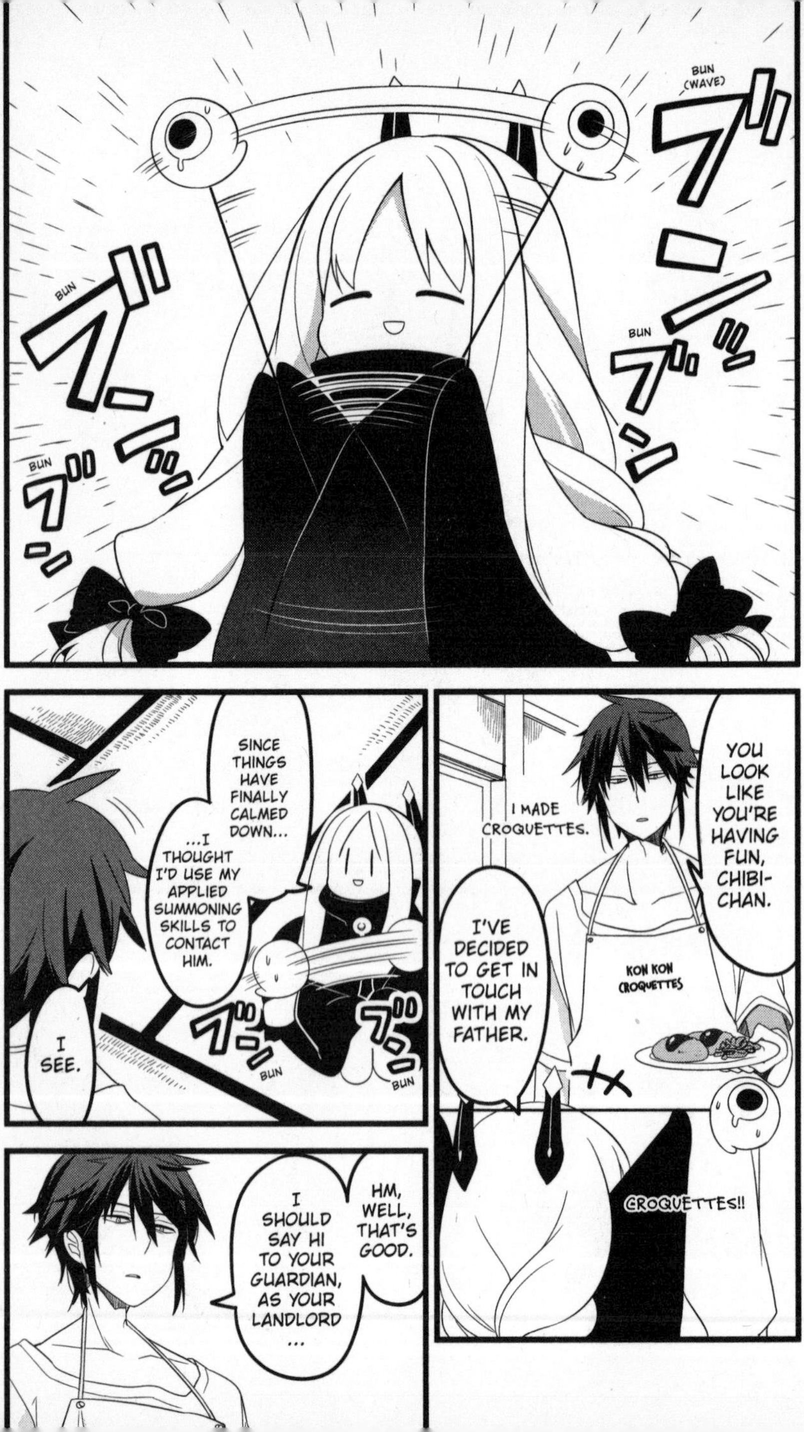
BUN (WAVE)
BUN
BUN
BUN
YOU LOOK LIKE YOU'RE HAVING FUN, CHIBI-CHAN.
I MADE CROQUETTES.
KON KON CROQUETTES
I'VE DECIDED TO GET IN TOUCH WITH MY FATHER.
CROQUETTES!!
SINCE THINGS HAVE FINALLY CALMED DOWN...
...I THOUGHT I'D USE MY APPLIED SUMMONING SKILLS TO CONTACT HIM.
BUN
BUN
I SEE.
HM, WELL, THAT'S GOOD.
I SHOULD SAY HI TO YOUR GUARDIAN, AS YOUR LANDLORD ...

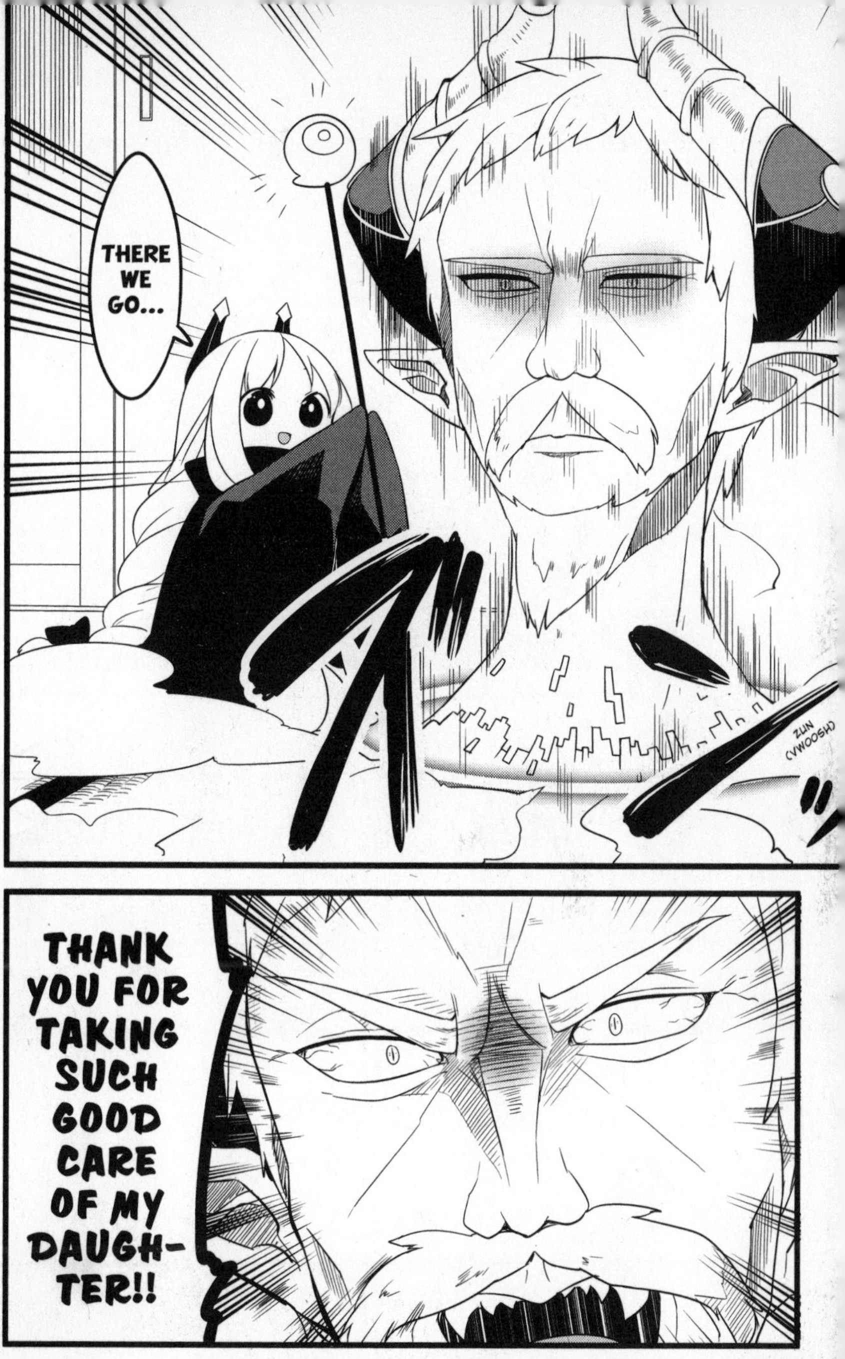
ZUN (VWOOSH)
THERE WE GO...
THANK YOU FOR TAKING SUCH GOOD CARE OF MY DAUGH-TER!!

CREATURE 3: MAKE YOUR CUTE LITTLE GIRL GO ON A JOURNEY

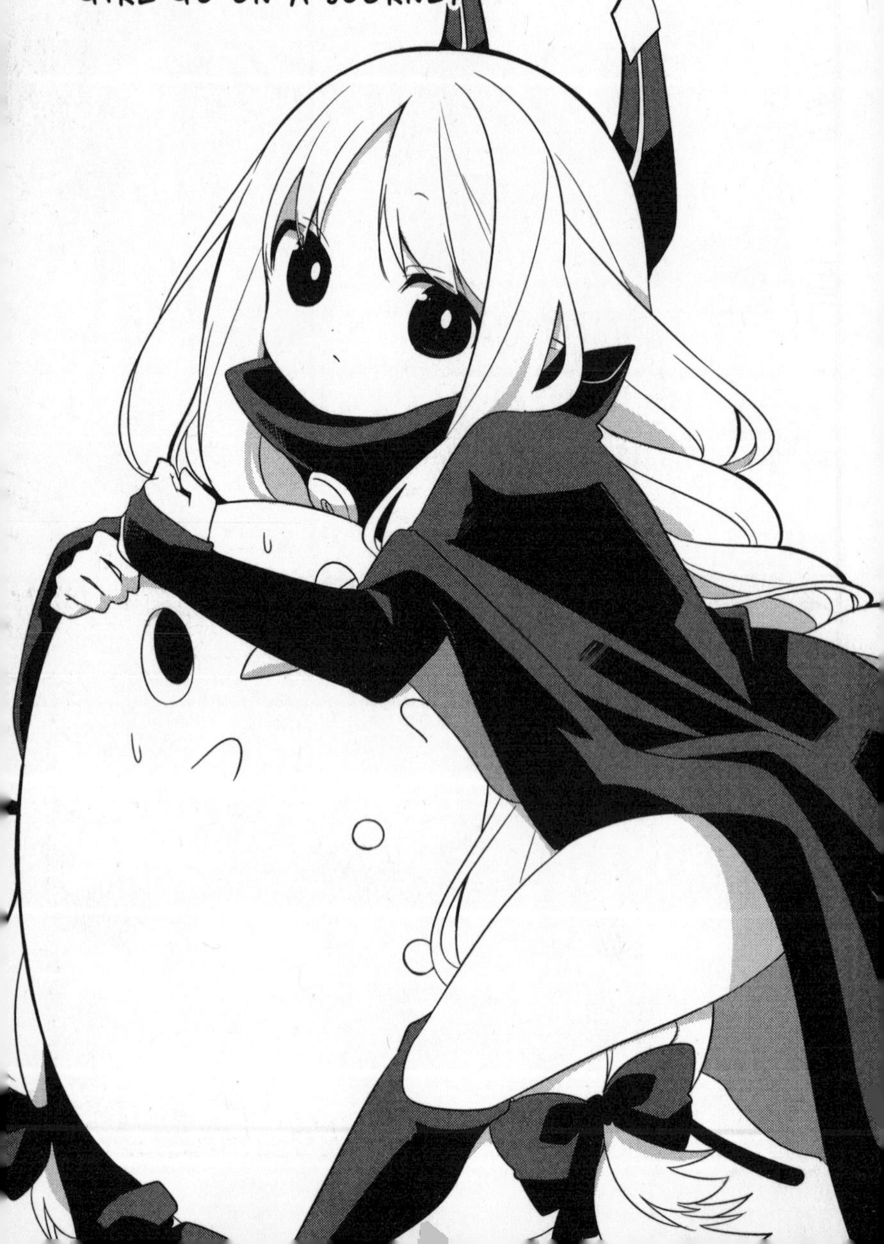

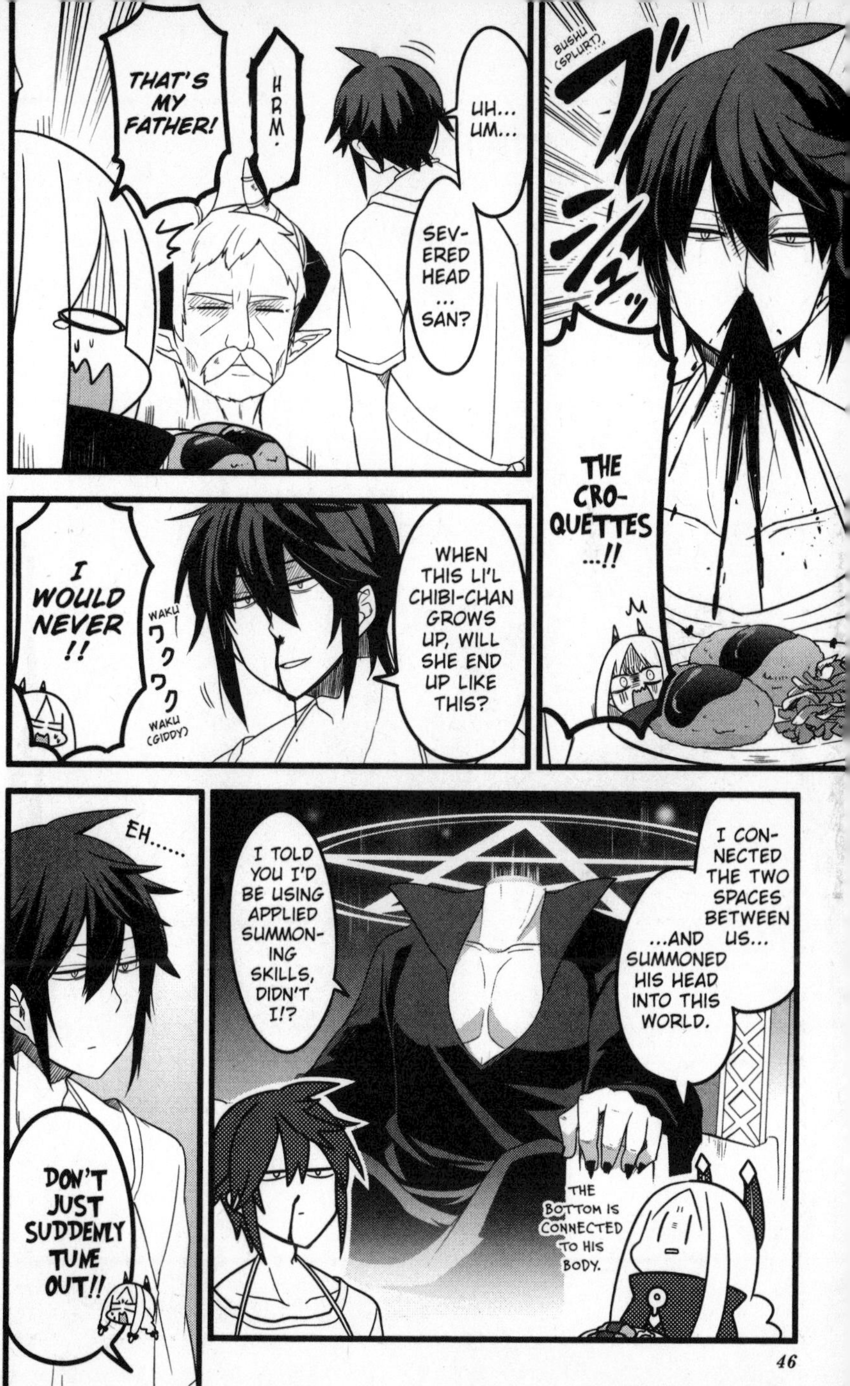
BUSHU (SPLURT)
THE CROQUETTES ...!!
UH... UM...
SEVERED HEAD ... SAN?
HRM.
THAT'S MY FATHER!
WHEN THIS LI'L CHIBI-CHAN GROWS UP, WILL SHE END UP LIKE THIS?
WAKU WAKU (GIDDY)
I WOULD NEVER!!
I CONNECTED THE TWO SPACES BETWEEN US...
...AND SUMMONED HIS HEAD INTO THIS WORLD.
I TOLD YOU I'D BE USING APPLIED SUMMONING SKILLS, DIDN'T I!?
THE BOTTOM IS CONNECTED TO HIS BODY.
EH......
DON'T JUST SUDDENLY TUNE OUT!!

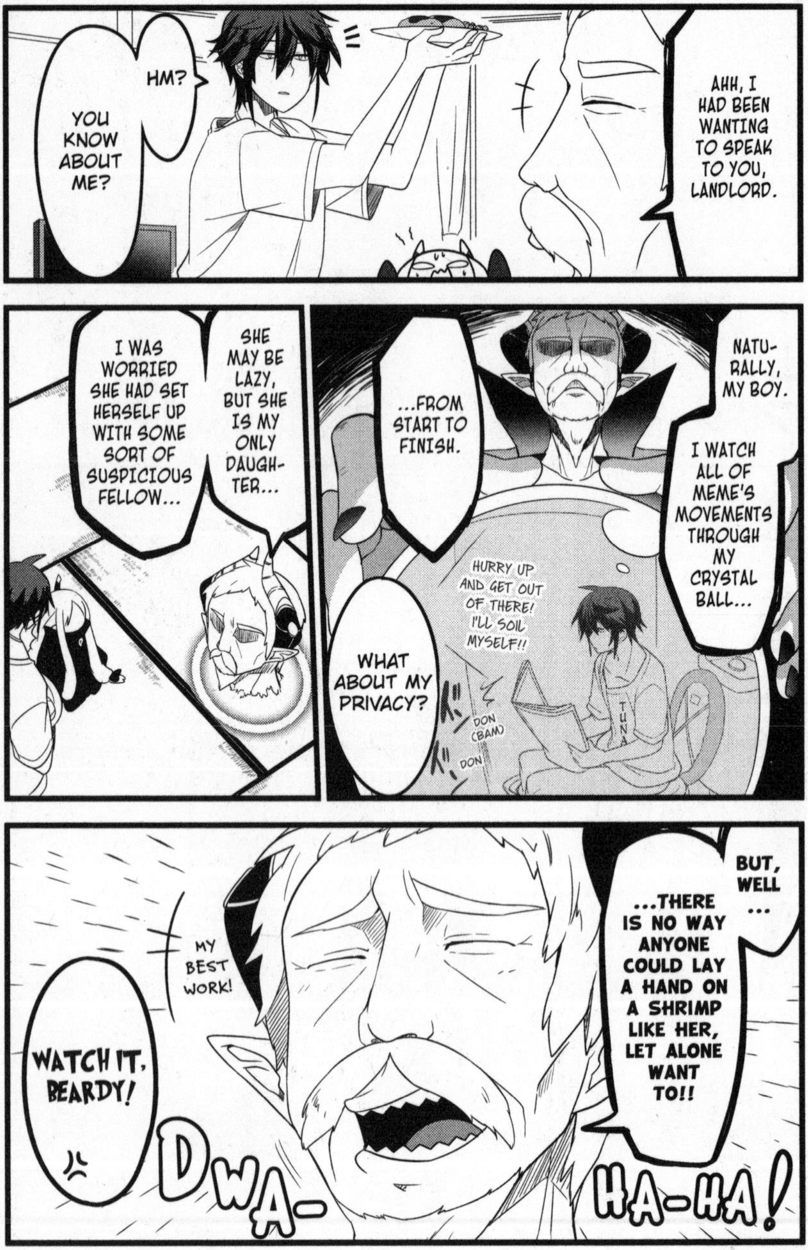
AHH, I HAD BEEN WANTING TO SPEAK TO YOU, LANDLORD.
HM?
YOU KNOW ABOUT ME?
NATURALLY, MY BOY.
I WATCH ALL OF MEME'S MOVEMENTS THROUGH MY CRYSTAL BALL...
...FROM START TO FINISH.
HURRY UP AND GET OUT OF THERE! I'LL SOIL MYSELF!!
DON (BAM)
DON
WHAT ABOUT MY PRIVACY?
SHE MAY BE LAZY, BUT SHE IS MY ONLY DAUGHTER...
I WAS WORRIED SHE HAD SET HERSELF UP WITH SOME SORT OF SUSPICIOUS FELLOW...
BUT, WELL...
...THERE IS NO WAY ANYONE COULD LAY A HAND ON A SHRIMP LIKE HER, LET ALONE WANT TO!!
DWA-HA-HA!
MY BEST WORK!
WATCH IT, BEARDY!

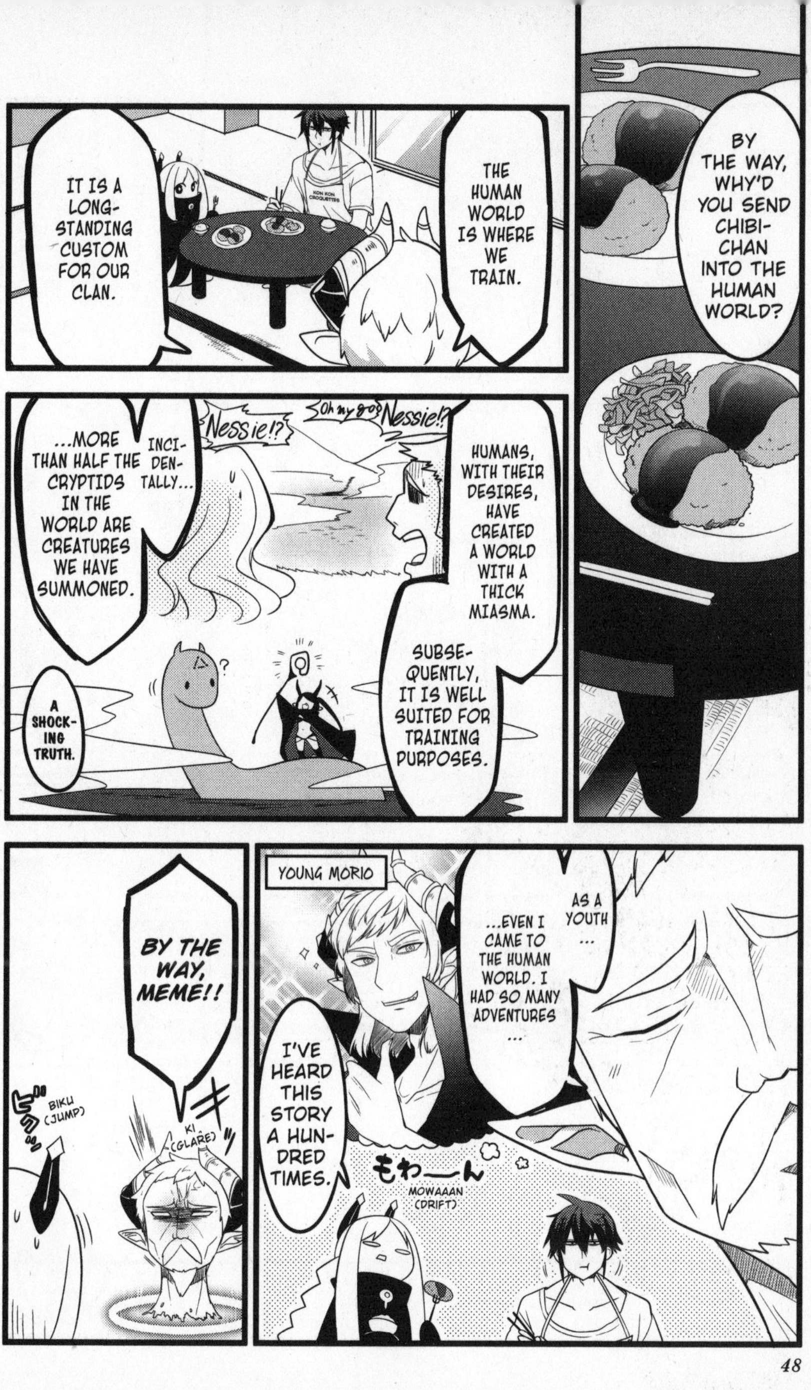

BY THE WAY, WHY'D YOU SEND CHIBI-CHAN INTO THE HUMAN WORLD?
THE HUMAN WORLD IS WHERE WE TRAIN.
IT IS A LONG-STANDING CUSTOM FOR OUR CLAN.
KON KON CROQUETTES
HUMANS, WITH THEIR DESIRES, HAVE CREATED A WORLD WITH A THICK MIASMA.
SUBSEQUENTLY, IT IS WELL SUITED FOR TRAINING PURPOSES.
Nessie!? Oh my god Nessie!?
INCIDENTALLY...
...MORE THAN HALF THE CRYPTIDS IN THE WORLD ARE CREATURES WE HAVE SUMMONED.
A SHOCKING TRUTH.
YOUNG MORIO
AS A YOUTH...
...EVEN I CAME TO THE HUMAN WORLD. I HAD SO MANY ADVENTURES...
I'VE HEARD THIS STORY A HUNDRED TIMES.
もわーん
MOWAAAN (DRIFT)
BY THE WAY, MEME!!
KI (GLARE)
BIKU (JUMP)

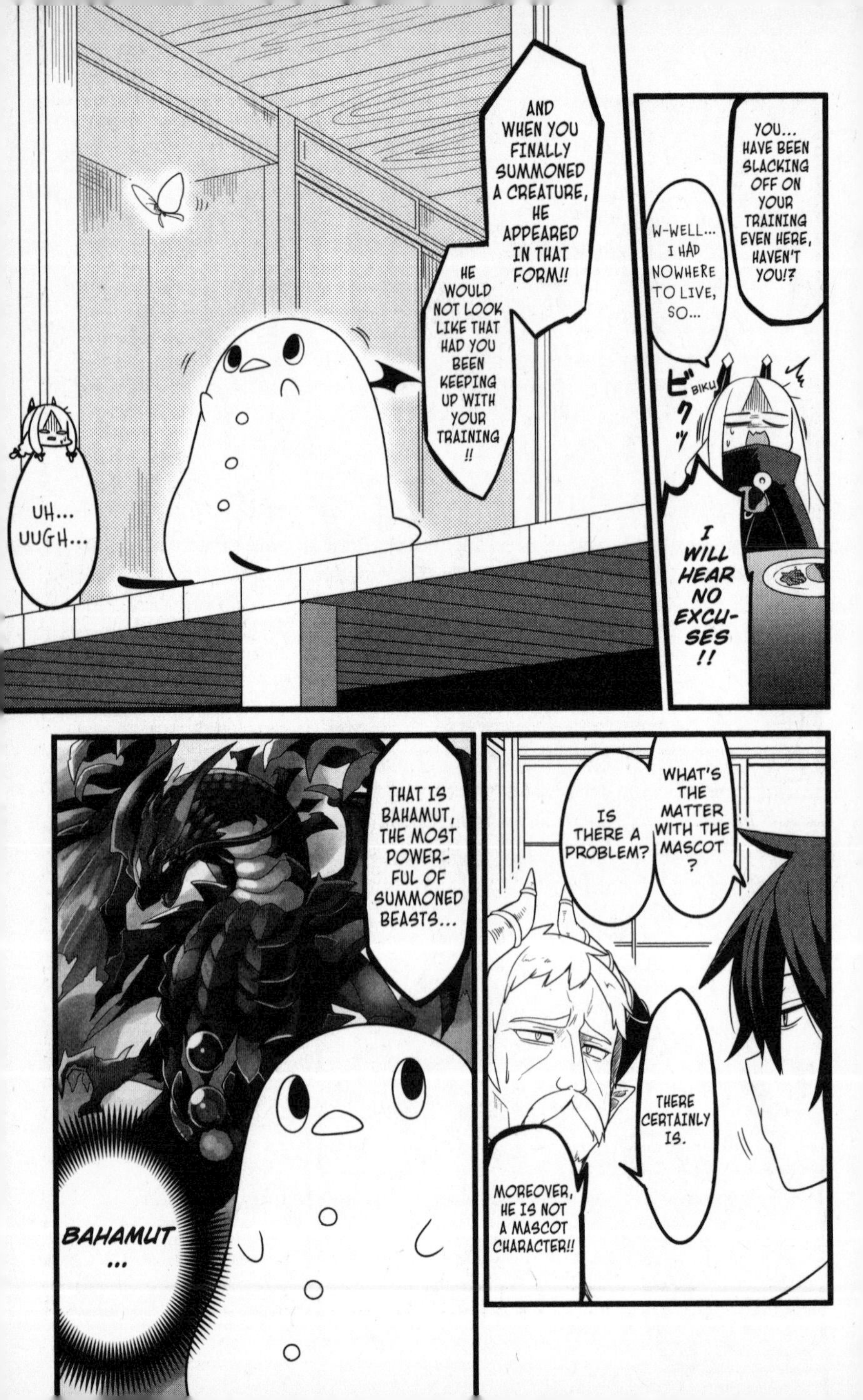
YOU... HAVE BEEN SLACKING OFF ON YOUR TRAINING EVEN HERE, HAVEN'T YOU!?
W-WELL... I HAD NOWHERE TO LIVE, SO...
ビクッ BIKU
I WILL HEAR NO EXCUSES!!
AND WHEN YOU FINALLY SUMMONED A CREATURE, HE APPEARED IN THAT FORM!!
HE WOULD NOT LOOK LIKE THAT HAD YOU BEEN KEEPING UP WITH YOUR TRAINING!!
UH... UUGH...
WHAT'S THE MATTER WITH THE MASCOT?
IS THERE A PROBLEM?
THERE CERTAINLY IS.
MOREOVER, HE IS NOT A MASCOT CHARACTER!!
THAT IS BAHAMUT, THE MOST POWERFUL OF SUMMONED BEASTS...
BAHAMUT...

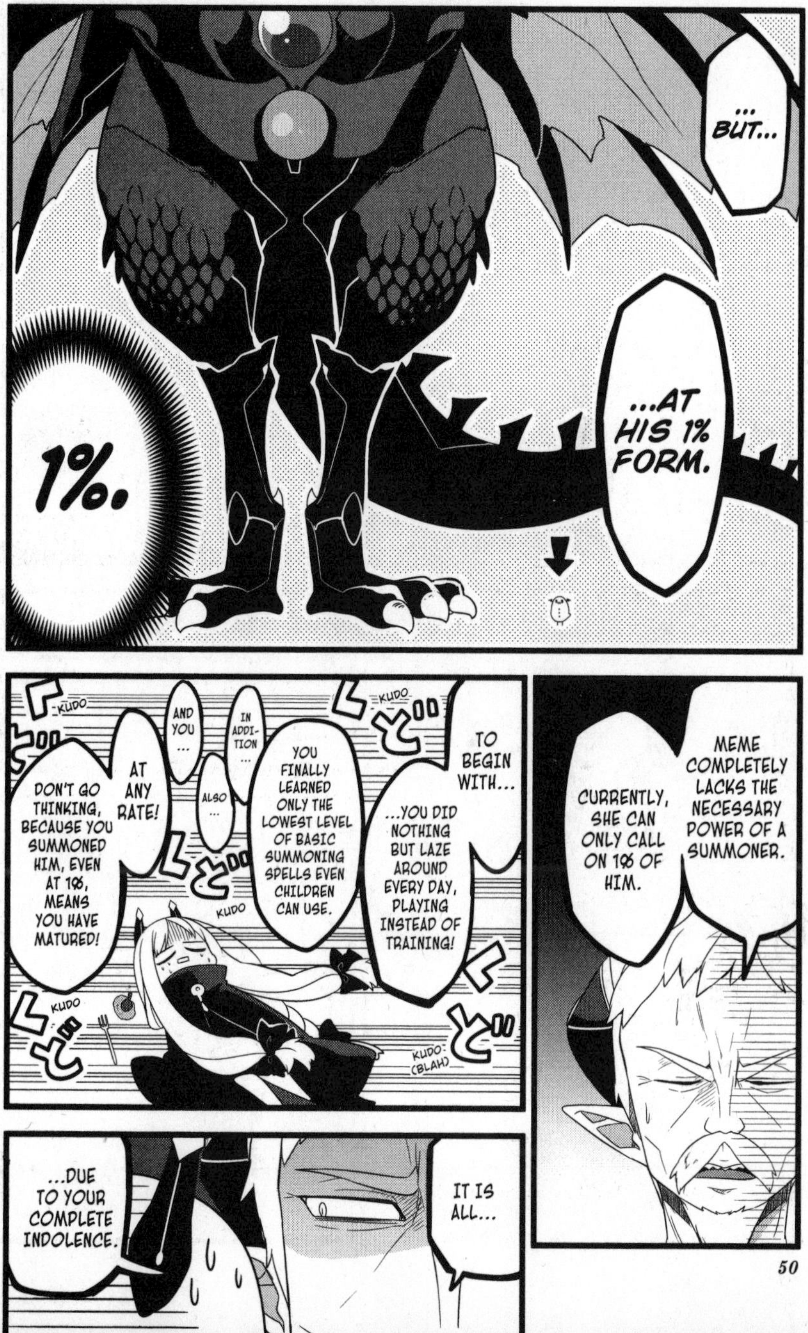

... BUT...
...AT HIS 1% FORM.
1%.
MEME COMPLETELY LACKS THE NECESSARY POWER OF A SUMMONER.
CURRENTLY, SHE CAN ONLY CALL ON 1% OF HIM.
KUDO
TO BEGIN WITH...
...YOU DID NOTHING BUT LAZE AROUND EVERY DAY, PLAYING INSTEAD OF TRAINING!
IN ADDITION...
YOU FINALLY LEARNED ONLY THE LOWEST LEVEL OF BASIC SUMMONING SPELLS EVEN CHILDREN CAN USE.
AND YOU...
ALSO...
KUDO
AT ANY RATE!
DON'T GO THINKING, BECAUSE YOU SUMMONED HIM, EVEN AT 1%, MEANS YOU HAVE MATURED!
KUDO
KUDO (BLAH)
KUDO
IT IS ALL...
...DUE TO YOUR COMPLETE INDOLENCE.

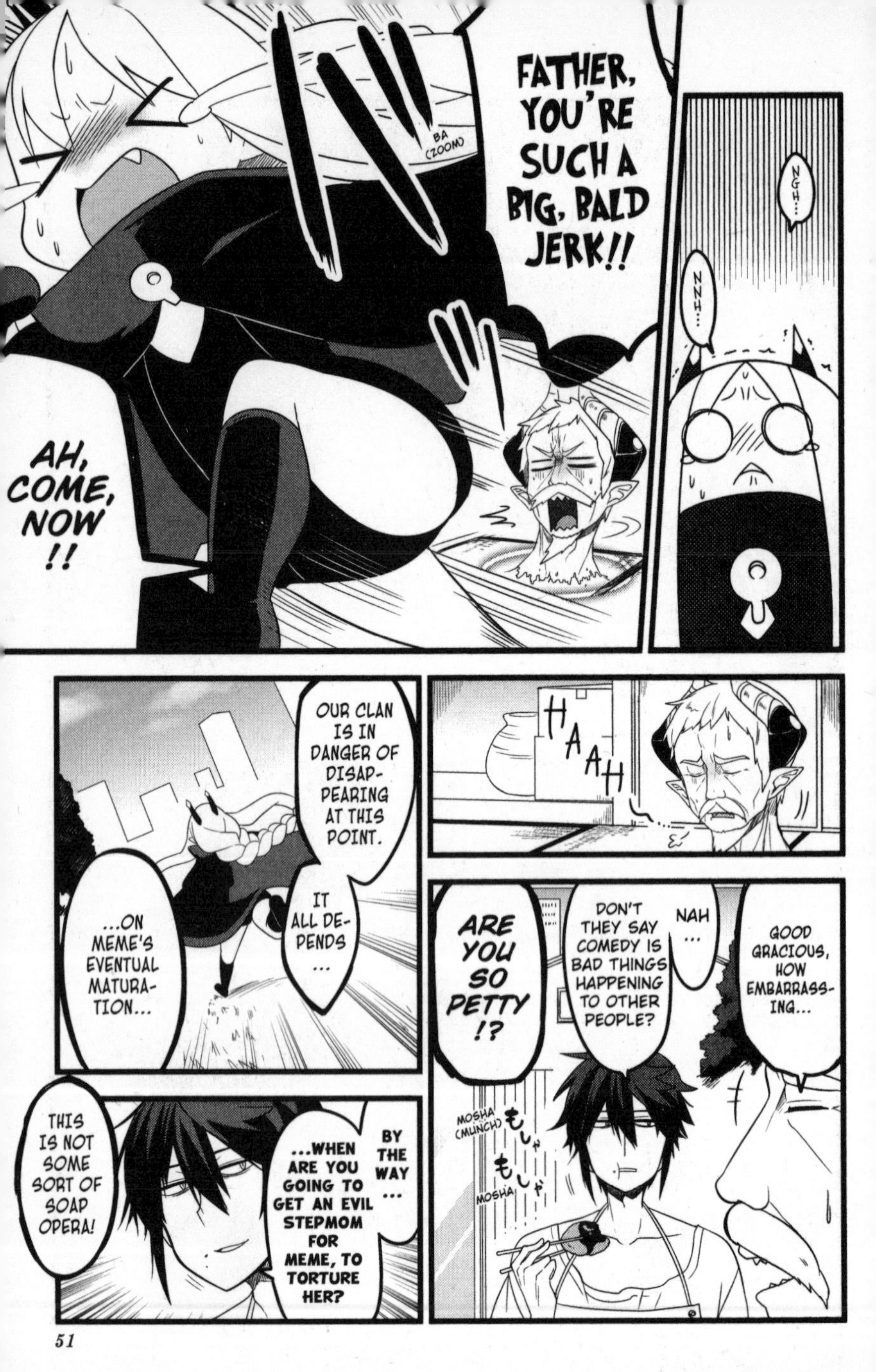
NGH...
NNH...
FATHER, YOU'RE SUCH A BIG, BALD JERK!!
BA (ZOOM)
AH, COME, NOW!!
HAAH
OUR CLAN IS IN DANGER OF DISAP-PEARING AT THIS POINT.
IT ALL DE-PENDS...
...ON MEME'S EVENTUAL MATURA-TION...
GOOD GRACIOUS, HOW EMBARRASS-ING...
NAH...
DON'T THEY SAY COMEDY IS BAD THINGS HAPPENING TO OTHER PEOPLE?
ARE YOU SO PETTY!?
MOSHA (MUNCH) もしゃ
もしゃ MOSHA
BY THE WAY...
...WHEN ARE YOU GOING TO GET AN EVIL STEPMOM FOR MEME, TO TORTURE HER?
THIS IS NOT SOME SORT OF SOAP OPERA!

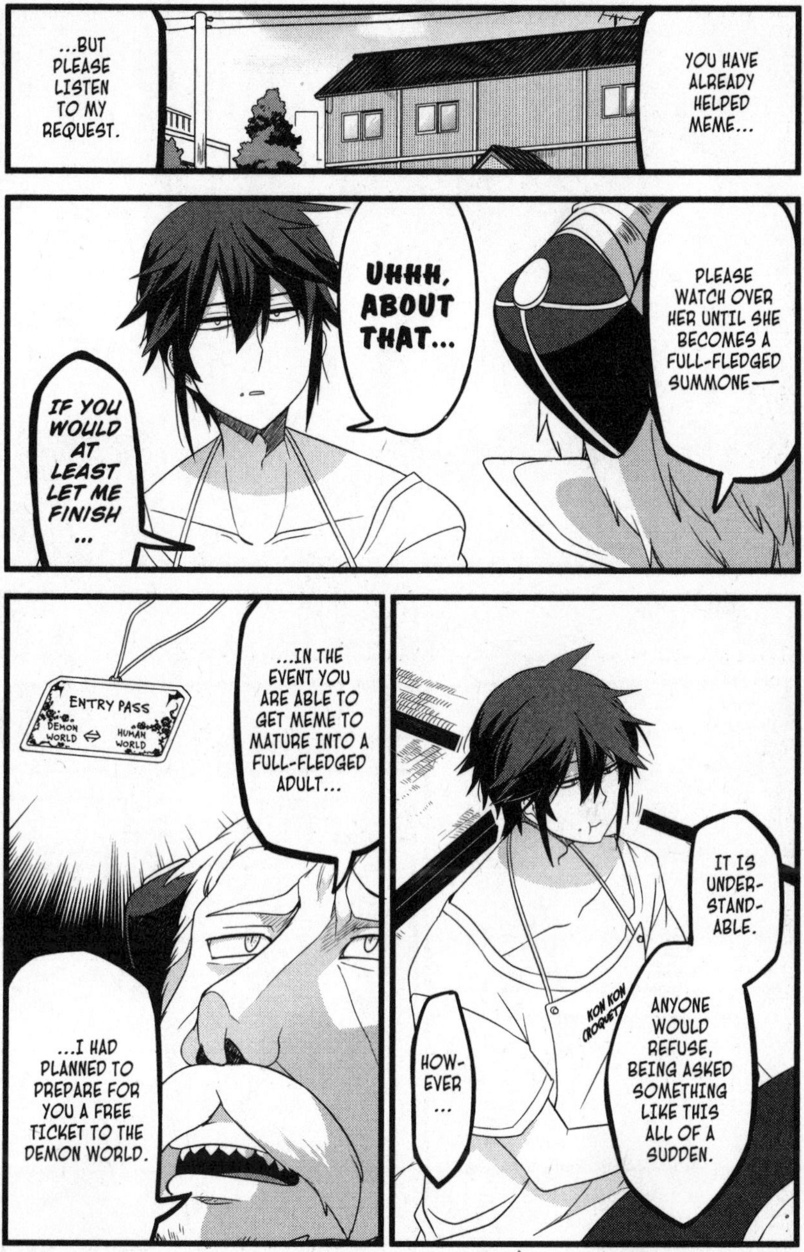
YOU HAVE ALREADY HELPED MEME...
...BUT PLEASE LISTEN TO MY REQUEST.
PLEASE WATCH OVER HER UNTIL SHE BECOMES A FULL-FLEDGED SUMMONE—
UHHH, ABOUT THAT...
IF YOU WOULD AT LEAST LET ME FINISH...
IT IS UNDERSTANDABLE.
ANYONE WOULD REFUSE, BEING ASKED SOMETHING LIKE THIS ALL OF A SUDDEN.
HOWEVER...
...IN THE EVENT YOU ARE ABLE TO GET MEME TO MATURE INTO A FULL-FLEDGED ADULT...
ENTRY PASS
DEMON WORLD ⇔ HUMAN WORLD
...I HAD PLANNED TO PREPARE FOR YOU A FREE TICKET TO THE DEMON WORLD.

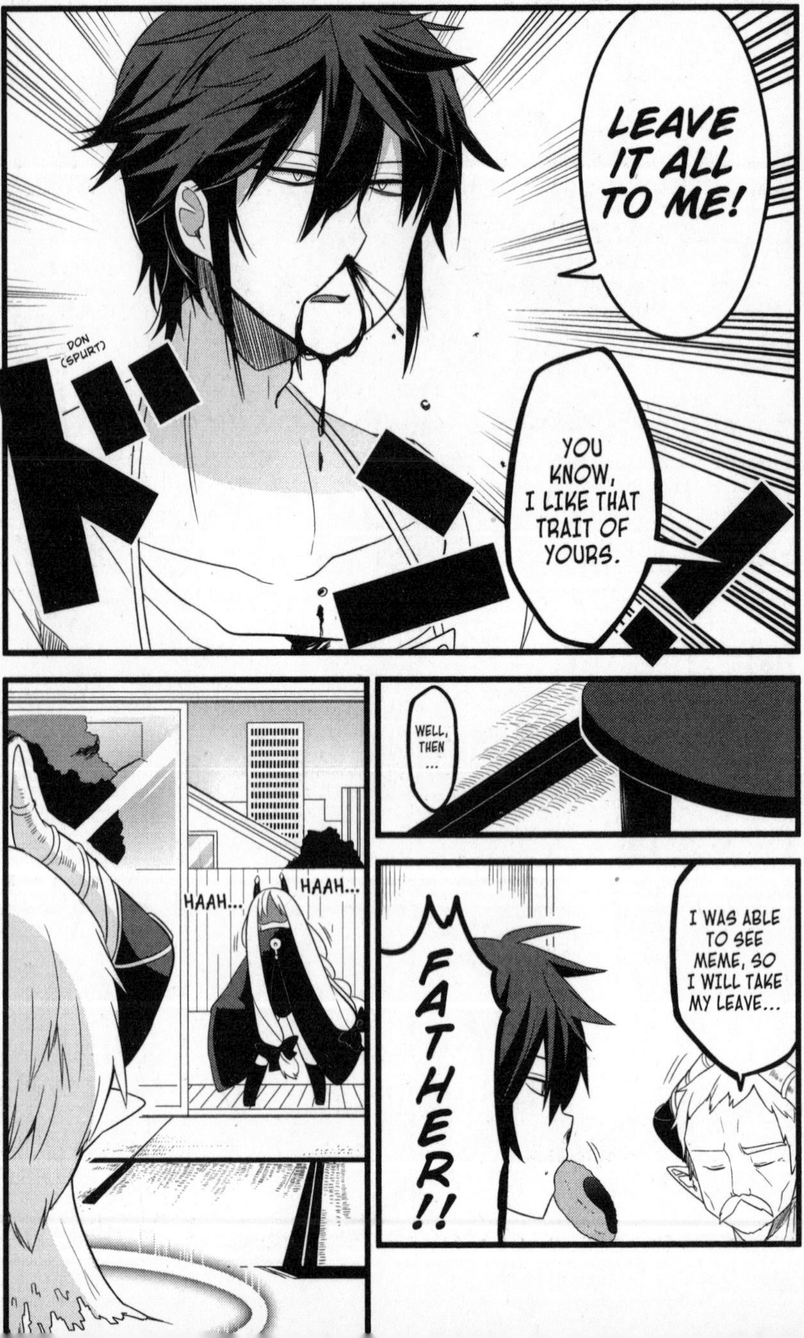
LEAVE IT ALL TO ME!
YOU KNOW, I LIKE THAT TRAIT OF YOURS.
DON (SPURT)
WELL, THEN ...
I WAS ABLE TO SEE MEME, SO I WILL TAKE MY LEAVE...
FATHER!!
HAAH... HAAH...

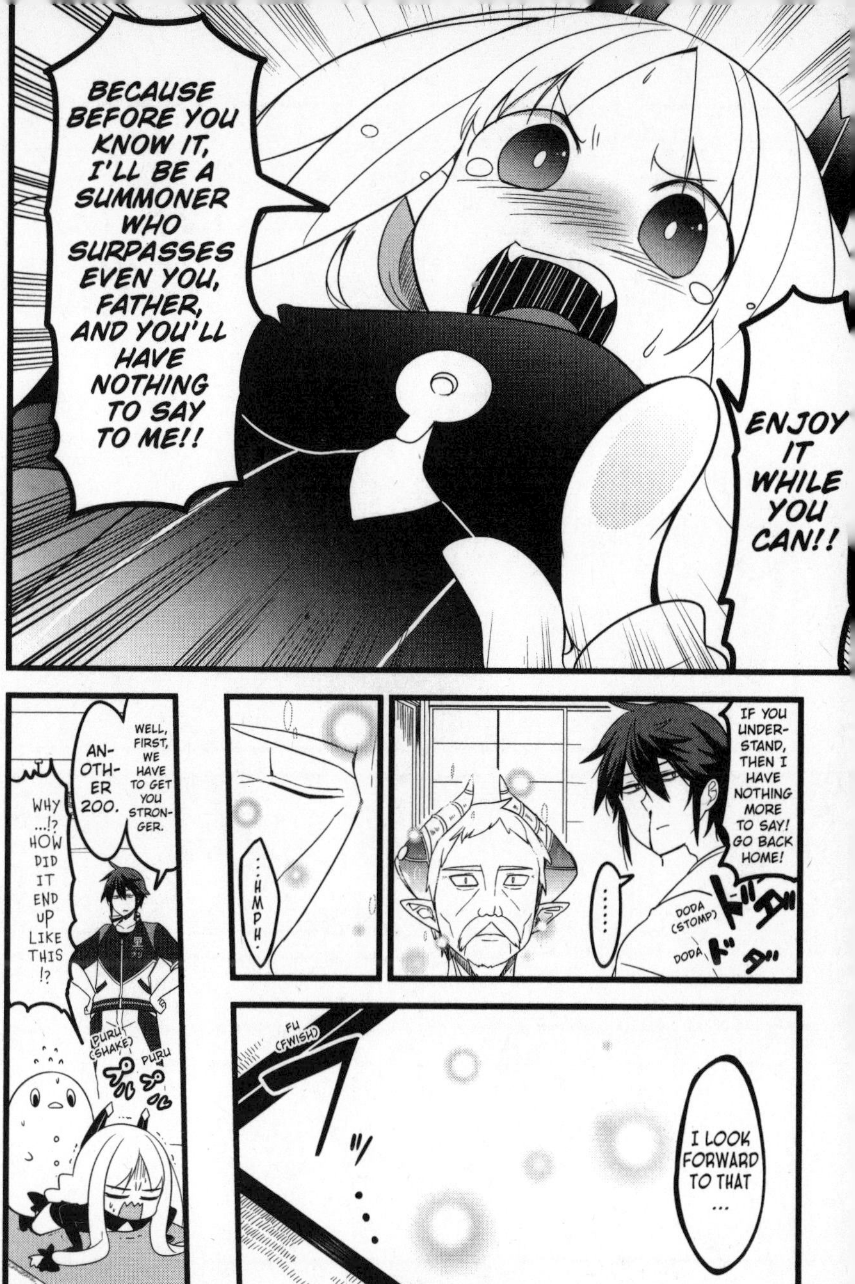
ENJOY IT WHILE YOU CAN!!
BECAUSE BEFORE YOU KNOW IT, I'LL BE A SUMMONER WHO SURPASSES EVEN YOU, FATHER, AND YOU'LL HAVE NOTHING TO SAY TO ME!!
IF YOU UNDER-STAND, THEN I HAVE NOTHING MORE TO SAY! GO BACK HOME!
DODA (STOMP)
DODA
......
...HMPH.
FU (FWISH)
I LOOK FORWARD TO THAT ...
...
WELL, FIRST, WE HAVE TO GET YOU STRON-GER.
AN-OTH-ER 200.
WHY ...!? HOW DID IT END UP LIKE THIS!?
PURU (SHAKE)
PURU

SHIRT: KUROYURI

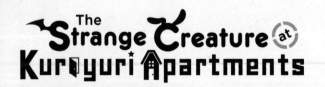

The Strange Creature at Kuroyuri Apartments

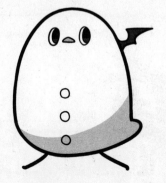

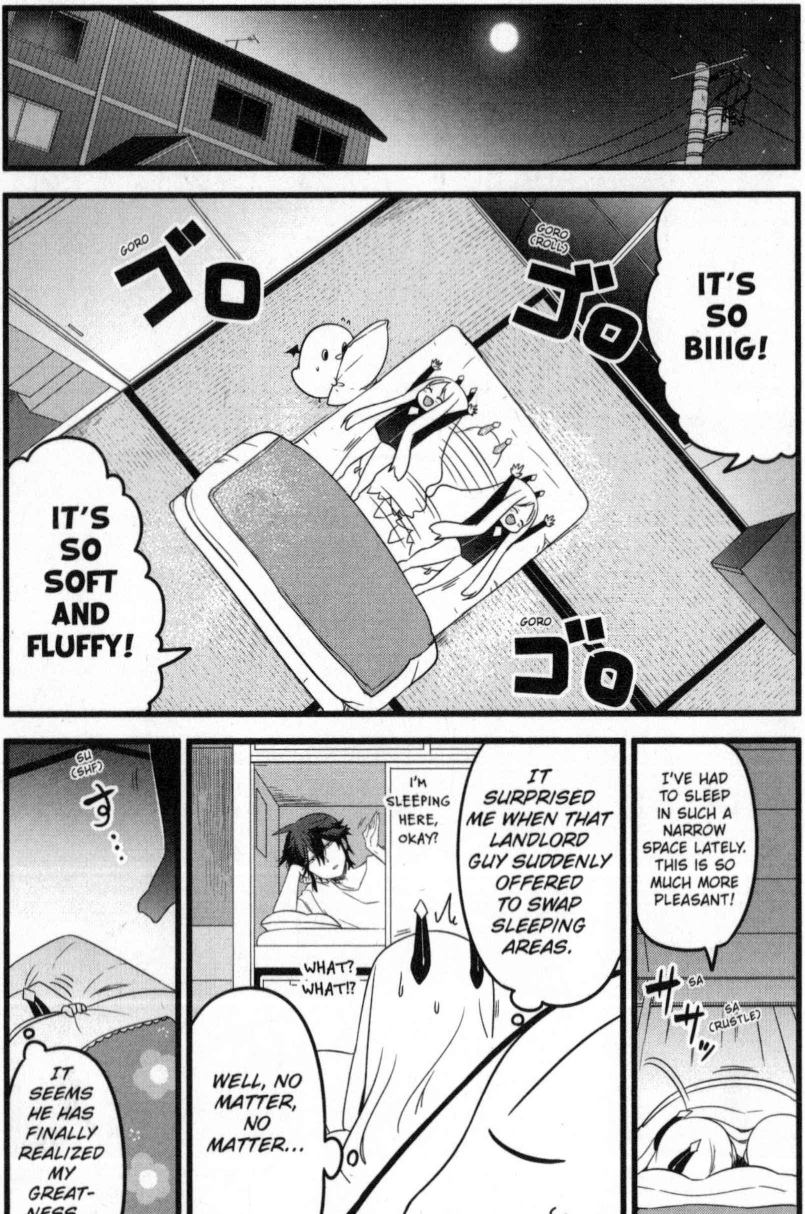
IT'S SO BIIIG!
GORO (ROLL)
ゴロ
GORO
ゴロ
IT'S SO SOFT AND FLUFFY!
GORO
ゴロ
I'VE HAD TO SLEEP IN SUCH A NARROW SPACE LATELY. THIS IS SO MUCH MORE PLEASANT!
SA
サ
SA (RUSTLE)
サッ
IT SURPRISED ME WHEN THAT LANDLORD GUY SUDDENLY OFFERED TO SWAP SLEEPING AREAS.
I'M SLEEPING HERE, OKAY?
WHAT? WHAT!?
WELL, NO MATTER, NO MATTER...
SU (SHF)
す…
IT SEEMS HE HAS FINALLY REALIZED MY GREAT-NESS...

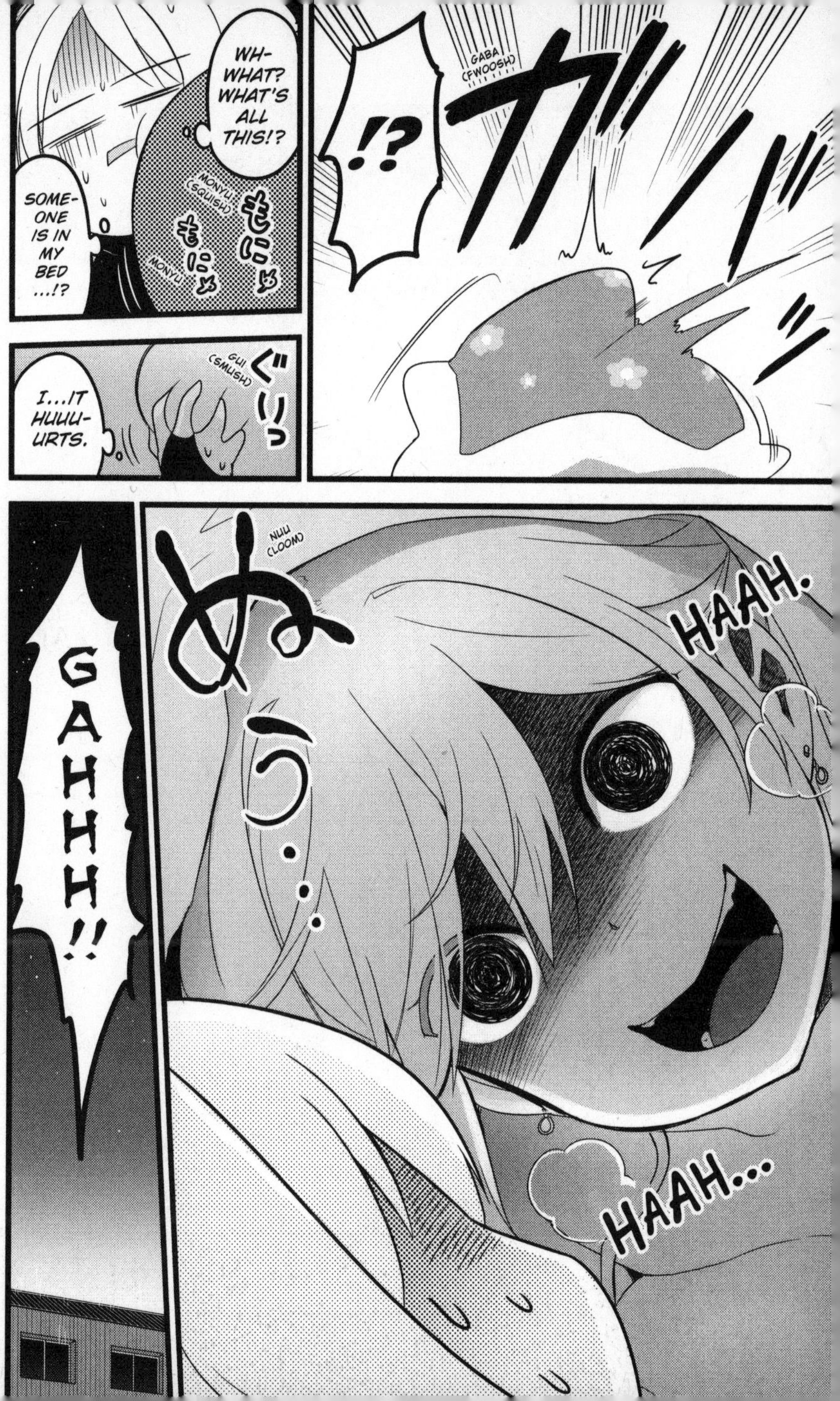
!?
GABA (FWOOSH)
WH-WHAT? WHAT'S ALL THIS!?
MONYU (SQUISH)
MONYU
SOME-ONE IS IN MY BED ...!?
GUI (SMUSH)
I...IT HUUU-URTS.
NUU (LOOM)
HAAH.
HAAH...
GAHHH!!

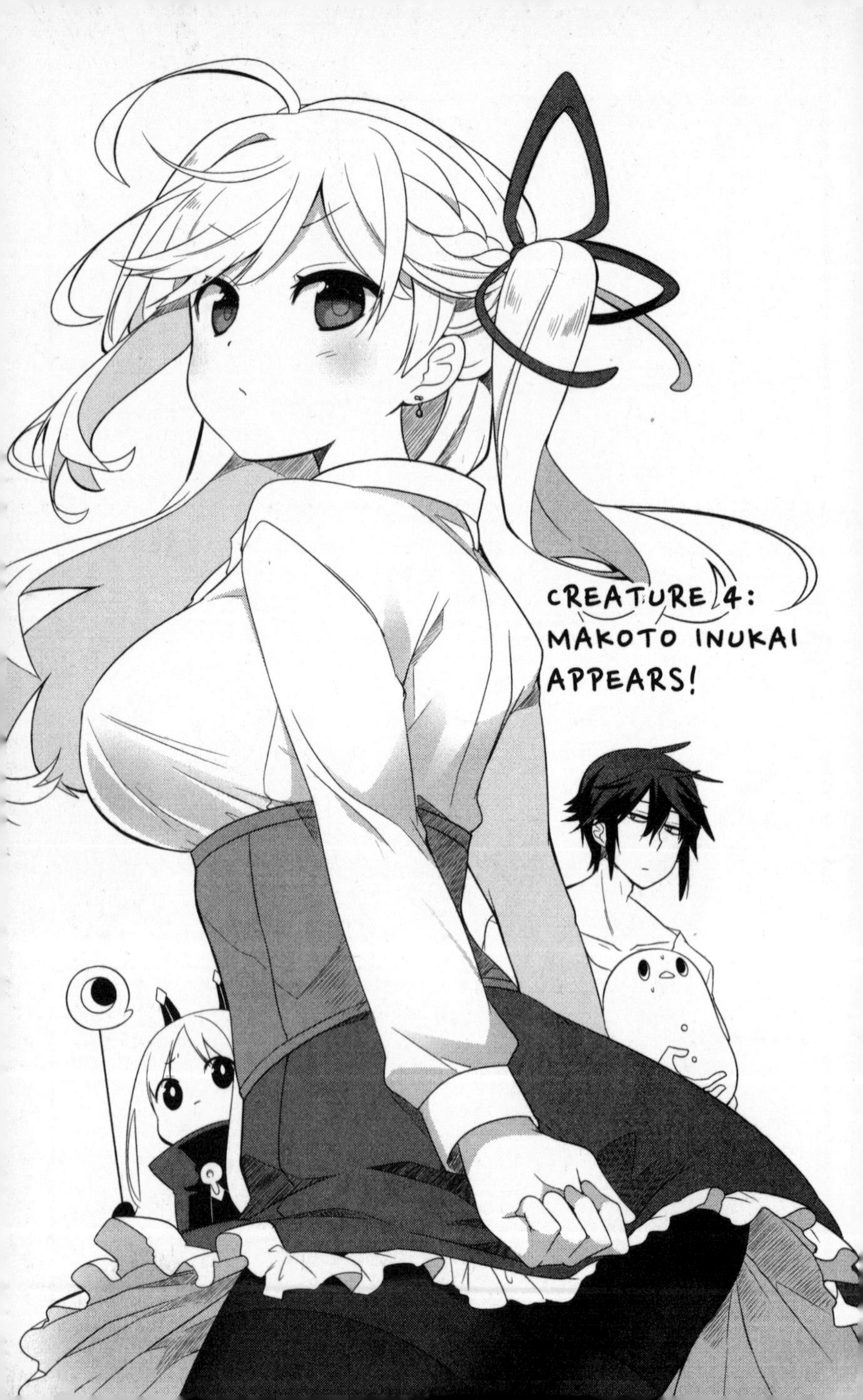
CREATURE 4:
MAKOTO INUKAI
APPEARS!

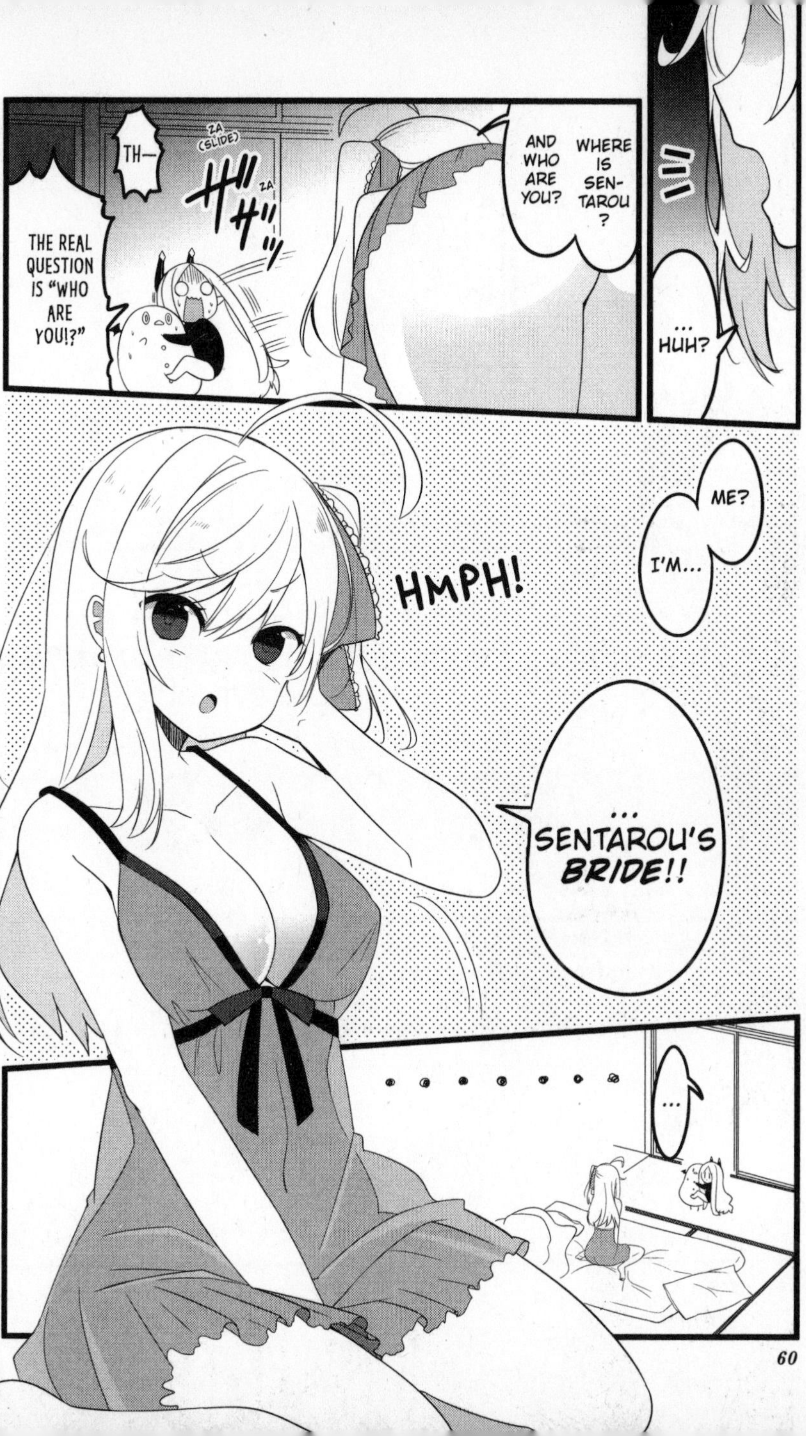
...HUH?
WHERE IS SEN-TAROU?
AND WHO ARE YOU?
ZA (SLIDE)
ZA
TH—
THE REAL QUESTION IS "WHO ARE YOU!?"
ME?
I'M...
HMPH!
...SENTAROU'S BRIDE!!
...

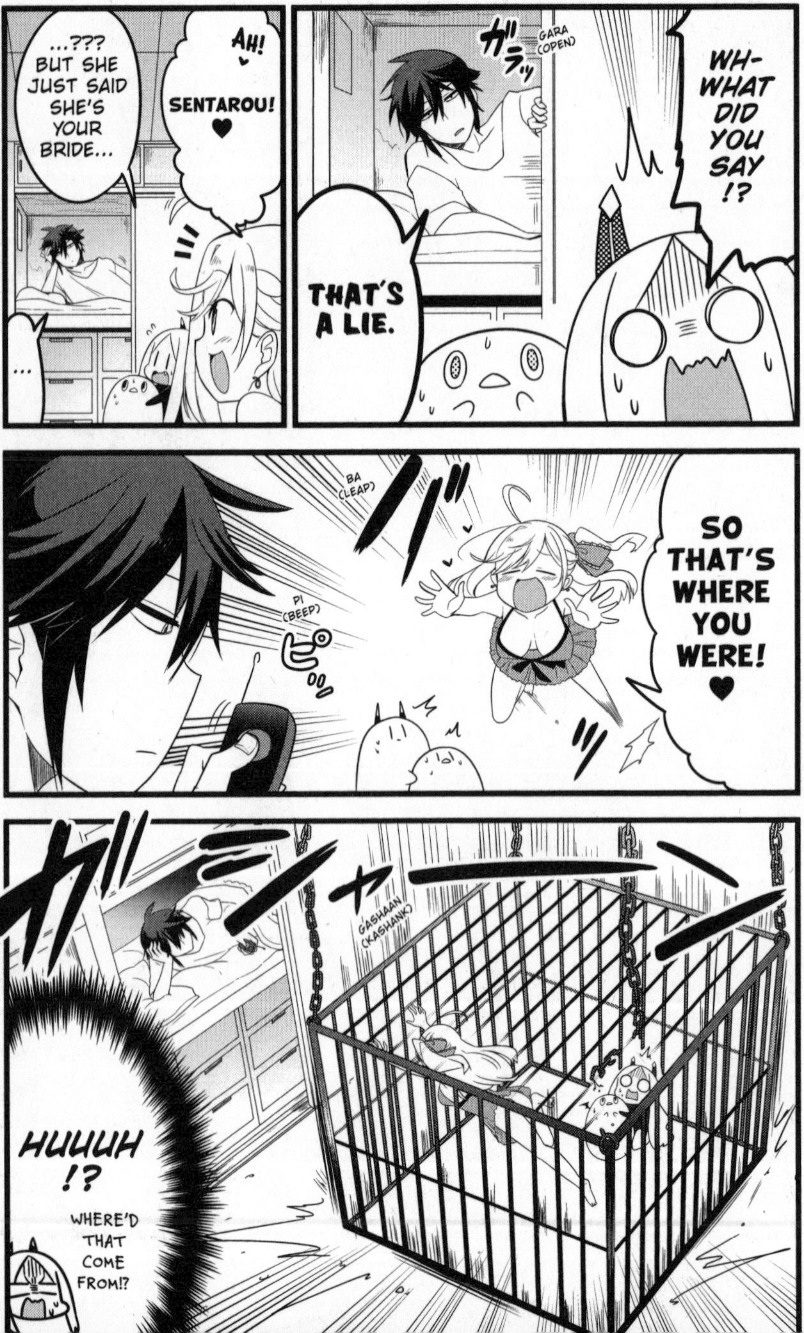
ガラッ
GARA (OPEN)
WH-WHAT DID YOU SAY!?
THAT'S A LIE.
AH! ♥
SENTAROU! ♥
...??? BUT SHE JUST SAID SHE'S YOUR BRIDE...
...
SO THAT'S WHERE YOU WERE! ♥
BA (LEAP)
PI (BEEP)
ピ
ガシャーン
GASHAAN (KASHANK)
HUUUH!?
WHERE'D THAT COME FROM!?

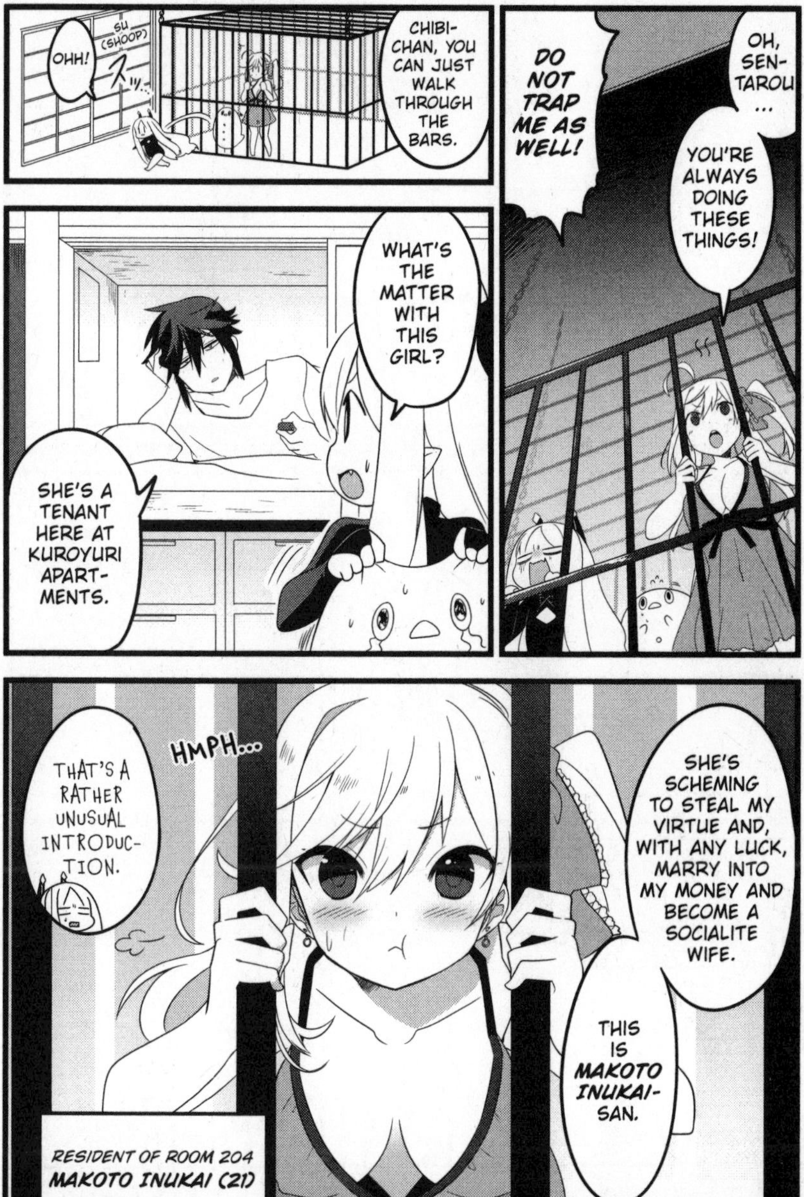
OH, SEN-TAROU...
YOU'RE ALWAYS DOING THESE THINGS!
DO NOT TRAP ME AS WELL!
CHIBI-CHAN, YOU CAN JUST WALK THROUGH THE BARS.
SU (SHOOP)
OHH!
WHAT'S THE MATTER WITH THIS GIRL?
SHE'S A TENANT HERE AT KUROYURI APARTMENTS.
SHE'S SCHEMING TO STEAL MY VIRTUE AND, WITH ANY LUCK, MARRY INTO MY MONEY AND BECOME A SOCIALITE WIFE.
THIS IS MAKOTO INUKAI-SAN.
HMPH...
THAT'S A RATHER UNUSUAL INTRODUCTION.
RESIDENT OF ROOM 204
MAKOTO INUKAI (21)

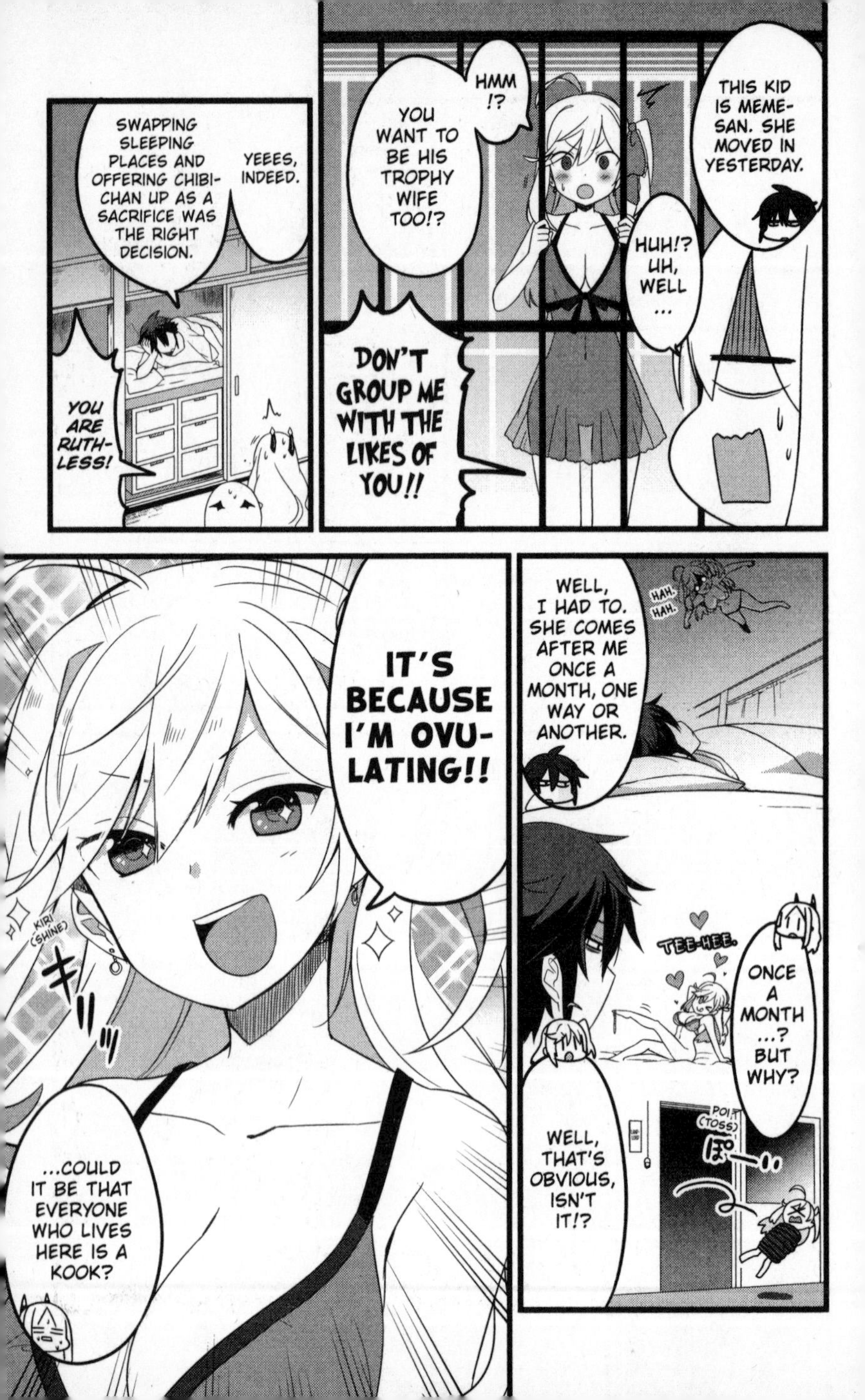
THIS KID IS MEME-SAN. SHE MOVED IN YESTERDAY.
HUH!? UH, WELL ...
HMM !?
YOU WANT TO BE HIS TROPHY WIFE TOO!?
DON'T GROUP ME WITH THE LIKES OF YOU!!
YEEES, INDEED.
SWAPPING SLEEPING PLACES AND OFFERING CHIBI-CHAN UP AS A SACRIFICE WAS THE RIGHT DECISION.
YOU ARE RUTHLESS!
HAH. HAH.
WELL, I HAD TO. SHE COMES AFTER ME ONCE A MONTH, ONE WAY OR ANOTHER.
TEE-HEE.
ONCE A MONTH ...? BUT WHY?
POI (TOSS)
WELL, THAT'S OBVIOUS, ISN'T IT!?
IT'S BECAUSE I'M OVULATING!!
KIRI (SHINE)
...COULD IT BE THAT EVERYONE WHO LIVES HERE IS A KOOK?

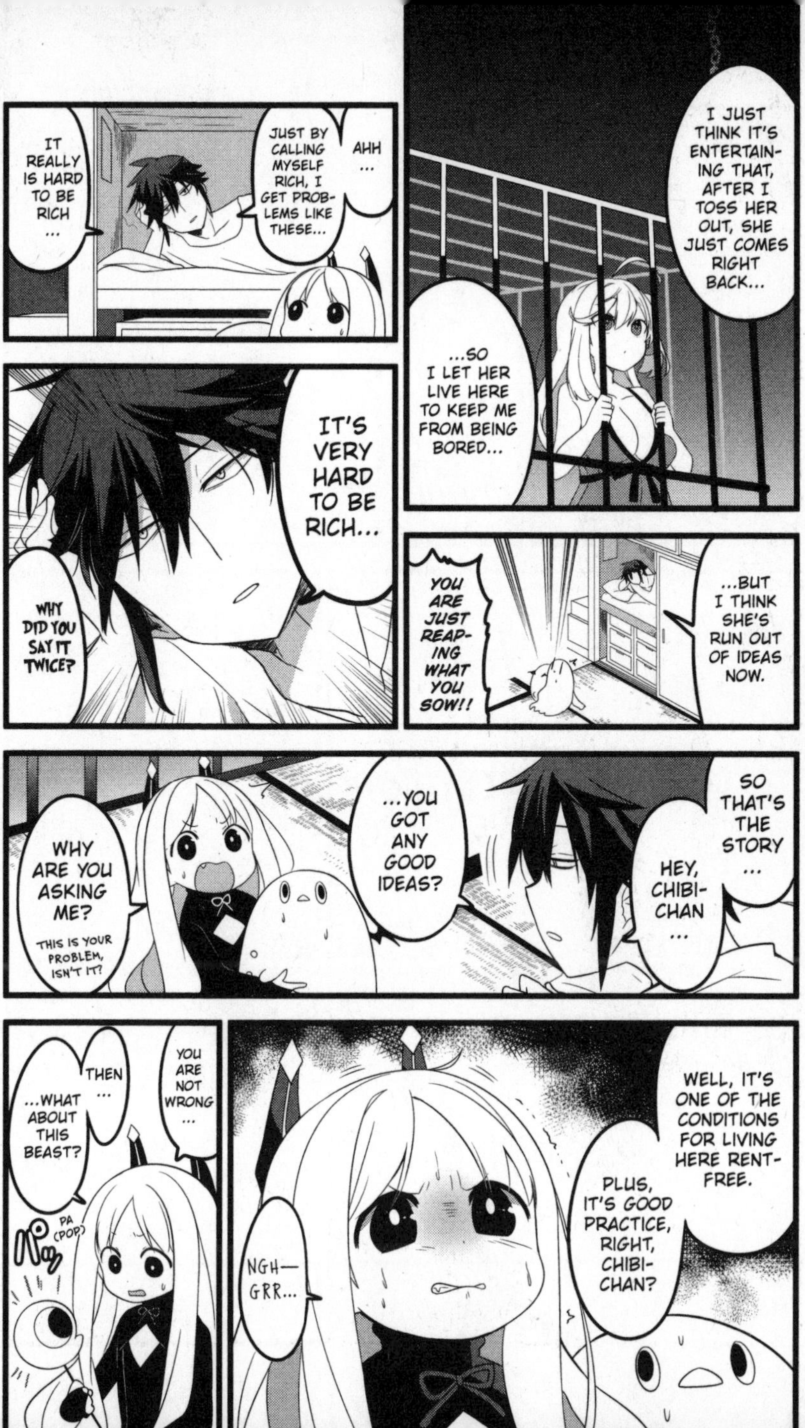
I JUST THINK IT'S ENTERTAINING THAT, AFTER I TOSS HER OUT, SHE JUST COMES RIGHT BACK...
...SO I LET HER LIVE HERE TO KEEP ME FROM BEING BORED...
...BUT I THINK SHE'S RUN OUT OF IDEAS NOW.
YOU ARE JUST REAPING WHAT YOU SOW!!
AHH...
JUST BY CALLING MYSELF RICH, I GET PROBLEMS LIKE THESE...
IT REALLY IS HARD TO BE RICH...
IT'S VERY HARD TO BE RICH...
WHY DID YOU SAY IT TWICE?
SO THAT'S THE STORY...
HEY, CHIBI-CHAN...
...YOU GOT ANY GOOD IDEAS?
WHY ARE YOU ASKING ME?
THIS IS YOUR PROBLEM, ISN'T IT?
WELL, IT'S ONE OF THE CONDITIONS FOR LIVING HERE RENT-FREE.
PLUS, IT'S GOOD PRACTICE, RIGHT, CHIBI-CHAN?
NGH— GRR...
YOU ARE NOT WRONG...
THEN...
...WHAT ABOUT THIS BEAST?
PA (POP)

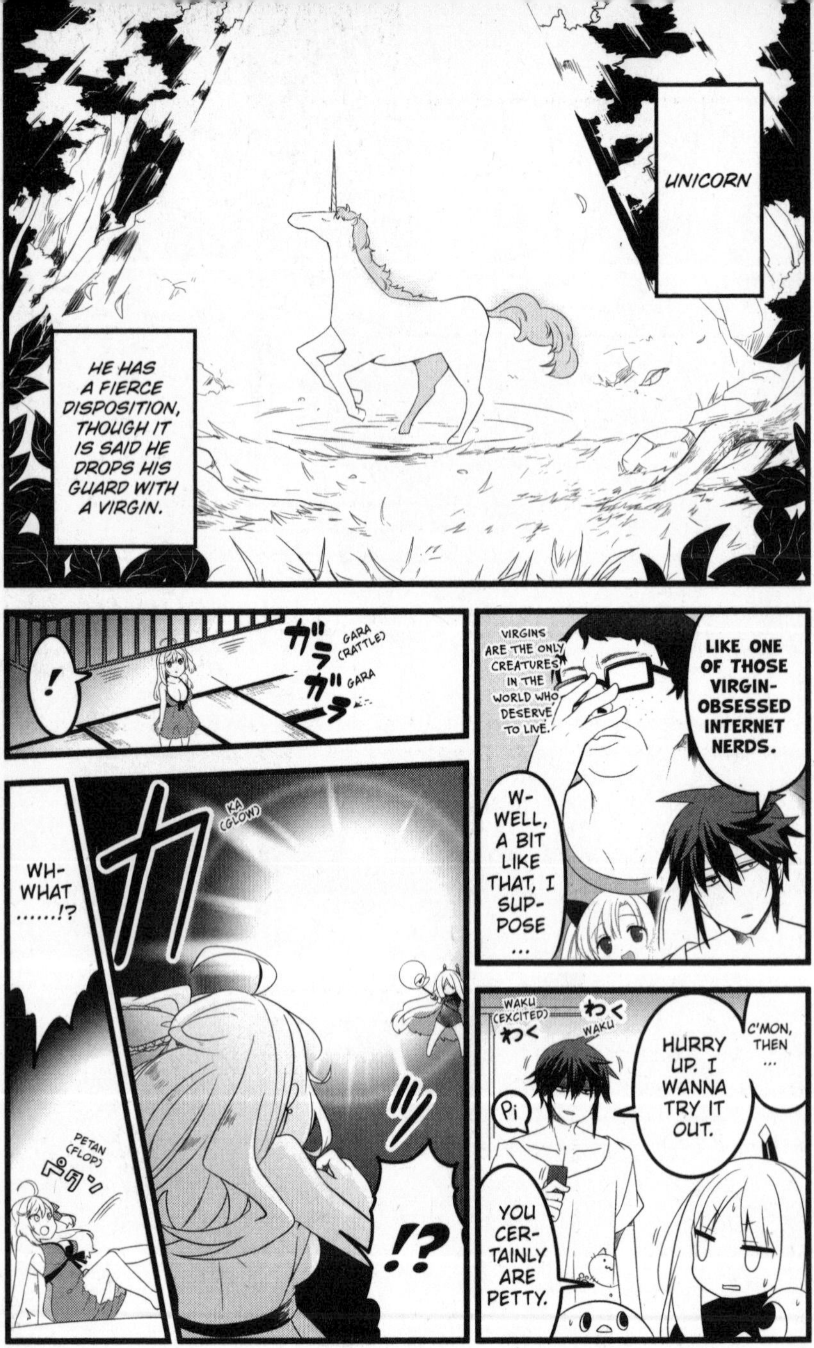
UNICORN
HE HAS A FIERCE DISPOSITION, THOUGH IT IS SAID HE DROPS HIS GUARD WITH A VIRGIN.
LIKE ONE OF THOSE VIRGIN-OBSESSED INTERNET NERDS.
VIRGINS ARE THE ONLY CREATURES IN THE WORLD WHO DESERVE TO LIVE.
W-WELL, A BIT LIKE THAT, I SUPPOSE...
C'MON, THEN...
HURRY UP. I WANNA TRY IT OUT.
わく WAKU
わく WAKU (EXCITED)
Pi
YOU CERTAINLY ARE PETTY.
ガラ GARA (RATTLE)
ガラ GARA
!
カ KA (GLOW)
WH-WHAT......!?
!?
ペタン PETAN (FLOP)

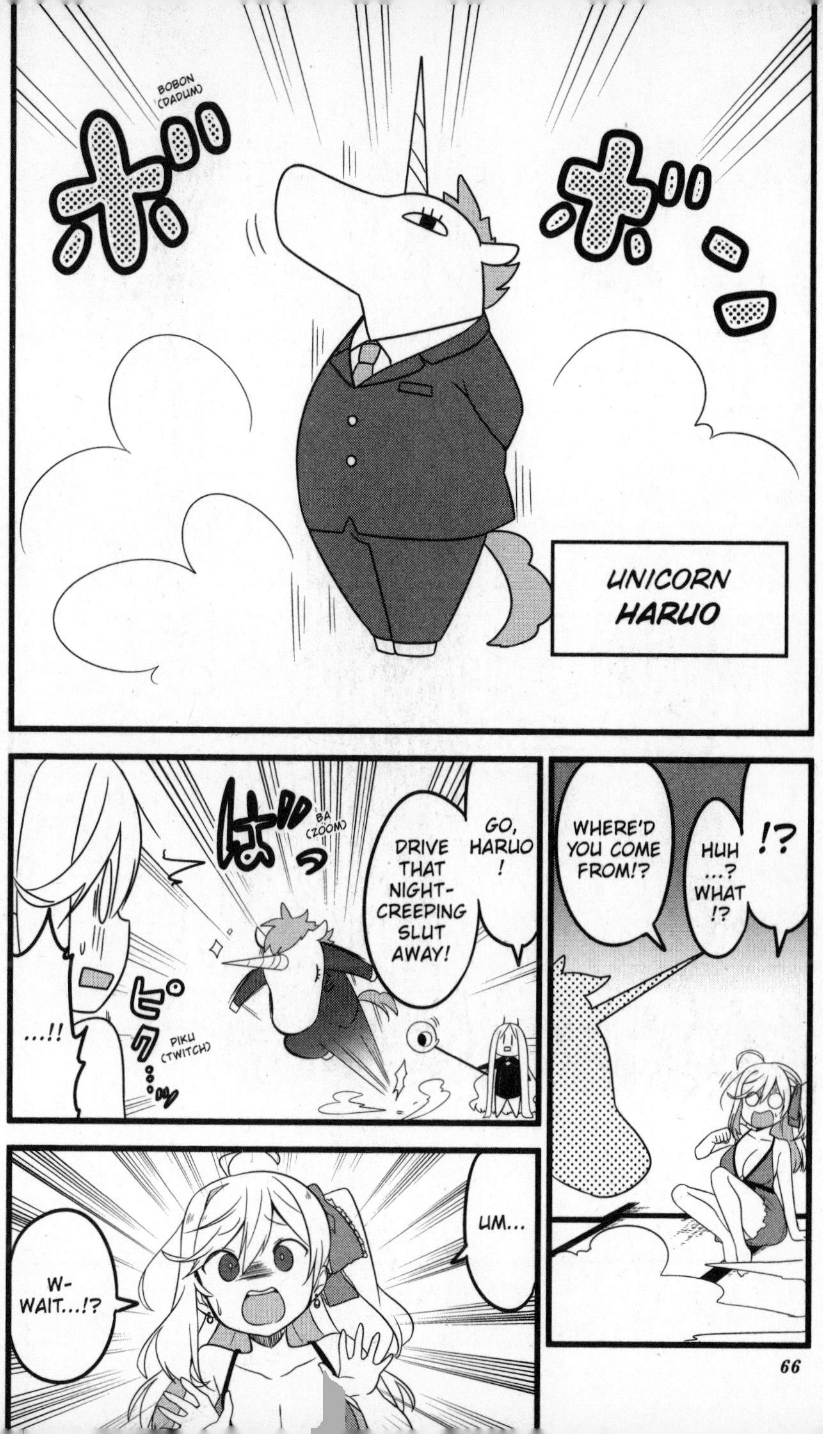
BOBON (DADUM)
UNICORN HARUO
!?
HUH ...? WHAT !?
WHERE'D YOU COME FROM!?
GO, HARUO!
DRIVE THAT NIGHT-CREEPING SLUT AWAY!
BA (ZOOM)
...!!
PIKU (TWITCH)
UM...
W-WAIT...!?

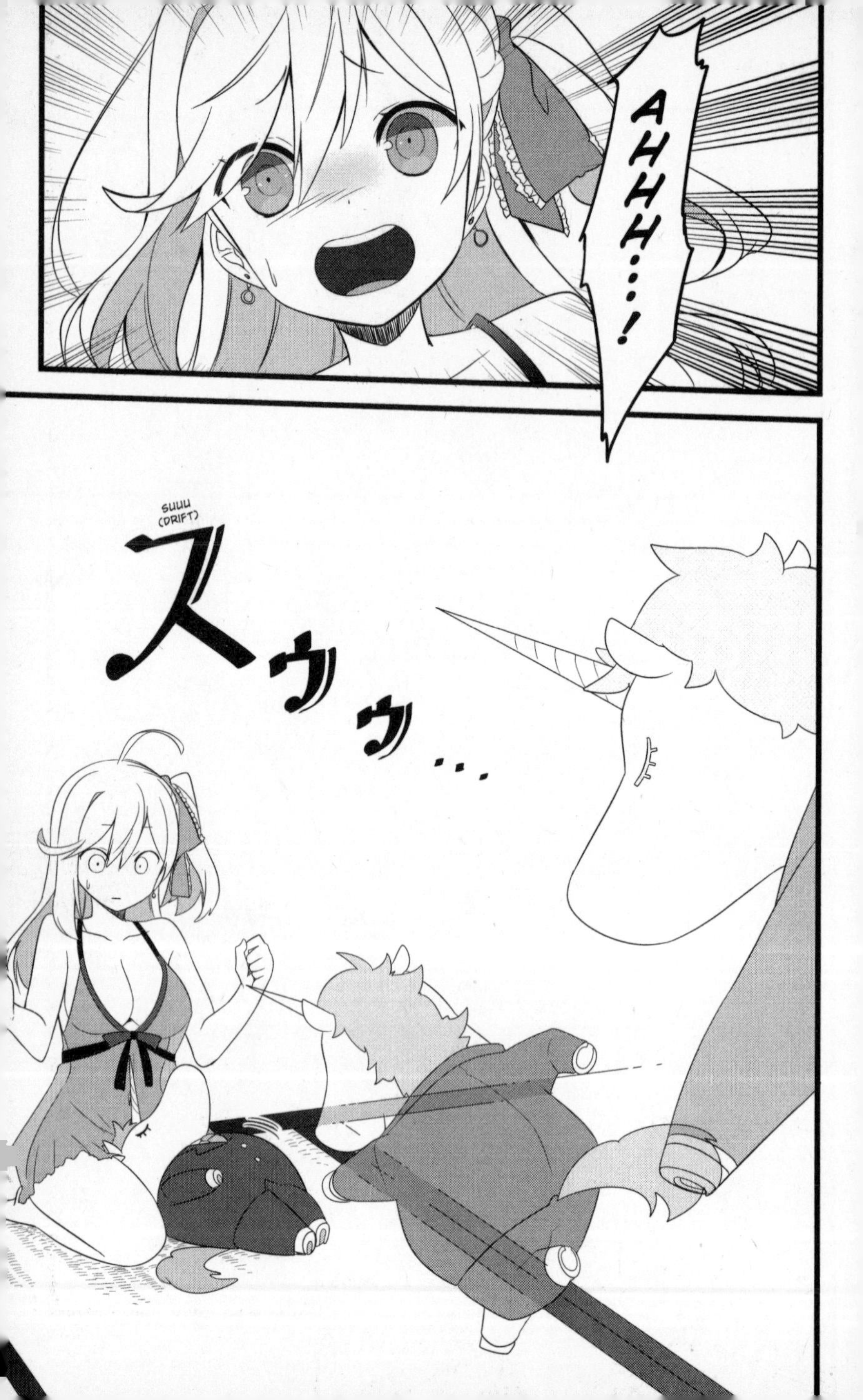
AHHHH...!
SUUU (DRIFT)
スゥゥ...

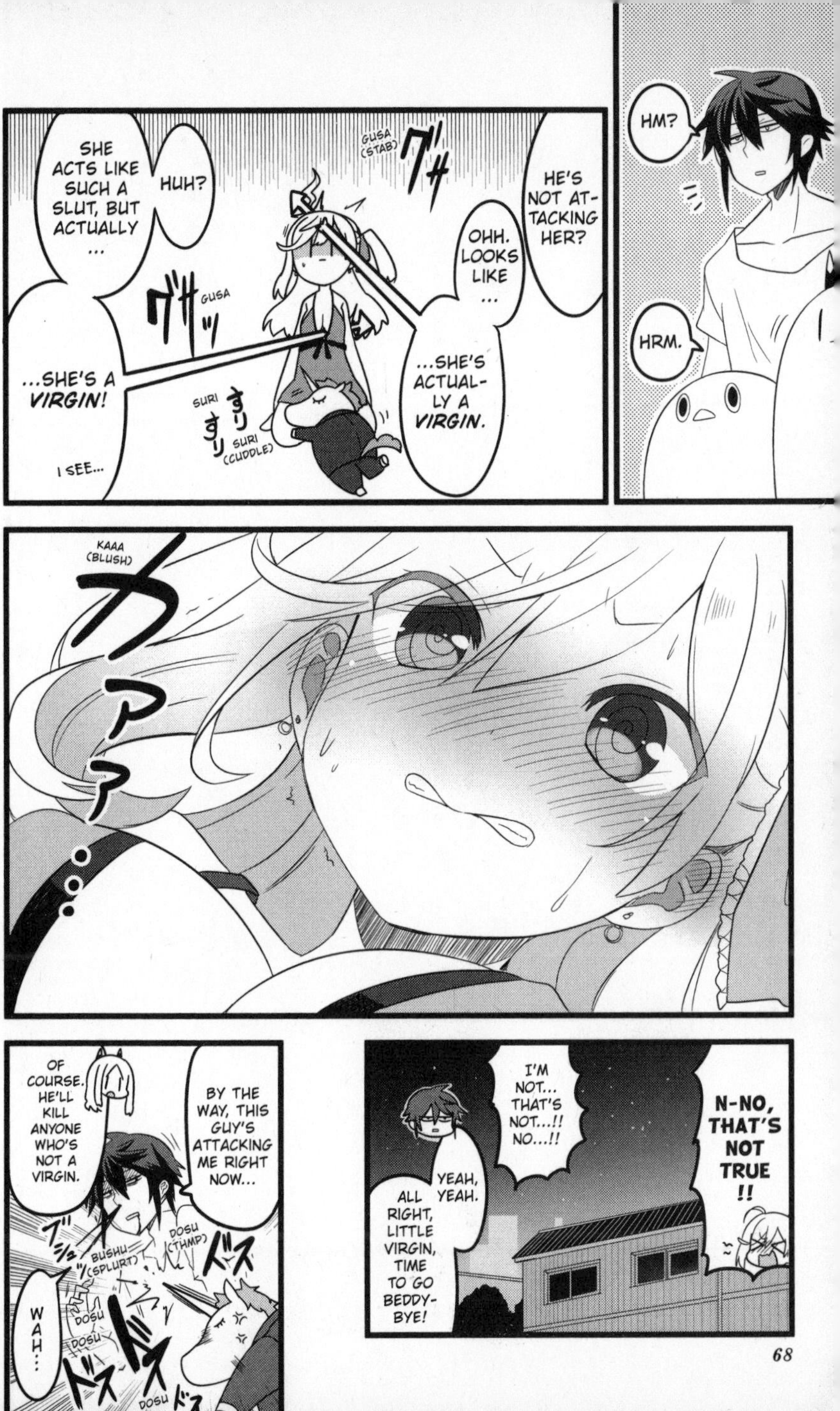
HM?
HRM.
HE'S NOT AT-TACKING HER?
GUSA (STAB)
OHH. LOOKS LIKE ...
HUH?
SHE ACTS LIKE SUCH A SLUT, BUT ACTUALLY ...
...SHE'S ACTUAL-LY A **VIRGIN**.
GUSA
SURI SURI (CUDDLE)
...SHE'S A **VIRGIN**!
I SEE...
KAAA (BLUSH)
N-NO, THAT'S NOT TRUE !!
I'M NOT... THAT'S NOT...!! NO...!!
YEAH, YEAH.
ALL RIGHT, LITTLE VIRGIN, TIME TO GO BEDDY-BYE!
BY THE WAY, THIS GUY'S ATTACKING ME RIGHT NOW...
OF COURSE. HE'LL KILL ANYONE WHO'S NOT A VIRGIN.
DOSU (THUMP)
BUSHU (SPLURT)
WAH...
DOSU
DOSU
DOSU

The Strange Creature at Kuroyuri Apartments

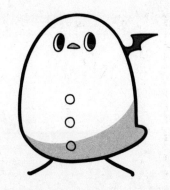

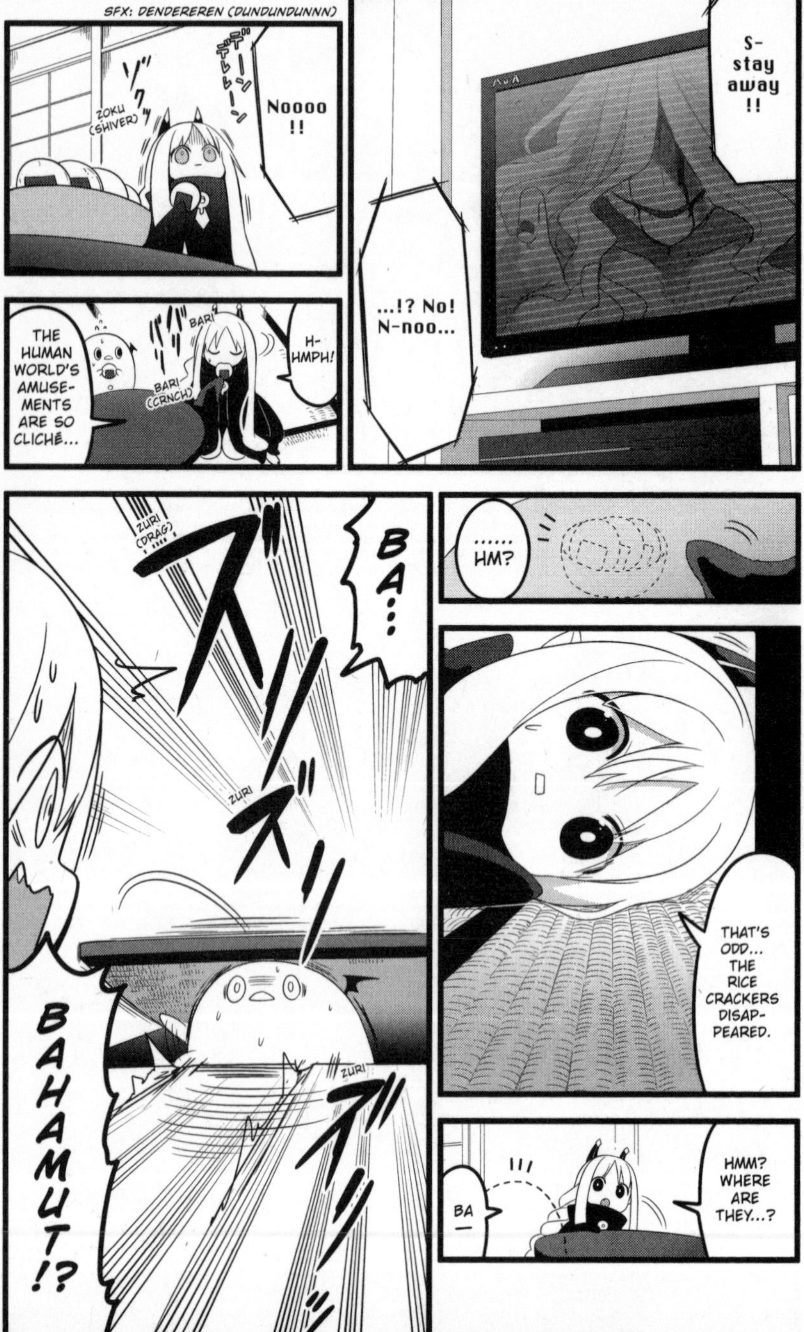
SFX: DENDERE REN (DUNDUNDUNNN)
S-stay away!!
...!? No! N-noo...
Noooo!!
ZOKU (SHIVER)
H-HMPH!
BARI
BARI (CRNCH)
THE HUMAN WORLD'S AMUSEMENTS ARE SO CLICHÉ...
......HM?
THAT'S ODD... THE RICE CRACKERS DISAPPEARED.
HMM? WHERE ARE THEY...?
BA—
BA...
ZURI (DRAG)
ZURI
ZURI
BAHAMUT!?

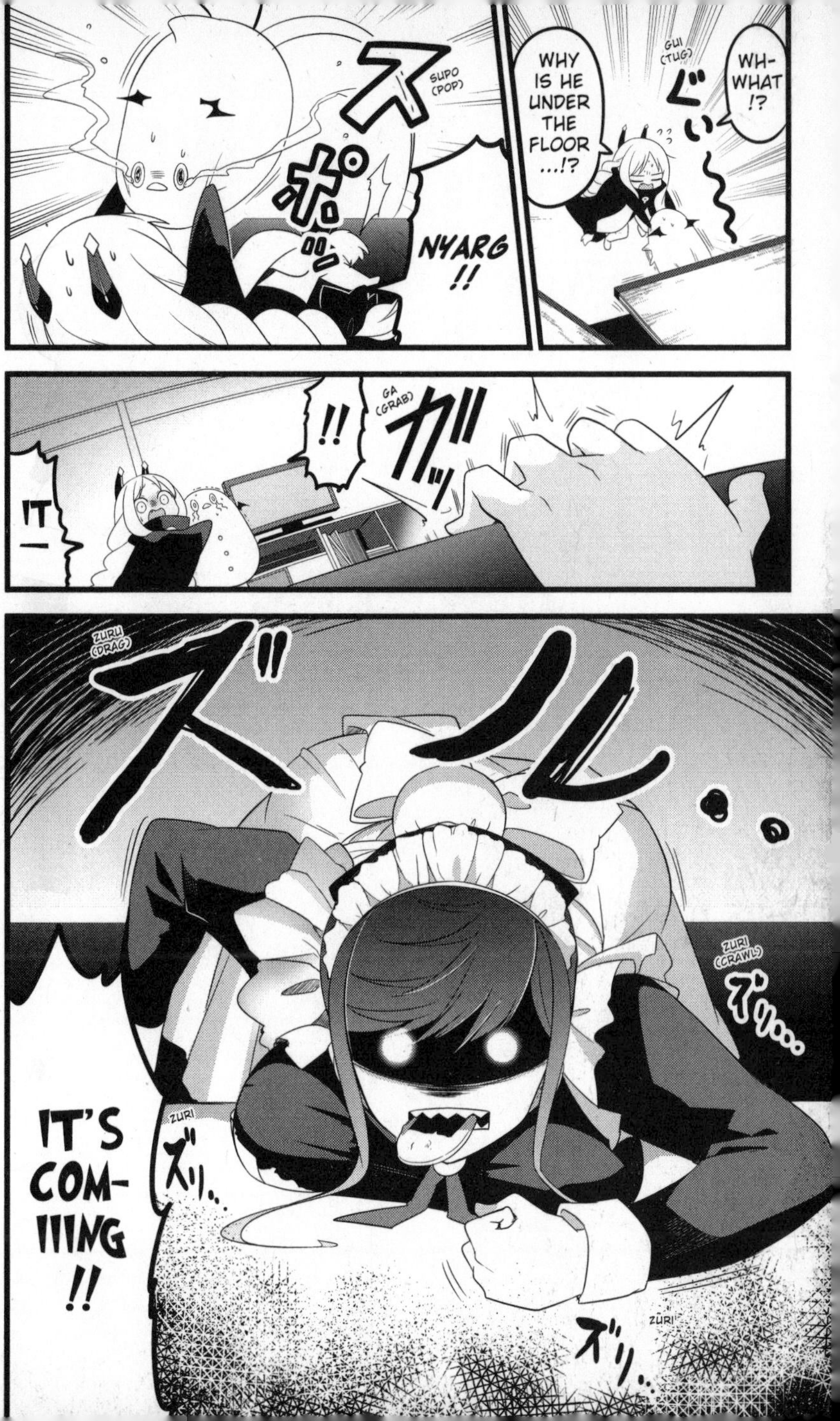
WH-WHAT!?
GUI (TUG)
ぐい
WHY IS HE UNDER THE FLOOR ...!?
SUPO (POP)
スポーン
NYARG!!
GA (GRAB)
ガッ
!!
IT—
ZURU (DRAG)
ズル…
ZURI (CRAWL)
ズリ…
ZURI
ズリ…
IT'S COM-IIIING!!
ZURI
ズリ…

CREATURE 5: THE INVINCIBLE MAID

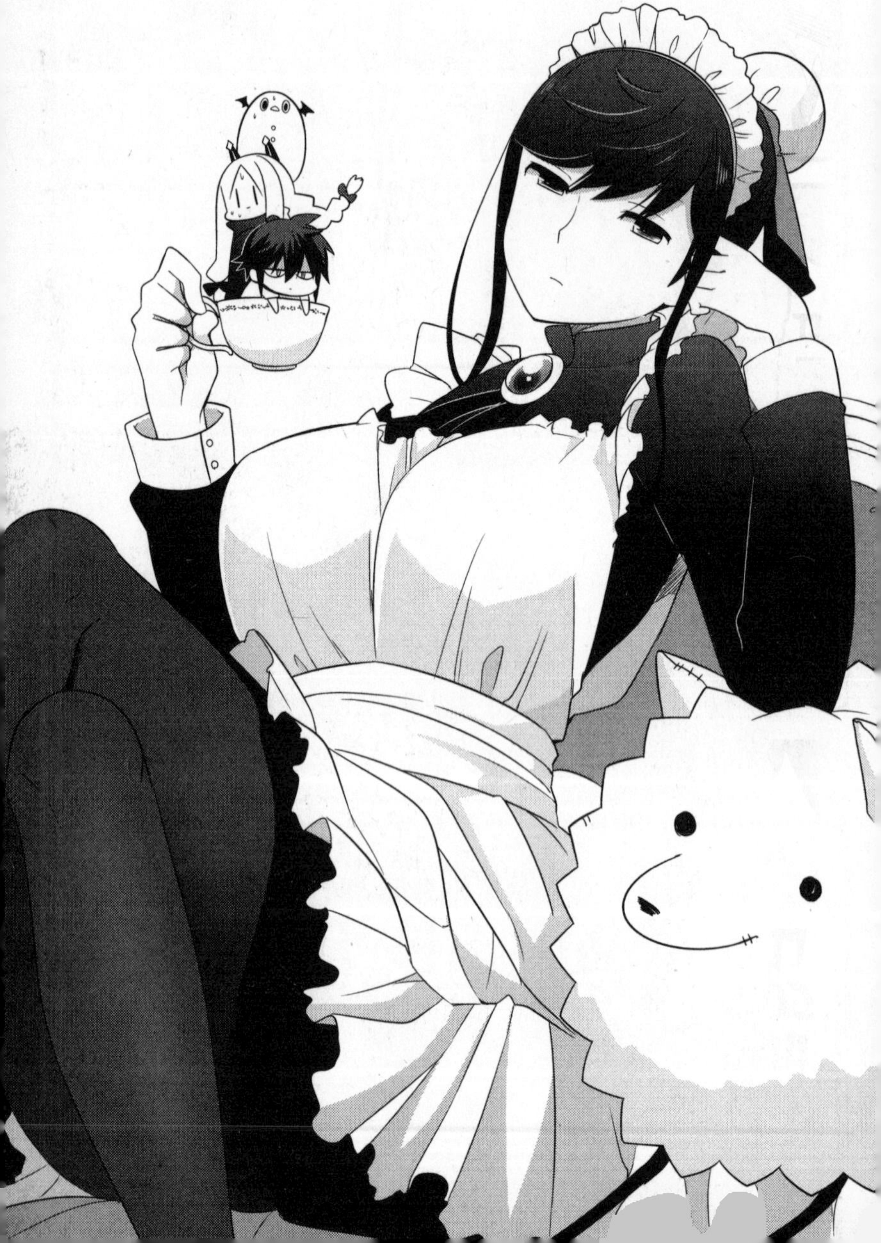

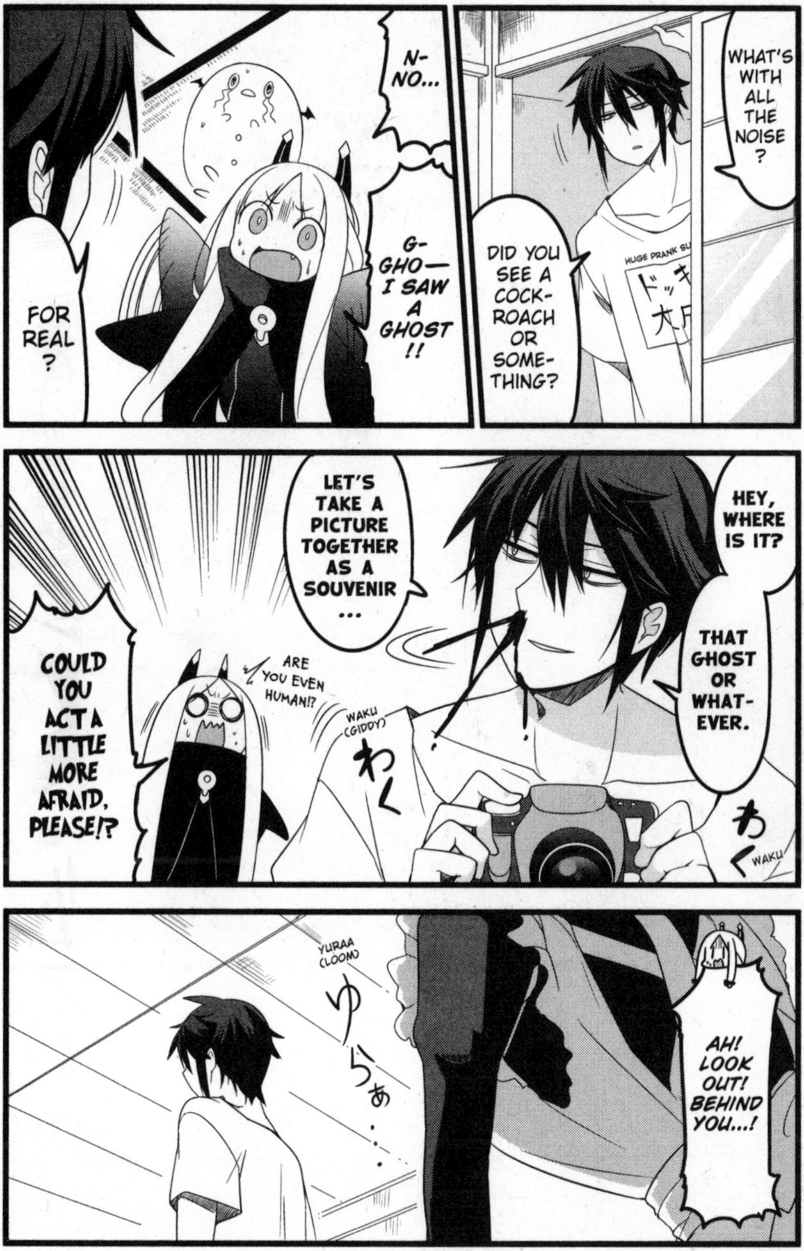
WHAT'S WITH ALL THE NOISE?
DID YOU SEE A COCKROACH OR SOMETHING?
N-NO...
G-GHO— I SAW A GHOST!!
FOR REAL?
HEY, WHERE IS IT?
THAT GHOST OR WHATEVER.
わく
WAKU
LET'S TAKE A PICTURE TOGETHER AS A SOUVENIR...
わく
WAKU (GIDDY)
ARE YOU EVEN HUMAN!?
COULD YOU ACT A LITTLE MORE AFRAID, PLEASE!?
AH! LOOK OUT! BEHIND YOU...!
ゆらぁ
YURAA (LOOM)

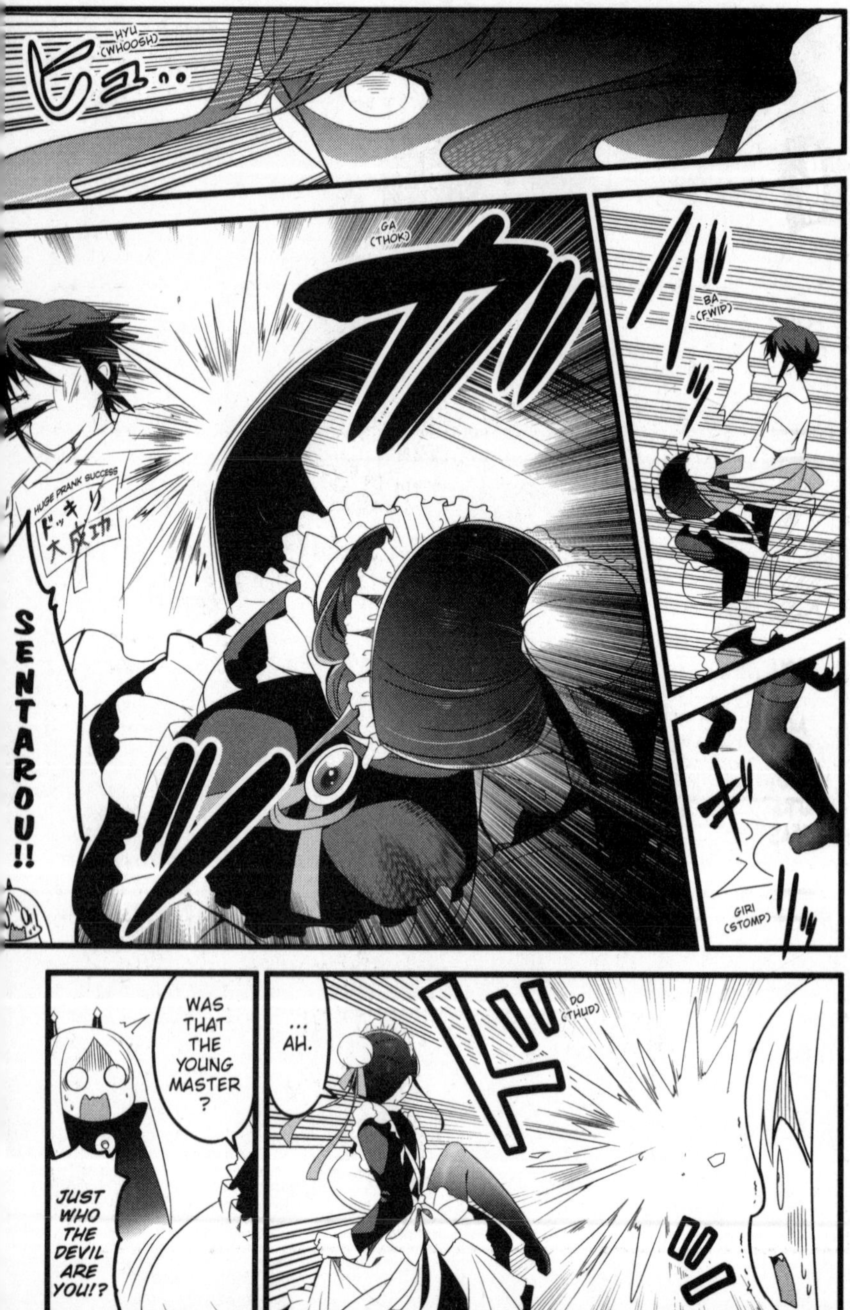
HYU (WHOOSH)
BA (FWIP)
GIRI (STOMP)
GA (THOK)
HUGE PRANK SUCCESS
SENTAROU!!
DO (THUD)
...AH.
WAS THAT THE YOUNG MASTER?
JUST WHO THE DEVIL ARE YOU!?

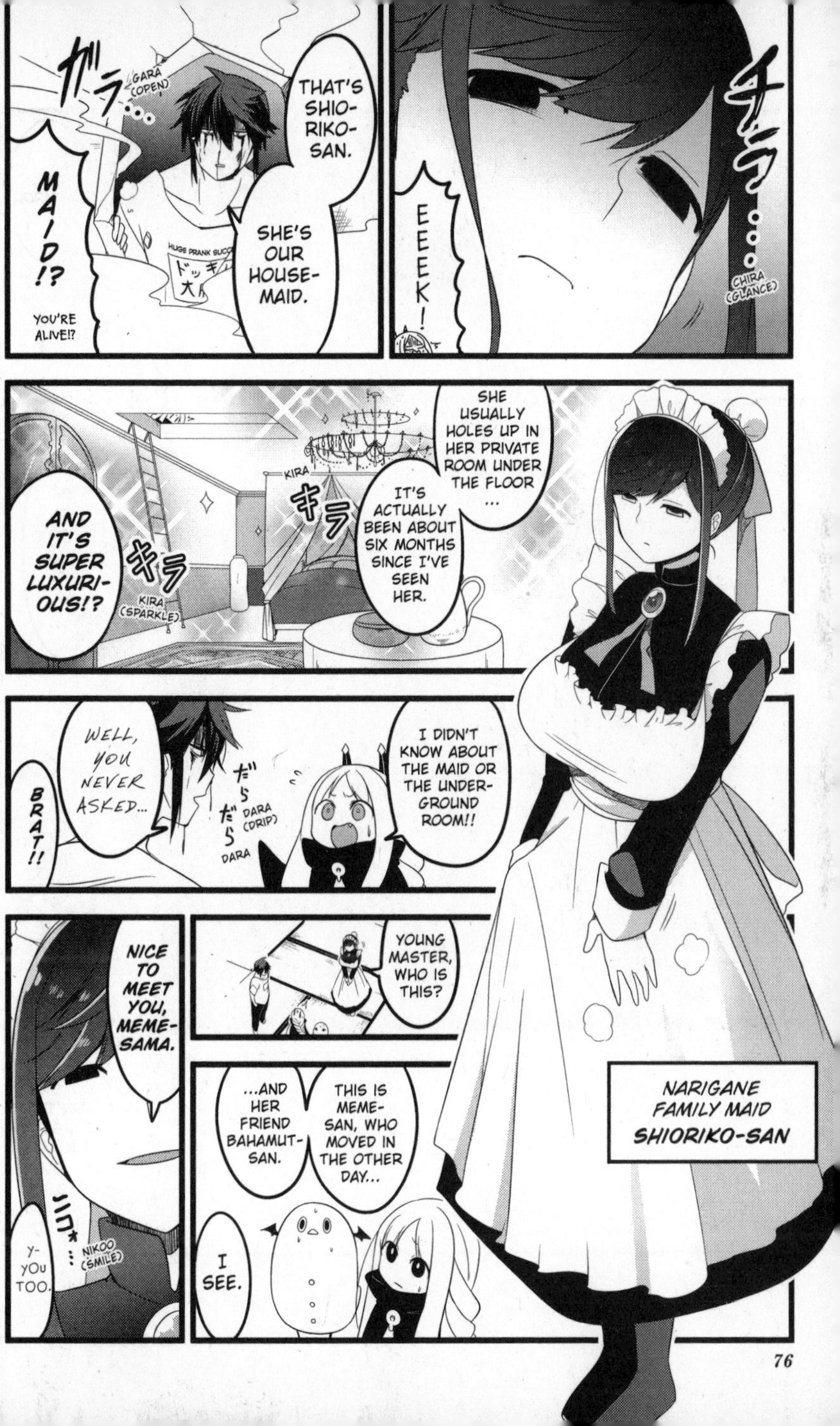
チラ…
CHIRA (GLANCE)
EEEK!
THAT'S SHIORIKO-SAN.
SHE'S OUR HOUSEMAID.
ガラ…
GARA (OPEN)
HUGE PRANK SUCC
ドッキ 大
MAID!?
YOU'RE ALIVE!?
SHE USUALLY HOLES UP IN HER PRIVATE ROOM UNDER THE FLOOR...
IT'S ACTUALLY BEEN ABOUT SIX MONTHS SINCE I'VE SEEN HER.
キラ
KIRA
キラ
KIRA (SPARKLE)
AND IT'S SUPER LUXURIOUS!?
NARIGANE FAMILY MAID SHIORIKO-SAN
I DIDN'T KNOW ABOUT THE MAID OR THE UNDERGROUND ROOM!!
だら
DARA (DRIP)
だら
DARA
WELL, YOU NEVER ASKED...
BRAT!!
YOUNG MASTER, WHO IS THIS?
THIS IS MEME-SAN, WHO MOVED IN THE OTHER DAY...
...AND HER FRIEND BAHAMUT-SAN.
I SEE.
NICE TO MEET YOU, MEME-SAMA.
ニコ…
NIKOO (SMILE)
Y-YOU TOO.

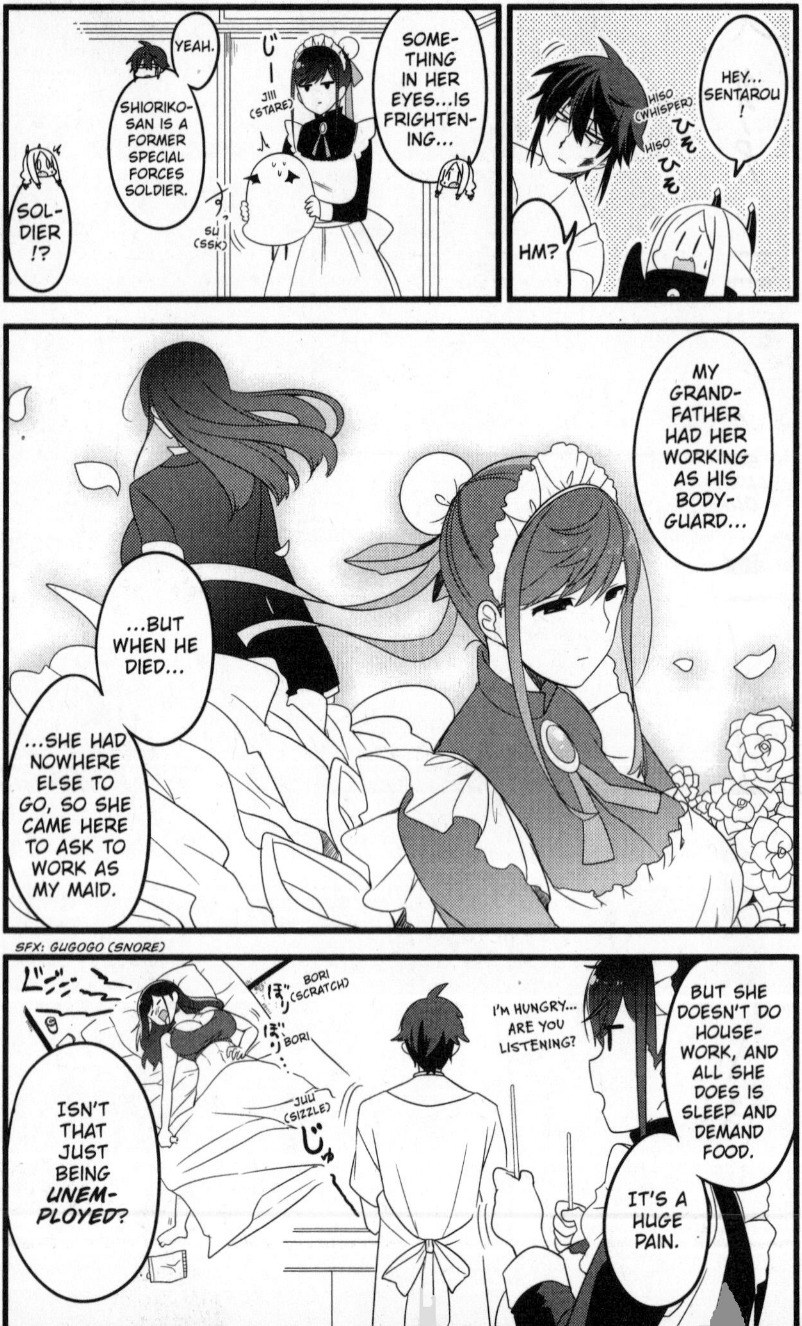
HEY... SENTAROU!
HISO (WHISPER) HISO
ひそひそ
HM?
SOMETHING IN HER EYES...IS FRIGHTENING...
じー
JIII (STARE)
YEAH.
SHIORIKO-SAN IS A FORMER SPECIAL FORCES SOLDIER.
す
SU (SSK)
SOLDIER!?
MY GRANDFATHER HAD HER WORKING AS HIS BODYGUARD...
...BUT WHEN HE DIED...
...SHE HAD NOWHERE ELSE TO GO, SO SHE CAME HERE TO ASK TO WORK AS MY MAID.
SFX: GUGOGO (SNORE)
BUT SHE DOESN'T DO HOUSEWORK, AND ALL SHE DOES IS SLEEP AND DEMAND FOOD.
IT'S A HUGE PAIN.
I'M HUNGRY... ARE YOU LISTENING?
JUU (SIZZLE)
じゅ~
BORI (SCRATCH)
ぼり
BORI
ぼり
ISN'T THAT JUST BEING ***UNEMPLOYED***?

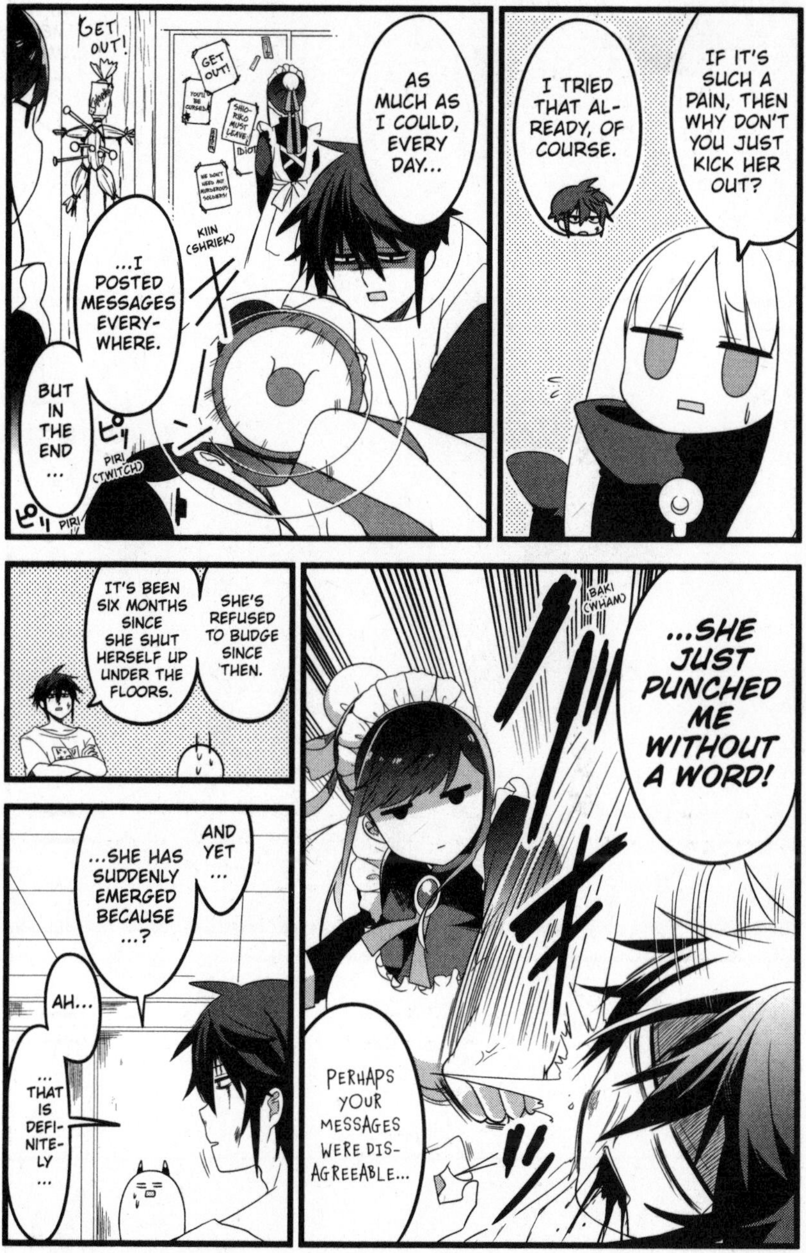
IF IT'S SUCH A PAIN, THEN WHY DON'T YOU JUST KICK HER OUT?
I TRIED THAT AL-READY, OF COURSE.
AS MUCH AS I COULD, EVERY DAY...
GET OUT!
GET OUT!
YOU'LL BE CURSED
SHIO-RIKO MUST LEAVE
IDIOT
WE DON'T NEED ANY MURDEROUS SOLDIERS!
KIIN (SHRIEK)
...I POSTED MESSAGES EVERY-WHERE.
BUT IN THE END...
ピッ
PIRI (TWITCH)
ピッ
PIRI
...SHE JUST PUNCHED ME WITHOUT A WORD!
BAKI (WHAM)
PERHAPS YOUR MESSAGES WERE DIS-AGREEABLE...
SHE'S REFUSED TO BUDGE SINCE THEN.
IT'S BEEN SIX MONTHS SINCE SHE SHUT HERSELF UP UNDER THE FLOORS.
AND YET...
...SHE HAS SUDDENLY EMERGED BECAUSE...?
AH...
...THAT IS DEFI-NITE-LY...

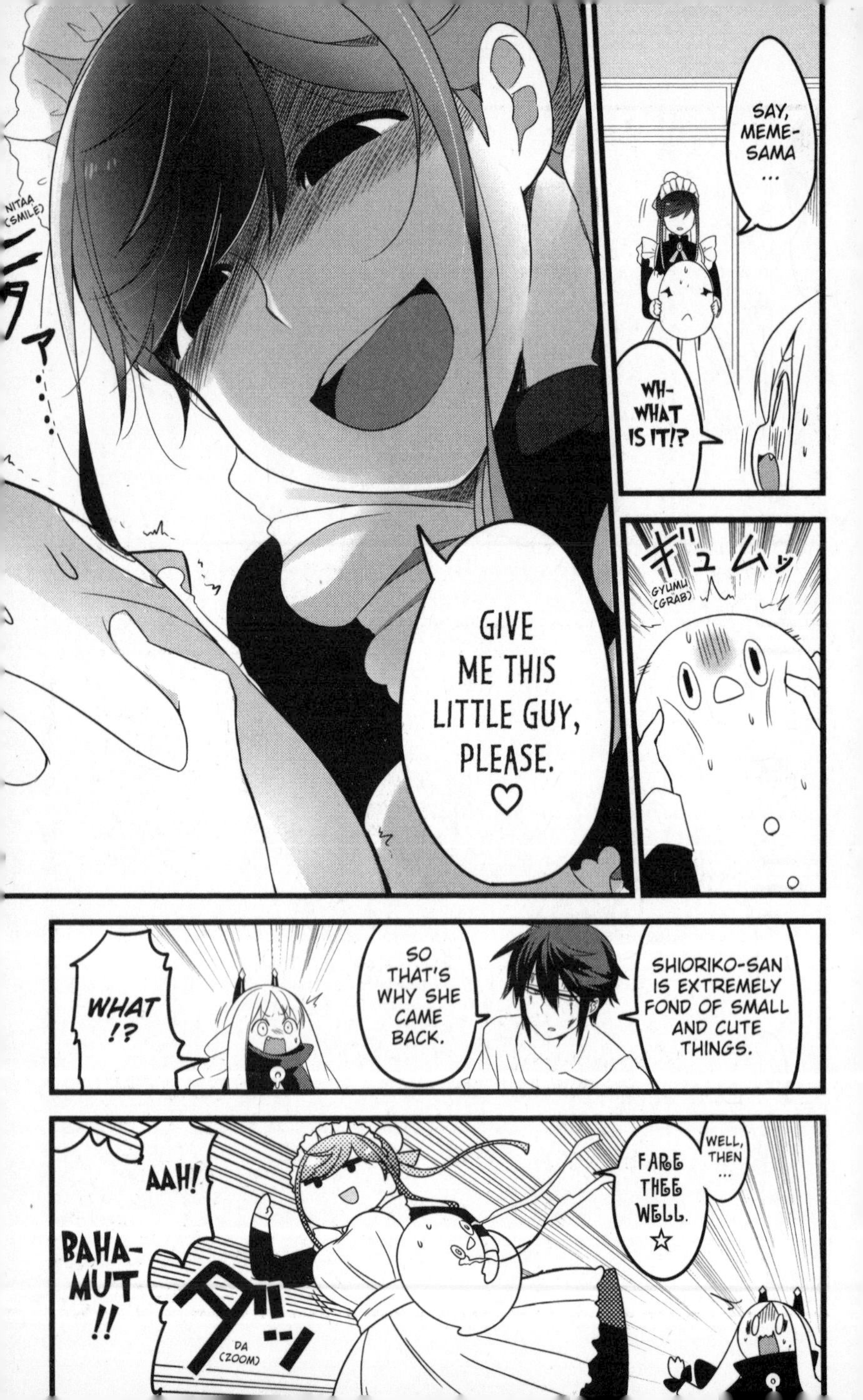
SAY, MEME-SAMA ...
WH-WHAT IS IT!?
ギュムッ
GYUMU (GRAB)
GIVE ME THIS LITTLE GUY, PLEASE. ♡
ニタア…
NITAA (SMILE)
SHIORIKO-SAN IS EXTREMELY FOND OF SMALL AND CUTE THINGS.
SO THAT'S WHY SHE CAME BACK.
WHAT !?
WELL, THEN ...
FARE THEE WELL. ☆
AAH!
BAHA-MUT !!
ダーッ
DA (ZOOM)

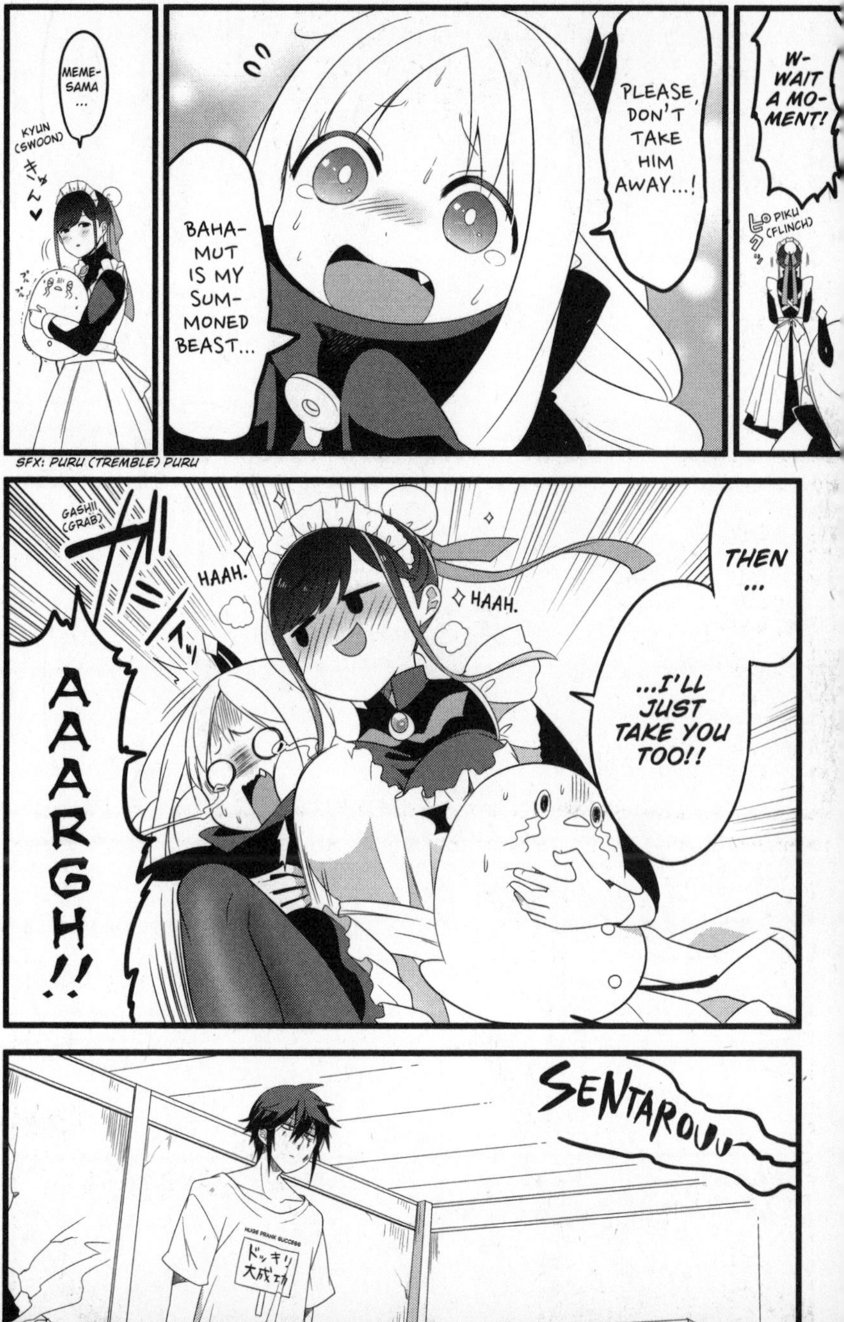
W-WAIT A MO-MENT!
PIKU (FLINCH)
PLEASE, DON'T TAKE HIM AWAY...!
BAHA-MUT IS MY SUM-MONED BEAST...
MEME-SAMA...
KYUN (SWOON)
SFX: PURU (TREMBLE) PURU
THEN...
...I'LL JUST TAKE YOU TOO!!
HAAH.
HAAH.
GASHI! (GRAB)
AAARGH!!
SENTAROUU
HUGE PRANK SUCCESS
ドッキリ大成功

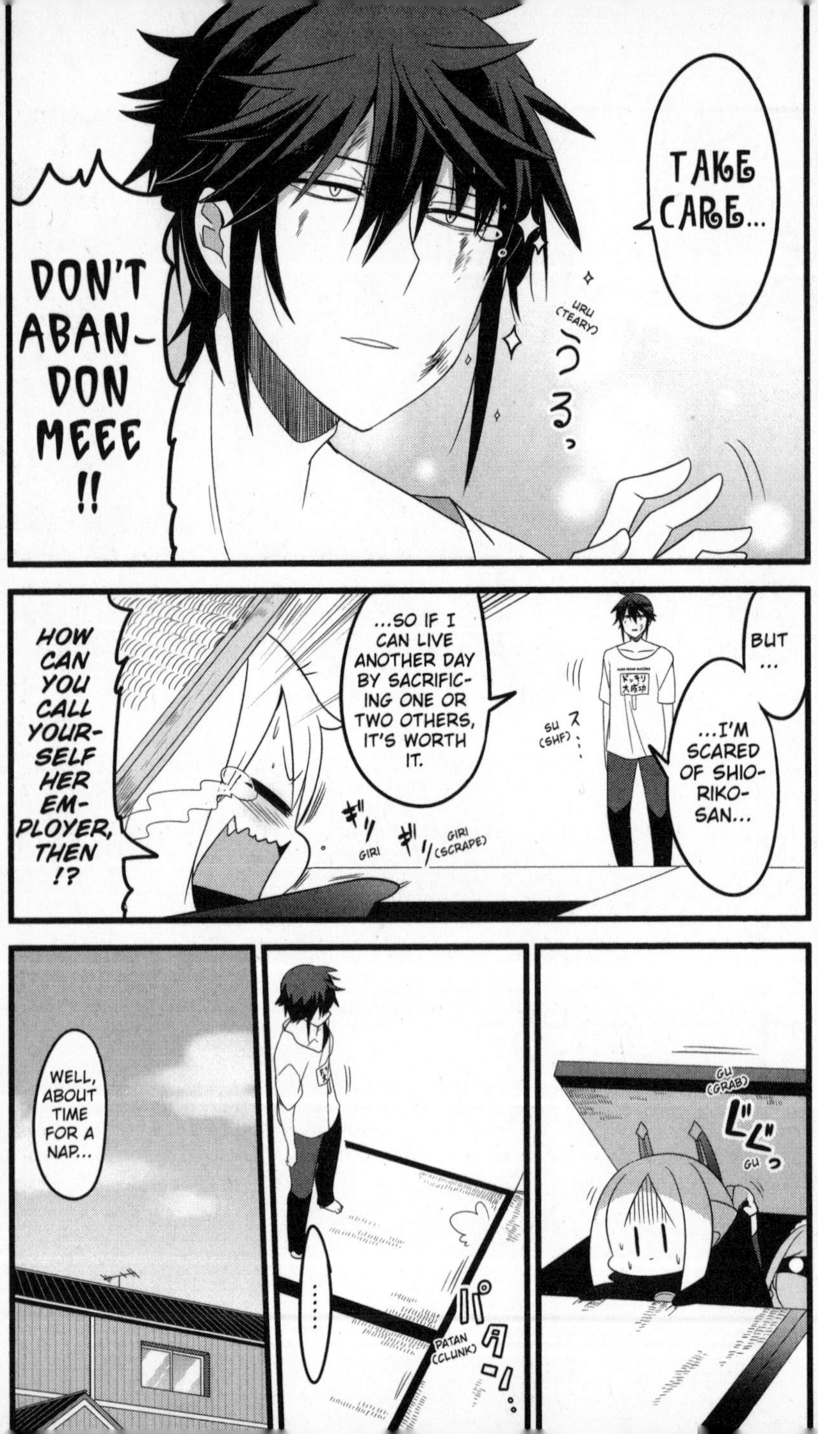
TAKE CARE...
URU (TEARY)
うるっ
DON'T ABAN-DON MEEE !!
BUT ...
...I'M SCARED OF SHIO-RIKO-SAN...
ドッキリ大成功
SU (SHF)
ス…
...SO IF I CAN LIVE ANOTHER DAY BY SACRIFICING ONE OR TWO OTHERS, IT'S WORTH IT.
ギリ
GIRI
ギリ
GIRI (SCRAPE)
HOW CAN YOU CALL YOURSELF HER EMPLOYER, THEN !?
GU (GRAB)
グッ
GU
……
パタン
PATAN (CLUNK)
WELL, ABOUT TIME FOR A NAP...

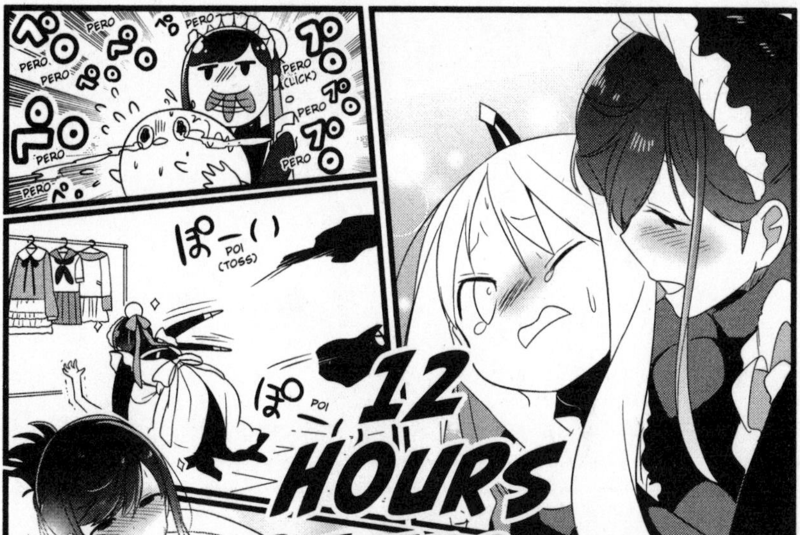
12 HOURS LATER...!
PERO
PERO
PERO
PERO (CLICK)
PERO
PERO
PERO
PERO
PERO
POI (TOSS)
POI
KASHA
KASHA
KASHA
KASHA
KASHA
KASHA (FLASH)

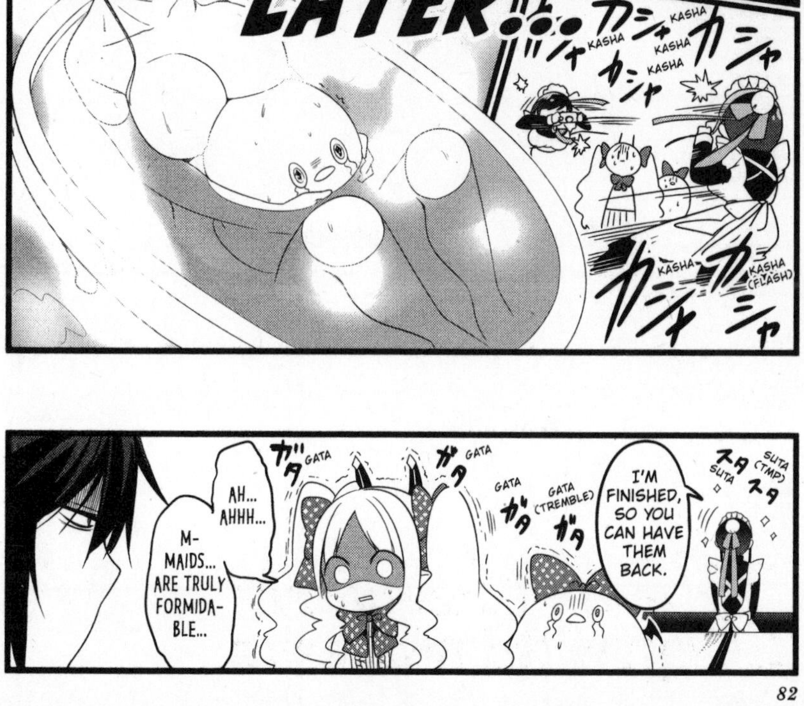
SUTA
SUTA (TMP)
I'M FINISHED, SO YOU CAN HAVE THEM BACK.
GATA (TREMBLE)
GATA
GATA
GATA
AH... AHHH...
M-MAIDS... ARE TRULY FORMIDA-BLE...

The Strange Creature at Kuroyuri Apartments

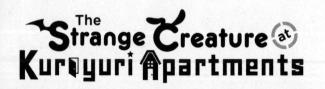

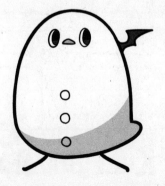

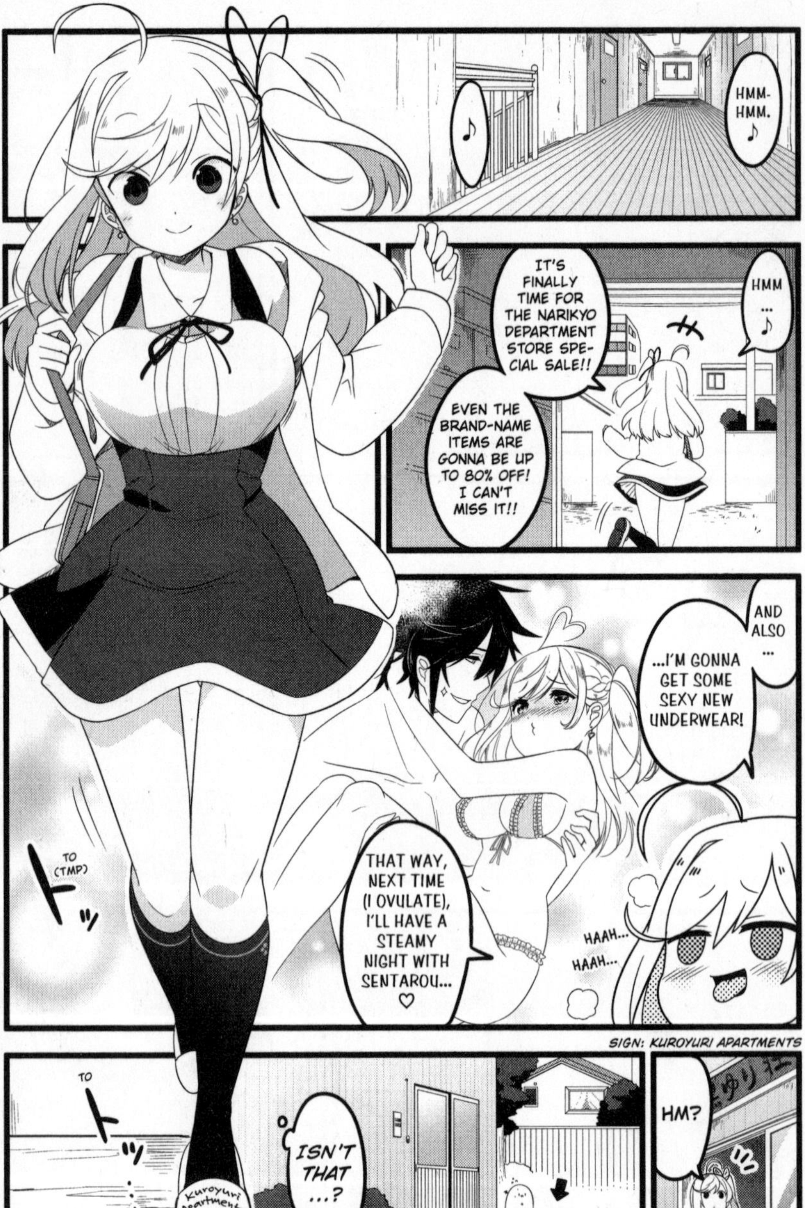
HMM-HMM. ♪
♪
HMM... ♪
IT'S FINALLY TIME FOR THE NARIKYO DEPARTMENT STORE SPECIAL SALE!!
EVEN THE BRAND-NAME ITEMS ARE GONNA BE UP TO 80% OFF! I CAN'T MISS IT!!
AND ALSO...
...I'M GONNA GET SOME SEXY NEW UNDERWEAR!
THAT WAY, NEXT TIME (I OVULATE), I'LL HAVE A STEAMY NIGHT WITH SENTAROU... ♡
HAAH... HAAH...
SIGN: KUROYURI APARTMENTS
HM?
ISN'T THAT ...?
Kuroyuri Apartments
TO (TMP)
TO

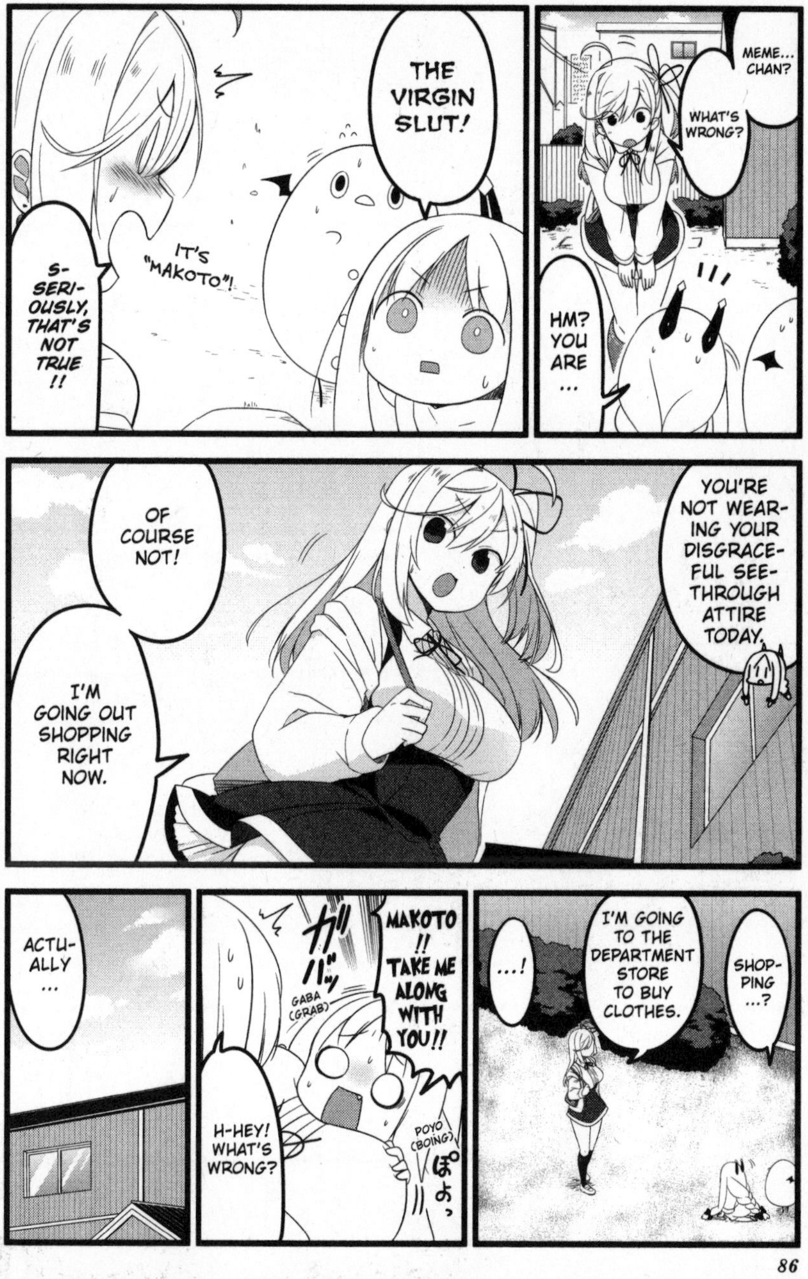
MEME... CHAN?
WHAT'S WRONG?
HM? YOU ARE ...
THE VIRGIN SLUT!
IT'S "MAKOTO"!
S-SERIOUSLY, THAT'S NOT TRUE!!
YOU'RE NOT WEARING YOUR DISGRACEFUL SEE-THROUGH ATTIRE TODAY.
OF COURSE NOT!
I'M GOING OUT SHOPPING RIGHT NOW.
SHOPPING...?
I'M GOING TO THE DEPARTMENT STORE TO BUY CLOTHES.
...!
MAKOTO!! TAKE ME ALONG WITH YOU!!
GABA (GRAB)
POYO (BOING)
H-HEY! WHAT'S WRONG?
ACTUALLY...

CREATURE 6: DEPARTMENT STORE CRISIS!! (PART 1)

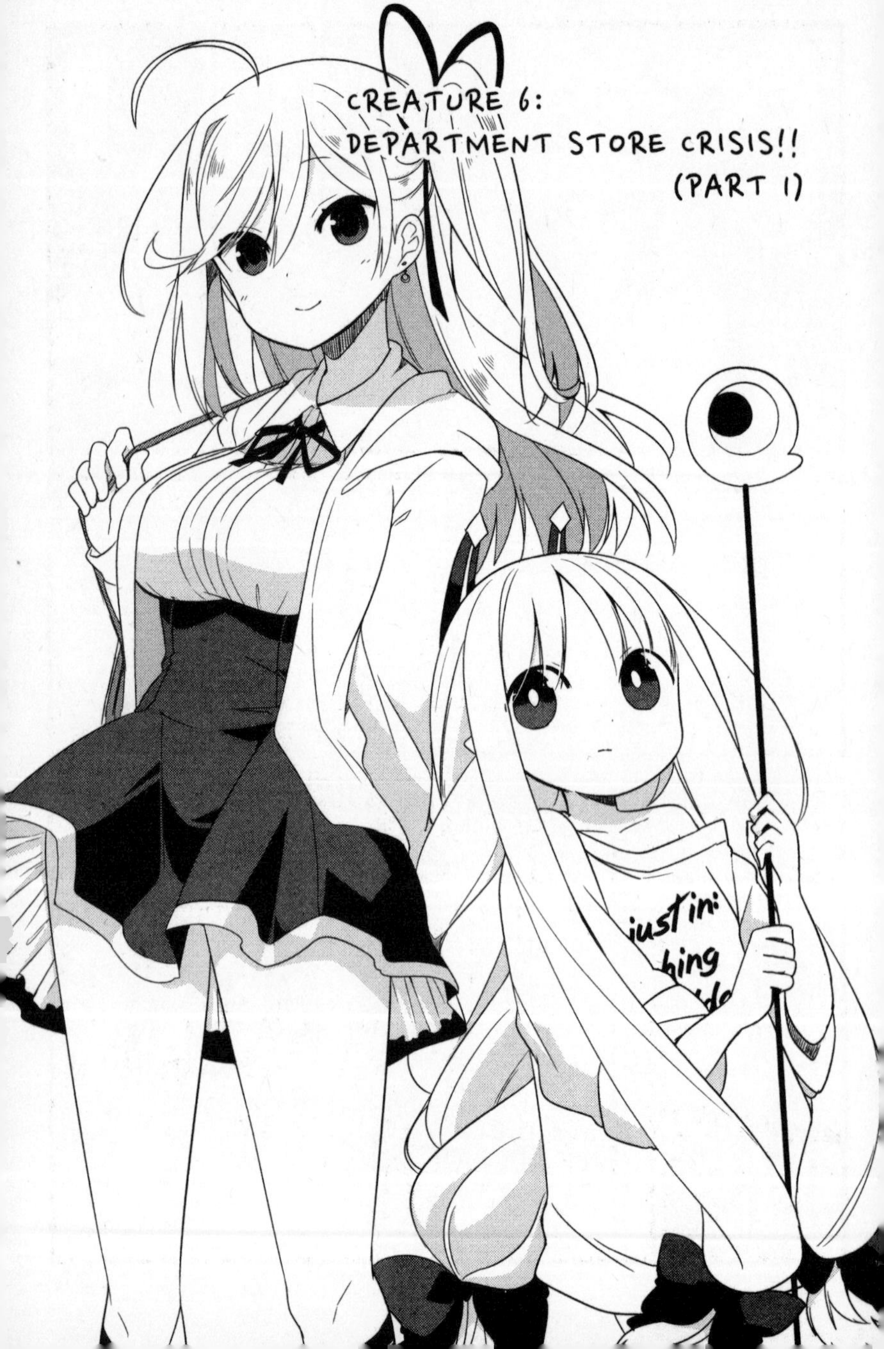

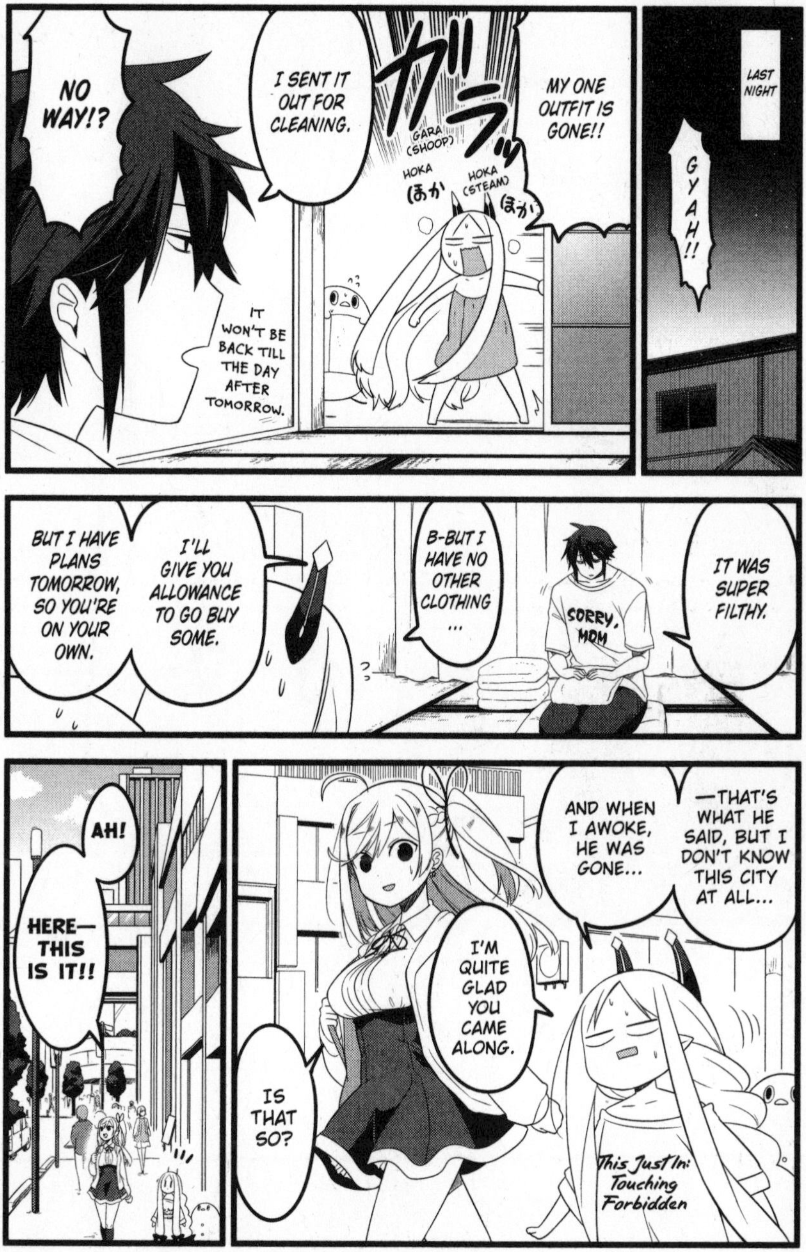
LAST NIGHT
GYAH!!
MY ONE OUTFIT IS GONE!!
ガラッ
GARA (SHOOP)
HOKA ほか HOKA (STEAM) ほかっ
I SENT IT OUT FOR CLEANING.
NO WAY!?
IT WON'T BE BACK TILL THE DAY AFTER TOMORROW.
IT WAS SUPER FILTHY.
SORRY, MOM
B-BUT I HAVE NO OTHER CLOTHING...
I'LL GIVE YOU ALLOWANCE TO GO BUY SOME.
BUT I HAVE PLANS TOMORROW, SO YOU'RE ON YOUR OWN.
—THAT'S WHAT HE SAID, BUT I DON'T KNOW THIS CITY AT ALL...
AND WHEN I AWOKE, HE WAS GONE...
I'M QUITE GLAD YOU CAME ALONG.
IS THAT SO?
This Just In: Touching Forbidden
AH!
HERE—THIS IS IT!!

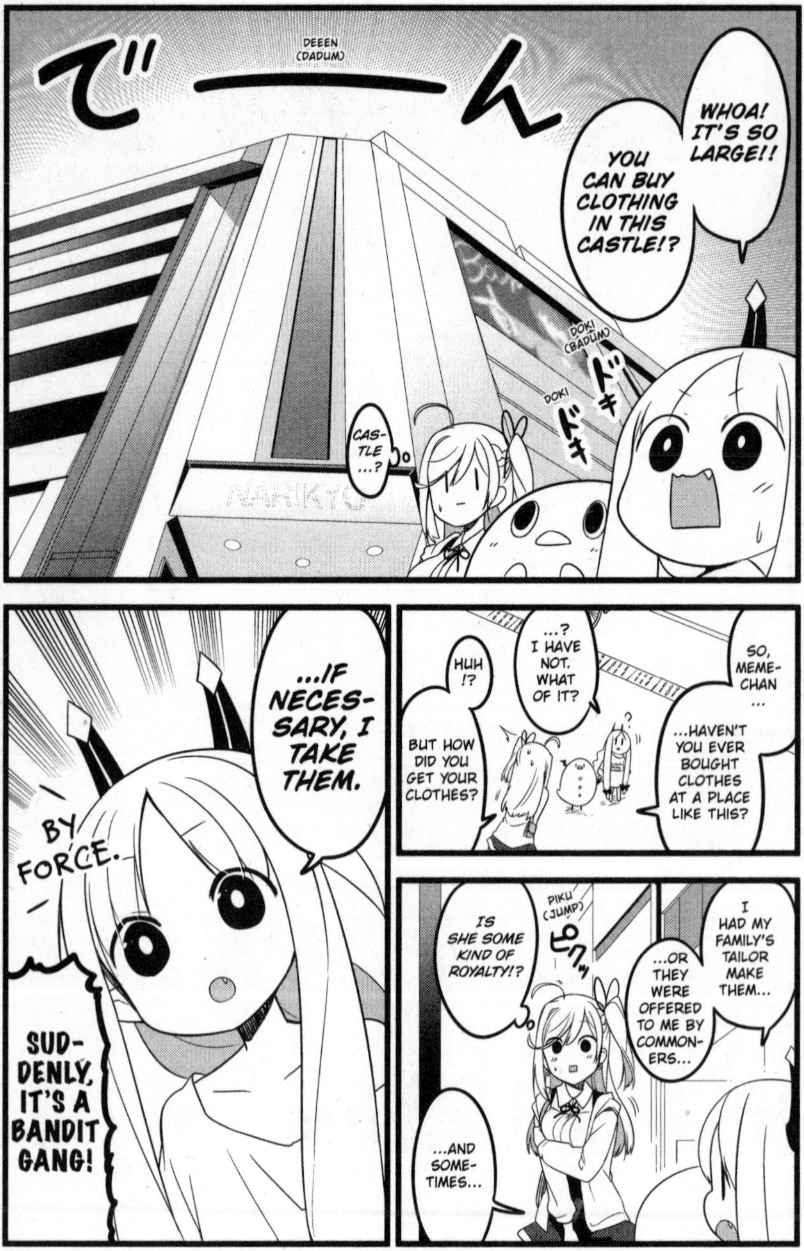
WHOA! IT'S SO LARGE!!
YOU CAN BUY CLOTHING IN THIS CASTLE!?
DEEEN (DADUM)
DOKI (BADUM)
DOKI
CASTLE ...?
SO, MEME-CHAN ...
...HAVEN'T YOU EVER BOUGHT CLOTHES AT A PLACE LIKE THIS?
...? I HAVE NOT. WHAT OF IT?
HUH!?
BUT HOW DID YOU GET YOUR CLOTHES?
I HAD MY FAMILY'S TAILOR MAKE THEM...
...OR THEY WERE OFFERED TO ME BY COMMONERS...
PIKU (JUMP)
IS SHE SOME KIND OF ROYALTY!?
...AND SOMETIMES...
...IF NECESSARY, I TAKE THEM.
BY FORCE.
SUDDENLY, IT'S A BANDIT GANG!

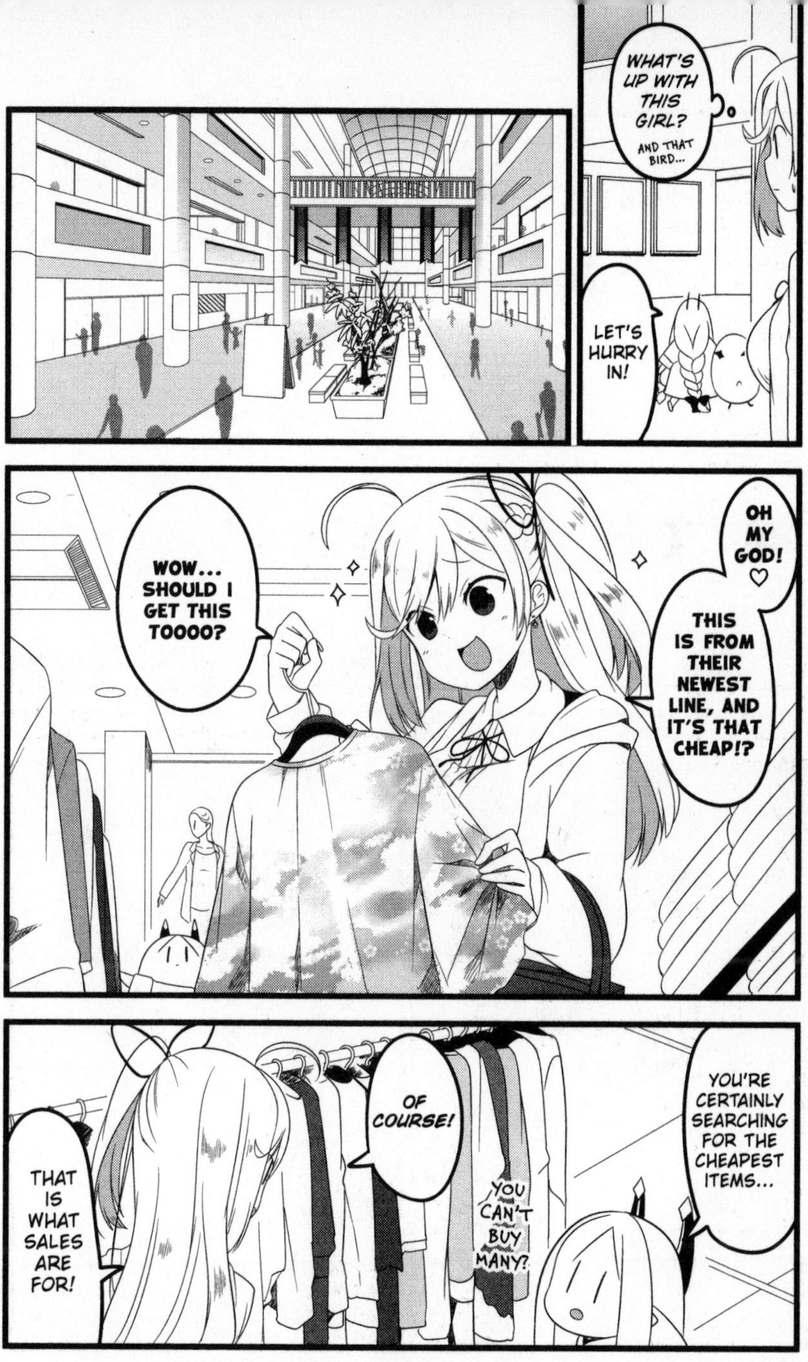
WHAT'S UP WITH THIS GIRL?
AND THAT BIRD...
LET'S HURRY IN!
OH MY GOD! ♡
THIS IS FROM THEIR NEWEST LINE, AND IT'S THAT CHEAP!?
WOW... SHOULD I GET THIS TOOOO?
YOU'RE CERTAINLY SEARCHING FOR THE CHEAPEST ITEMS...
OF COURSE!
YOU CAN'T BUY MANY?
THAT IS WHAT SALES ARE FOR!

FLIER: SPECIAL SALE!! / SIGN: ONIONS, 3 FOR 99 YEN

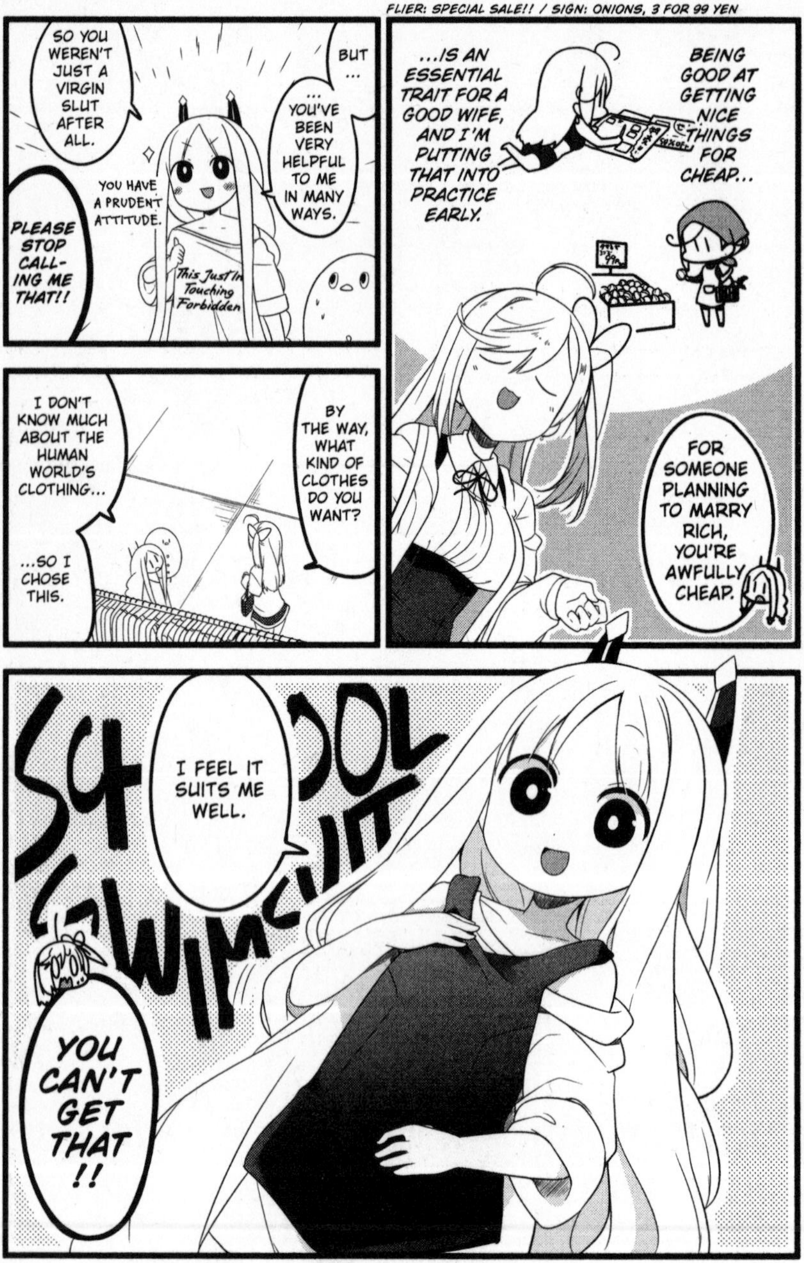
BEING GOOD AT GETTING NICE THINGS FOR CHEAP...
...IS AN ESSENTIAL TRAIT FOR A GOOD WIFE, AND I'M PUTTING THAT INTO PRACTICE EARLY.
FOR SOMEONE PLANNING TO MARRY RICH, YOU'RE AWFULLY CHEAP.
BUT ... ... YOU'VE BEEN VERY HELPFUL TO ME IN MANY WAYS.
SO YOU WEREN'T JUST A VIRGIN SLUT AFTER ALL.
YOU HAVE A PRUDENT ATTITUDE.
This Just In Touching Forbidden
PLEASE STOP CALLING ME THAT!!
BY THE WAY, WHAT KIND OF CLOTHES DO YOU WANT?
I DON'T KNOW MUCH ABOUT THE HUMAN WORLD'S CLOTHING...
...SO I CHOSE THIS.
SCHOOL SWIMSUIT
I FEEL IT SUITS ME WELL.
YOU CAN'T GET THAT!!

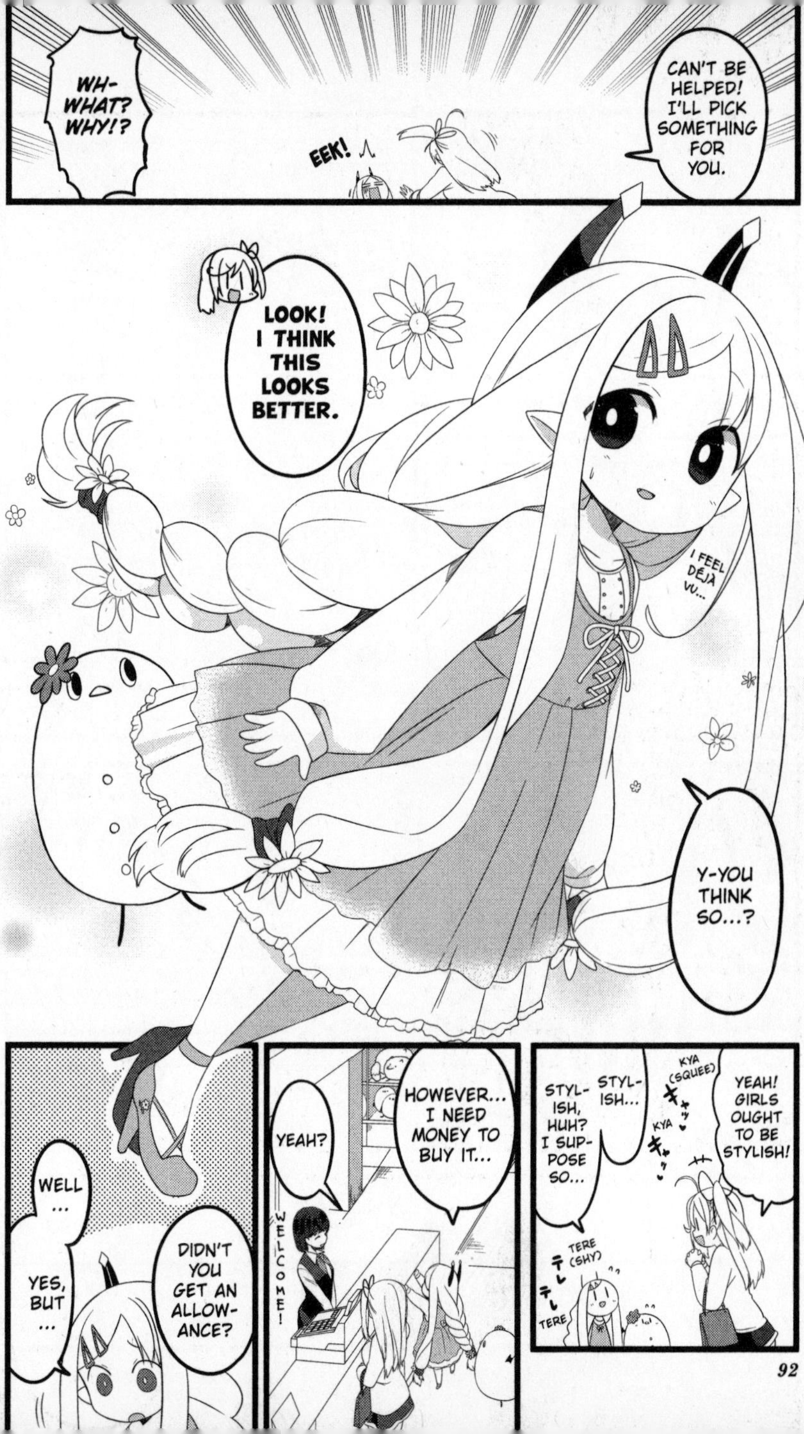

CAN'T BE HELPED! I'LL PICK SOMETHING FOR YOU.
EEK!
WH-WHAT? WHY!?
LOOK! I THINK THIS LOOKS BETTER.
I FEEL DÉJÀ VU...
Y-YOU THINK SO...?
YEAH! GIRLS OUGHT TO BE STYLISH!
KYA (SQUEE)
KYA
STYL-ISH...
STYL-ISH, HUH? I SUP-POSE SO...
TERE (SHY)
TERE
HOWEVER... I NEED MONEY TO BUY IT...
YEAH?
WELCOME!
DIDN'T YOU GET AN ALLOW-ANCE?
WELL ...
YES, BUT ...

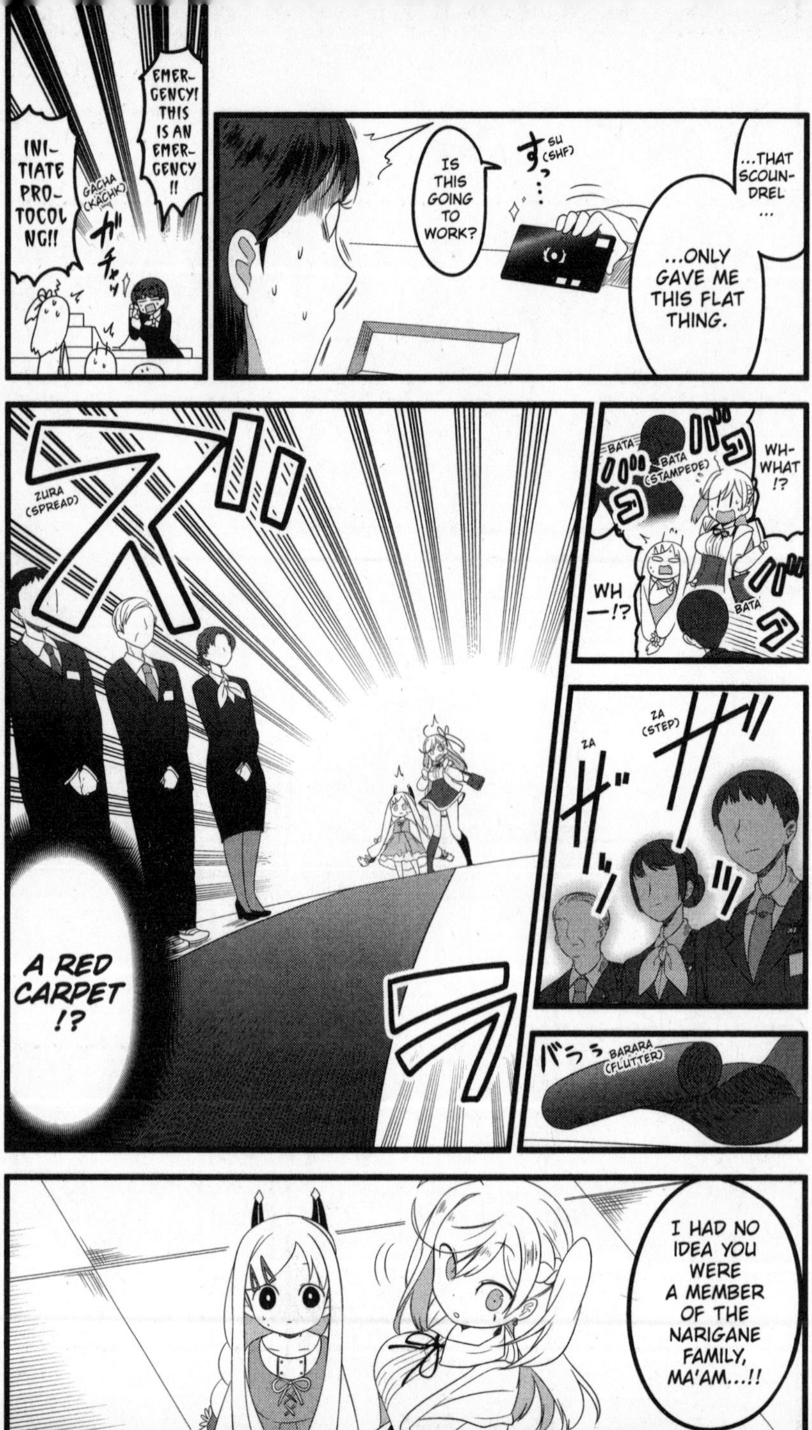
...THAT SCOUNDREL...
...ONLY GAVE ME THIS FLAT THING.
SU (SHF)
IS THIS GOING TO WORK?
EMERGENCY! THIS IS AN EMERGENCY!!
INITIATE PROTOCOL NG!!
GACHA (KACHK)
WH-WHAT!?
BATA
BATA (STAMPEDE)
BATA
WH—!?
ZA (STEP)
ZA
BARARA (FLUTTER)
ZURA (SPREAD)
A RED CARPET!?
I HAD NO IDEA YOU WERE A MEMBER OF THE NARIGANE FAMILY, MA'AM...!!

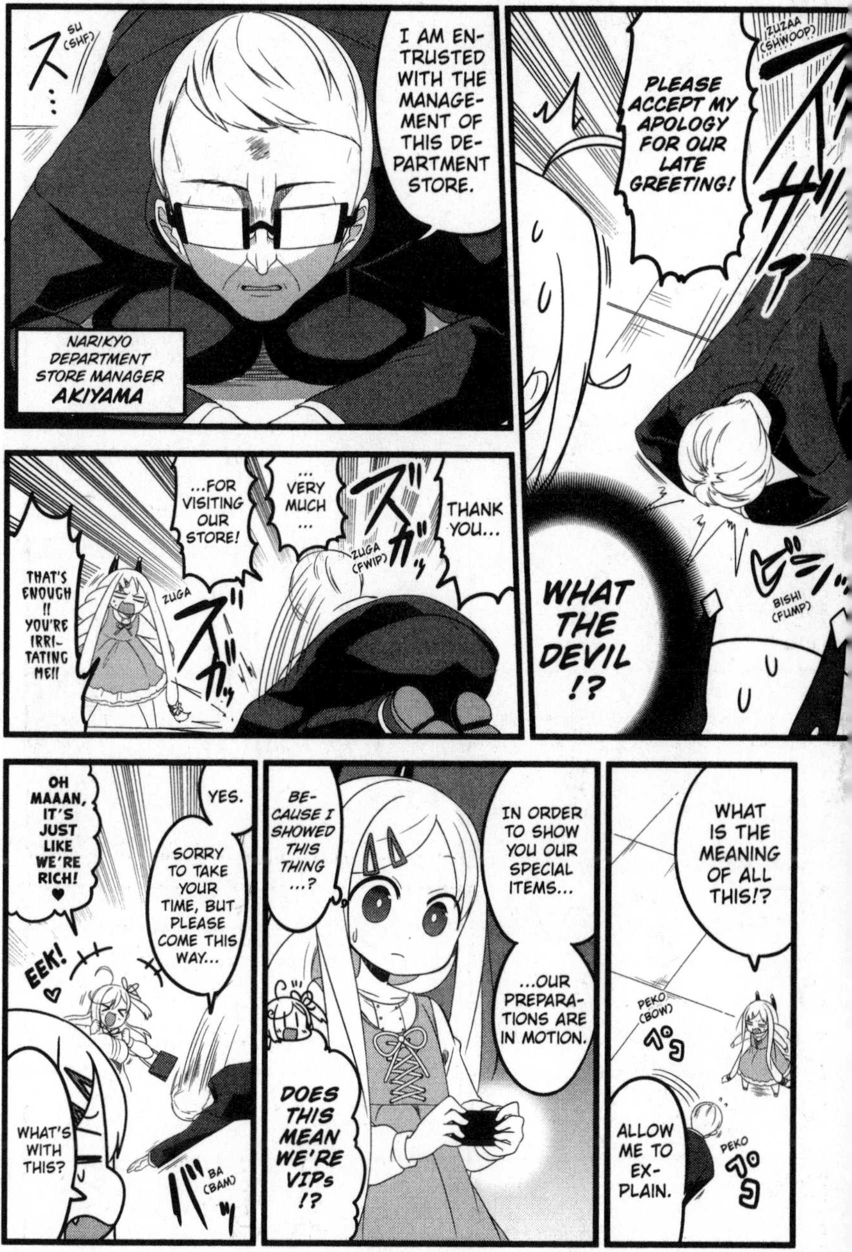
ZUZAA (SHWOOP)
PLEASE ACCEPT MY APOLOGY FOR OUR LATE GREETING!
WHAT THE DEVIL!?
BISHI (FUMP)
SU (SHF)
I AM ENTRUSTED WITH THE MANAGEMENT OF THIS DEPARTMENT STORE.
NARIKYO DEPARTMENT STORE MANAGER AKIYAMA
THANK YOU...
ZUGA (FWIP)
...VERY MUCH...
...FOR VISITING OUR STORE!
ZUGA
THAT'S ENOUGH!! YOU'RE IRRITATING ME!!
WHAT IS THE MEANING OF ALL THIS!?
PEKO (BOW)
ALLOW ME TO EXPLAIN.
PEKO
IN ORDER TO SHOW YOU OUR SPECIAL ITEMS...
...OUR PREPARATIONS ARE IN MOTION.
BECAUSE I SHOWED THIS THING...?
DOES THIS MEAN WE'RE VIPs!?
YES.
SORRY TO TAKE YOUR TIME, BUT PLEASE COME THIS WAY...
OH MAAAN, IT'S JUST LIKE WE'RE RICH! ♥
EEK! ♥
WHAT'S WITH THIS?
BA (BAM)

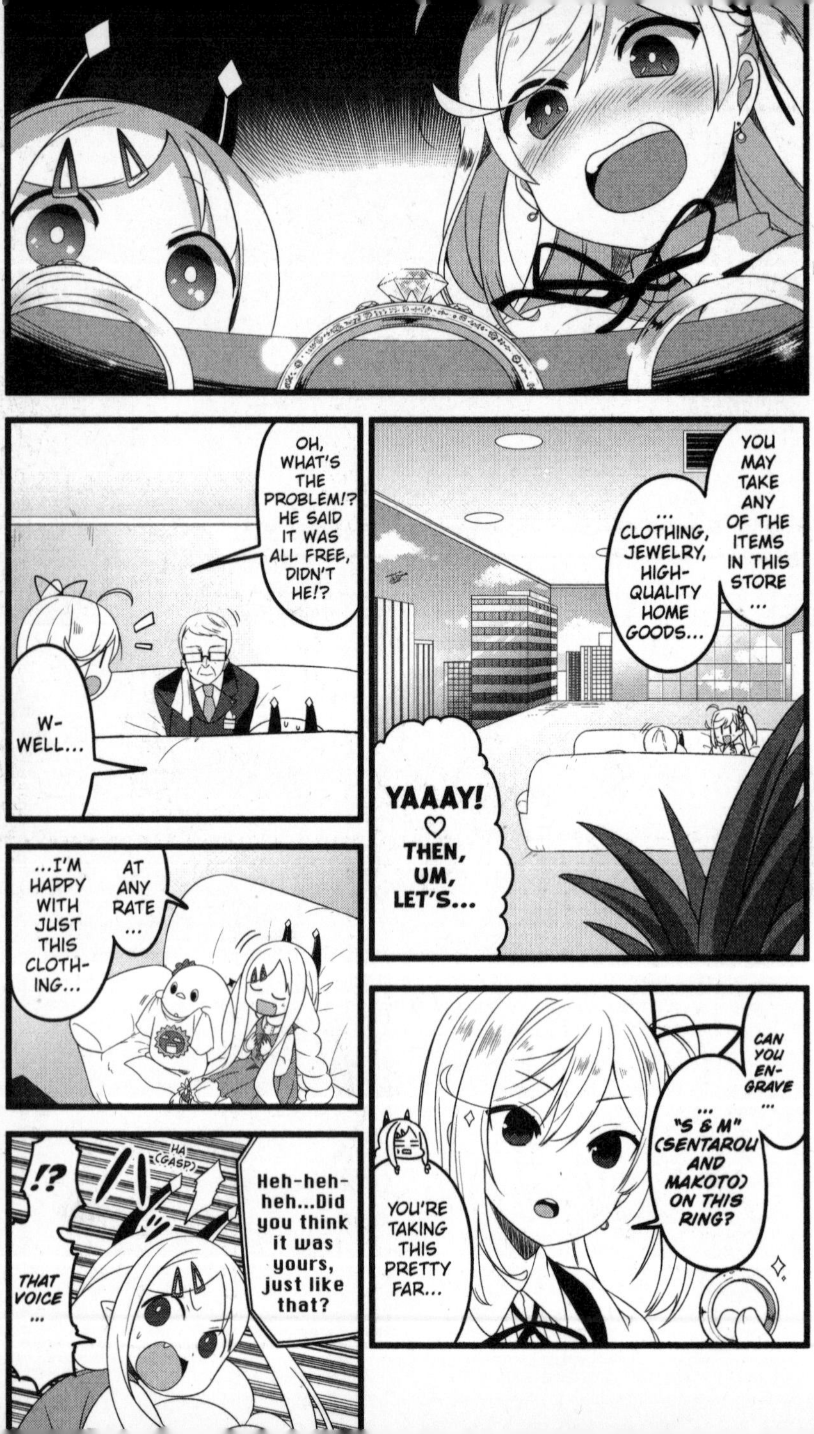
YOU MAY TAKE ANY OF THE ITEMS IN THIS STORE...
...CLOTHING, JEWELRY, HIGH-QUALITY HOME GOODS...
YAAAY! ♡ THEN, UM, LET'S...
OH, WHAT'S THE PROBLEM!? HE SAID IT WAS ALL FREE, DIDN'T HE!?
W-WELL...
AT ANY RATE...
...I'M HAPPY WITH JUST THIS CLOTHING...
CAN YOU ENGRAVE...
..."S & M" (SENTAROU AND MAKOTO) ON THIS RING?
YOU'RE TAKING THIS PRETTY FAR...
Heh-heh-heh...Did you think it was yours, just like that?
HA (GASP)
!?
THAT VOICE...

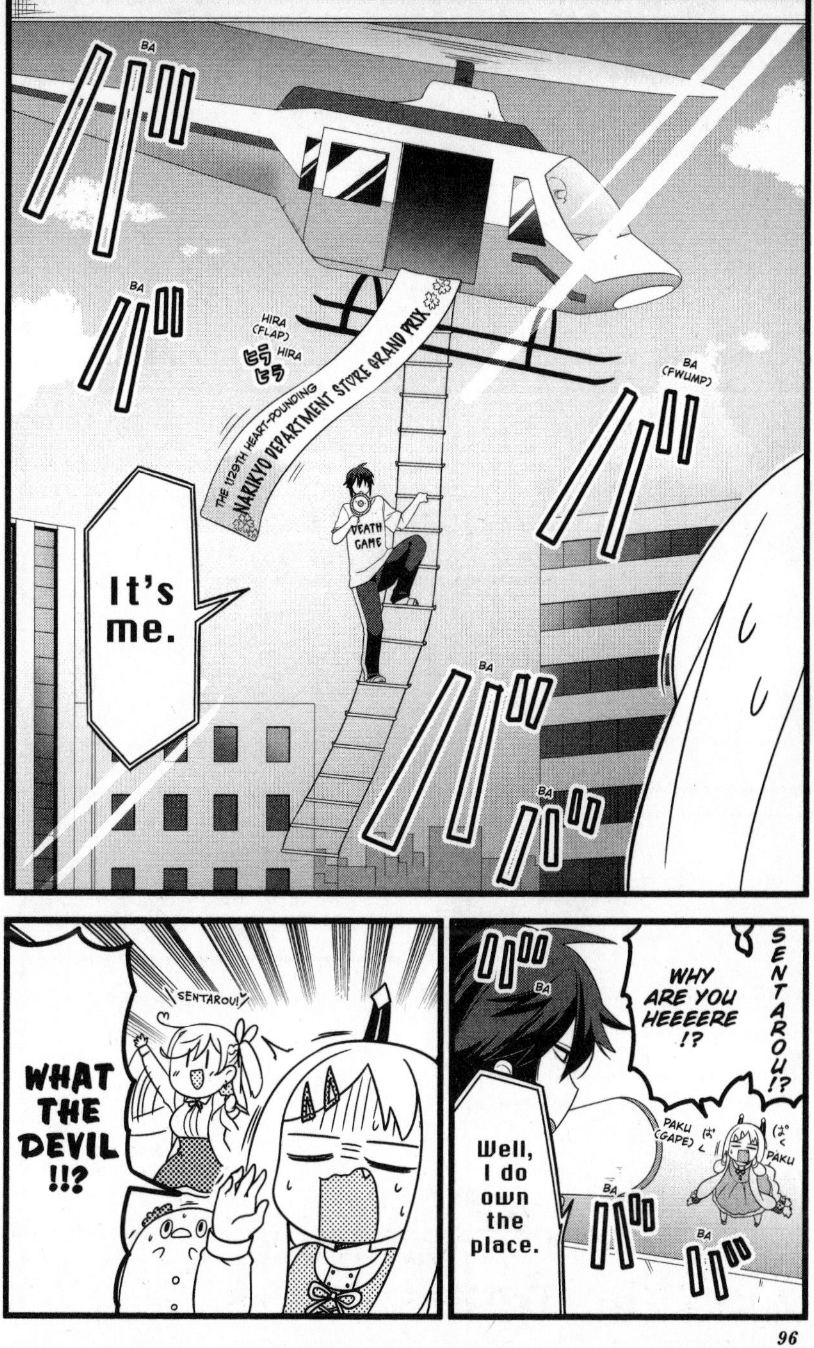
BA
BA
HIRA (FLAP) HIRA
THE 1129TH HEART-POUNDING NARIKYO DEPARTMENT STORE GRAND PRIX
BA (FWUMP)
DEATH GAME
It's me.
BA
BA
SENTAROU!?
WHY ARE YOU HEEEERE!?
BA
Well, I do own the place.
PAKU (GAPE) PAKU
BA
BA
SENTAROU!
WHAT THE DEVIL!!?

The Strange Creature at Kuroyuri Apartments

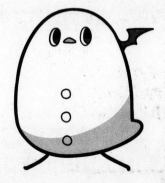

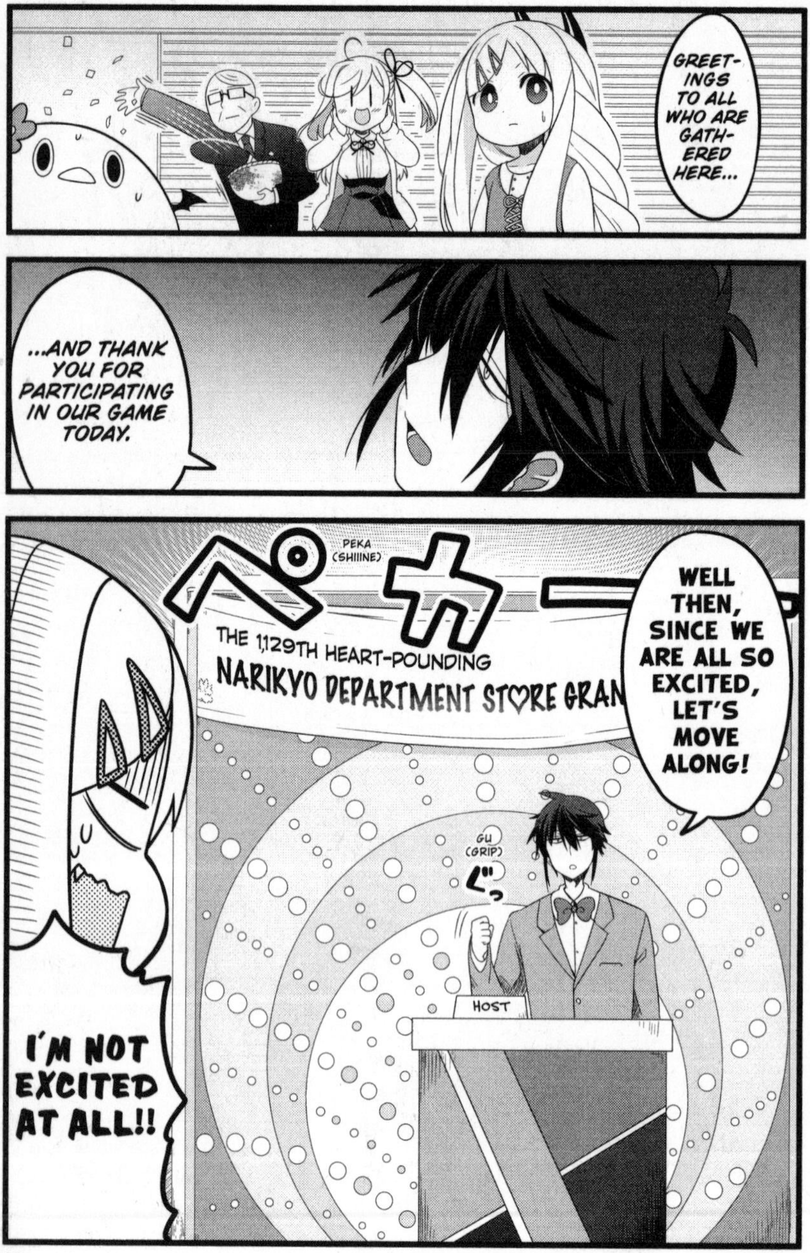
GREET-INGS TO ALL WHO ARE GATH-ERED HERE...
...AND THANK YOU FOR PARTICIPATING IN OUR GAME TODAY.
ペカー
PEKA (SHIIINE)
WELL THEN, SINCE WE ARE ALL SO EXCITED, LET'S MOVE ALONG!
THE 1,129TH HEART-POUNDING
NARIKYO DEPARTMENT STORE GRAN
GU (GRIP)
ぐっ
HOST
I'M NOT EXCITED AT ALL!!

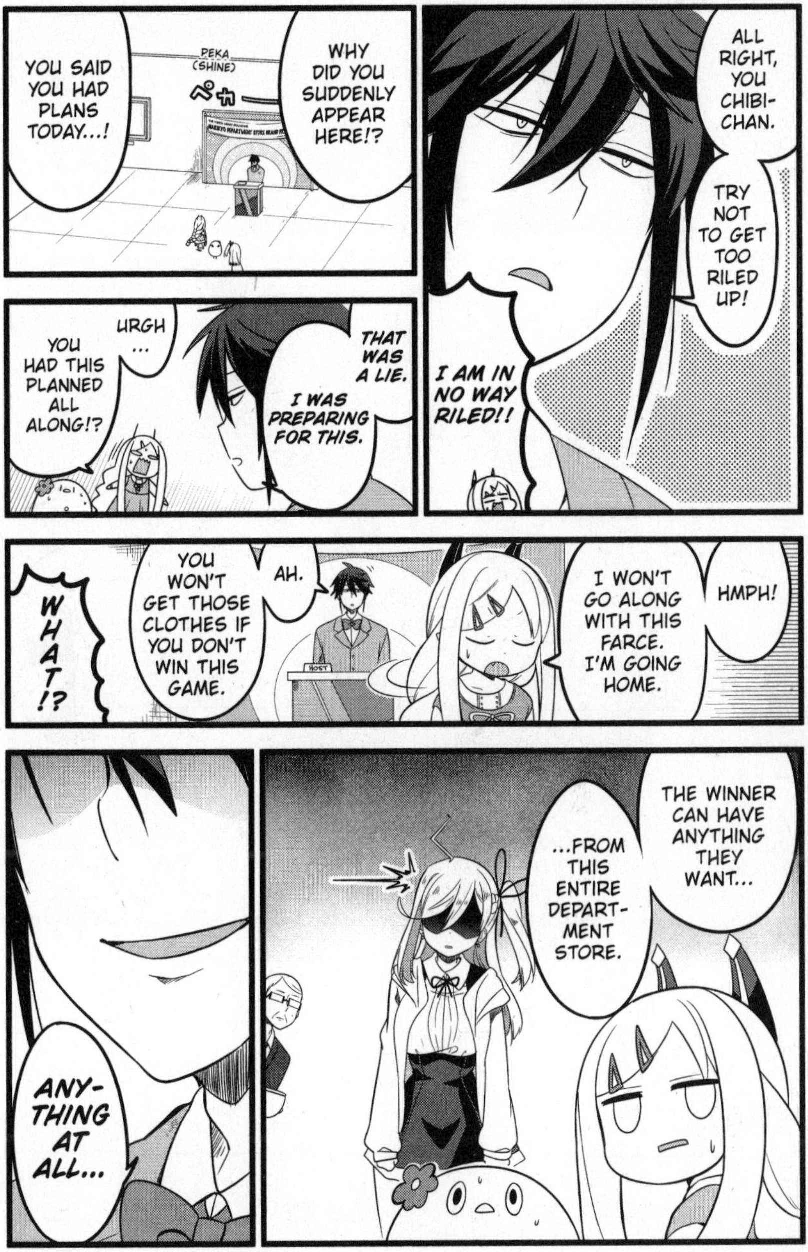
ALL RIGHT, YOU CHIBI-CHAN.
TRY NOT TO GET TOO RILED UP!
I AM IN NO WAY RILED!!
WHY DID YOU SUDDENLY APPEAR HERE!?
PEKA (SHINE)
YOU SAID YOU HAD PLANS TODAY...!
THAT WAS A LIE.
I WAS PREPARING FOR THIS.
URGH...
YOU HAD THIS PLANNED ALL ALONG!?
HMPH!
I WON'T GO ALONG WITH THIS FARCE. I'M GOING HOME.
AH.
HOST
YOU WON'T GET THOSE CLOTHES IF YOU DON'T WIN THIS GAME.
WHAT!?
THE WINNER CAN HAVE ANYTHING THEY WANT...
...FROM THIS ENTIRE DEPARTMENT STORE.
ANYTHING AT ALL...

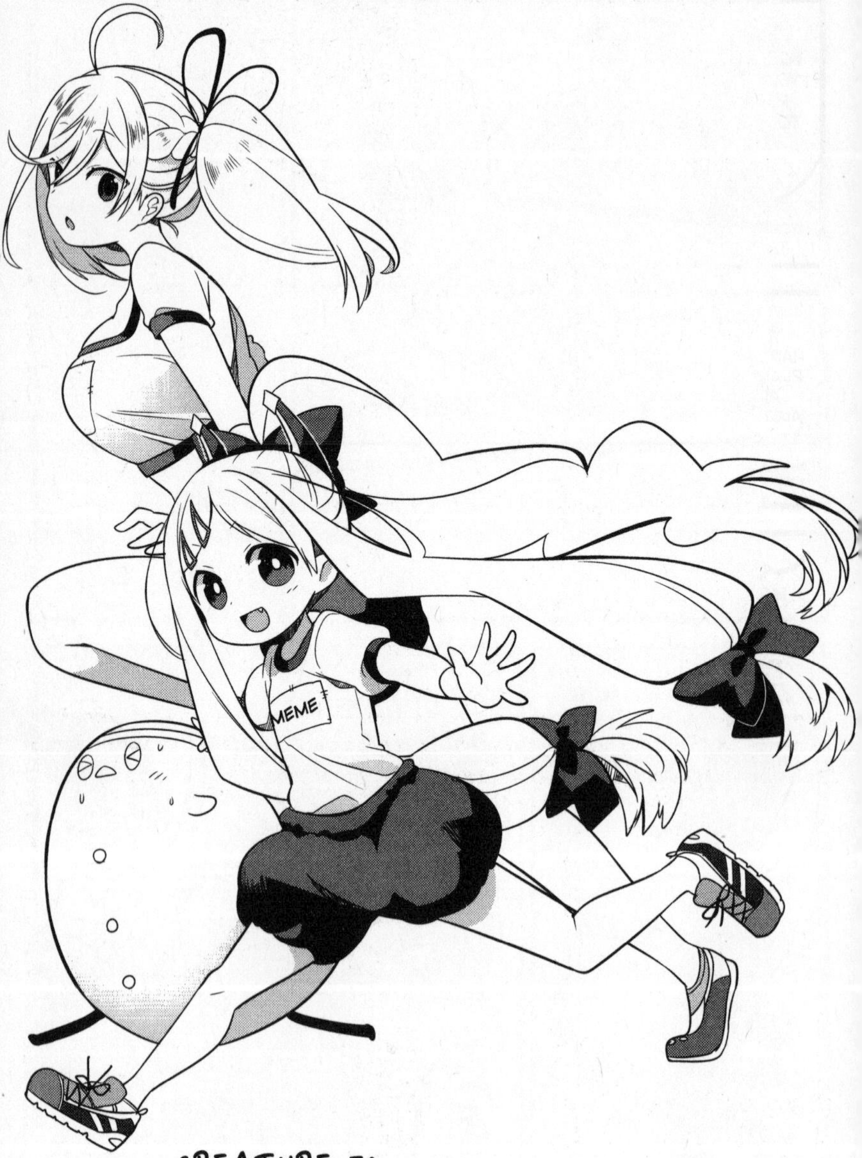
MEME

CREATURE 7:
DEPARTMENT STORE CRISIS!! (PART 2)

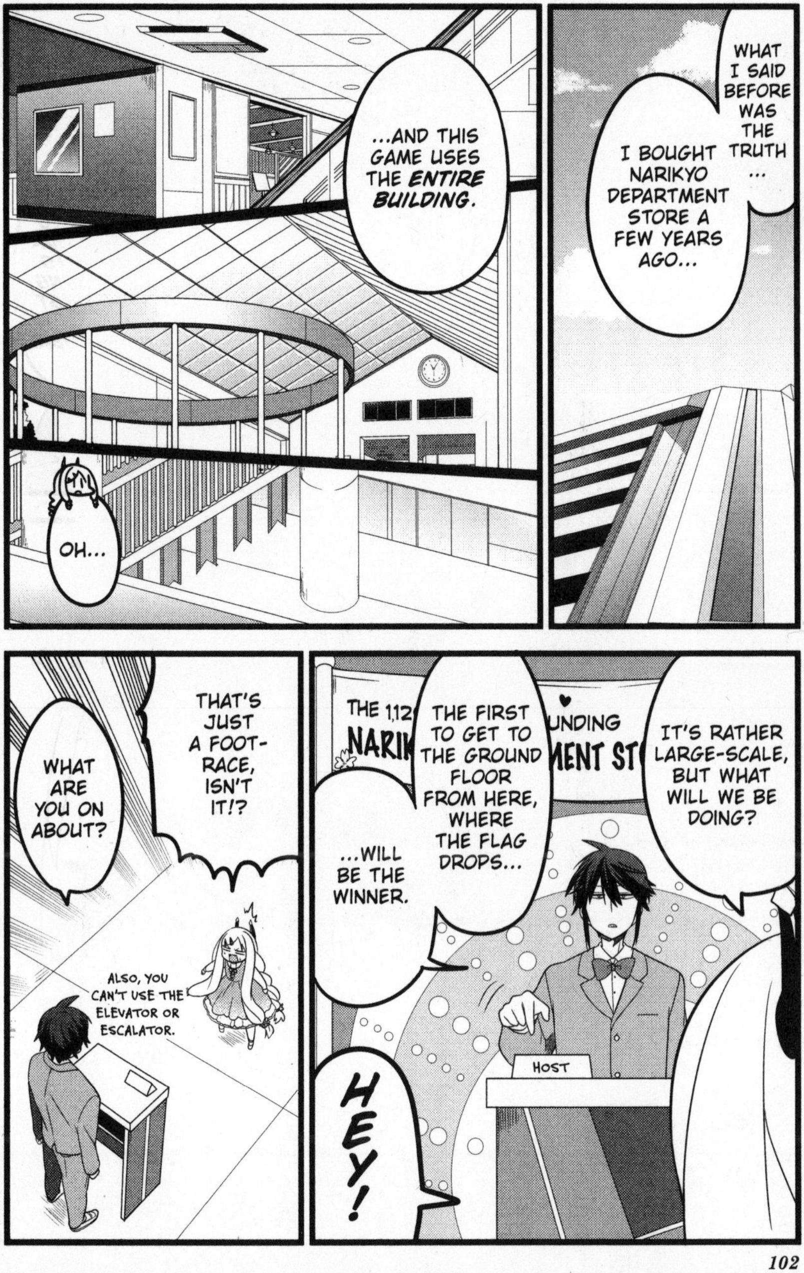
WHAT I SAID BEFORE WAS THE TRUTH...
I BOUGHT NARIKYO DEPARTMENT STORE A FEW YEARS AGO...
...AND THIS GAME USES THE ENTIRE BUILDING.
OH...
IT'S RATHER LARGE-SCALE, BUT WHAT WILL WE BE DOING?
THE FIRST TO GET TO THE GROUND FLOOR FROM HERE, WHERE THE FLAG DROPS...
...WILL BE THE WINNER.
HOST
HEY!
THAT'S JUST A FOOT-RACE, ISN'T IT!?
WHAT ARE YOU ON ABOUT?
ALSO, YOU CAN'T USE THE ELEVATOR OR ESCALATOR.

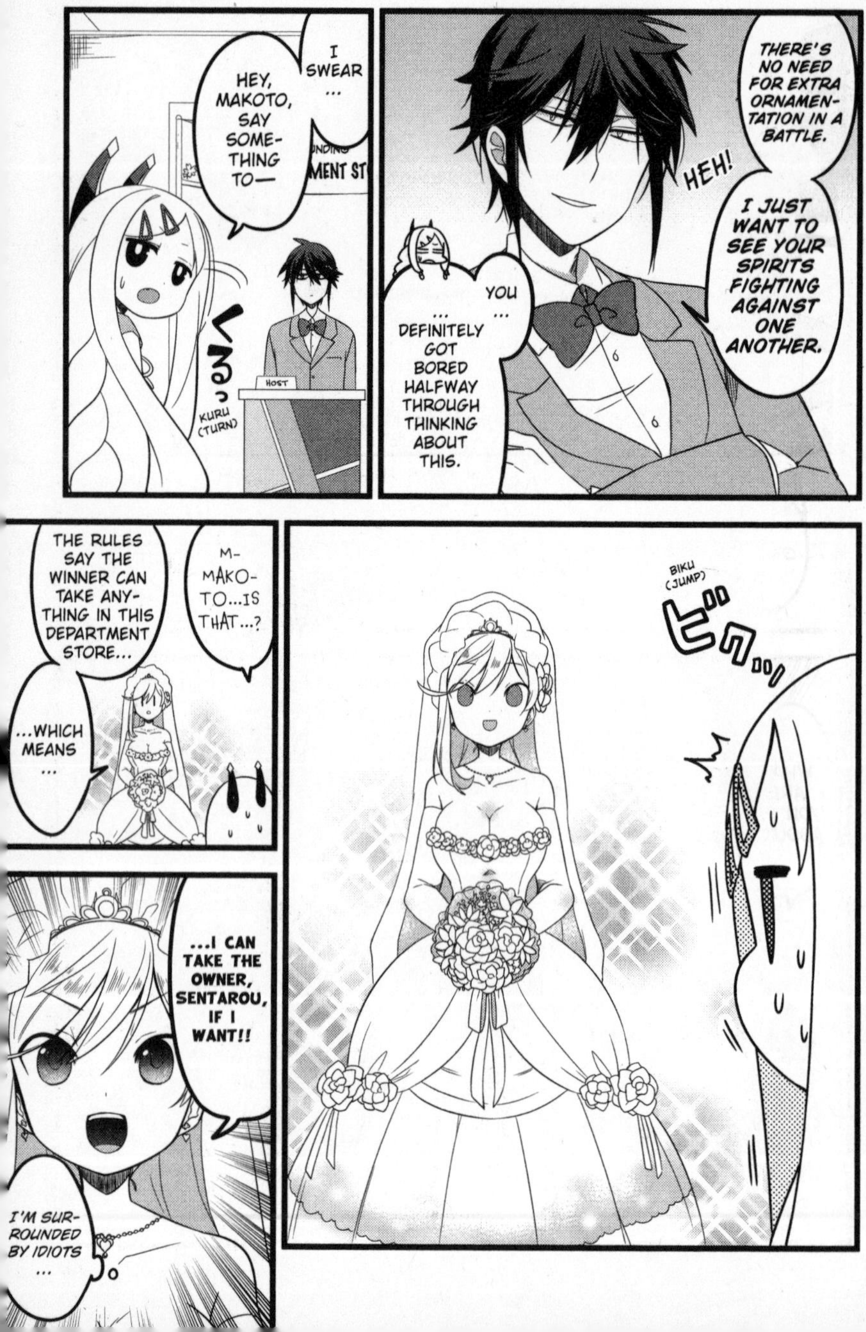
THERE'S NO NEED FOR EXTRA ORNAMENTATION IN A BATTLE.
HEH!
I JUST WANT TO SEE YOUR SPIRITS FIGHTING AGAINST ONE ANOTHER.
YOU... DEFINITELY GOT BORED HALFWAY THROUGH THINKING ABOUT THIS.
I SWEAR...
HEY, MAKOTO, SAY SOMETHING TO—
HOST
KURU (TURN)
BIKU (JUMP)
M-MAKOTO...IS THAT...?
THE RULES SAY THE WINNER CAN TAKE ANYTHING IN THIS DEPARTMENT STORE...
...WHICH MEANS...
...I CAN TAKE THE OWNER, SENTAROU, IF I WANT!!
I'M SURROUNDED BY IDIOTS...

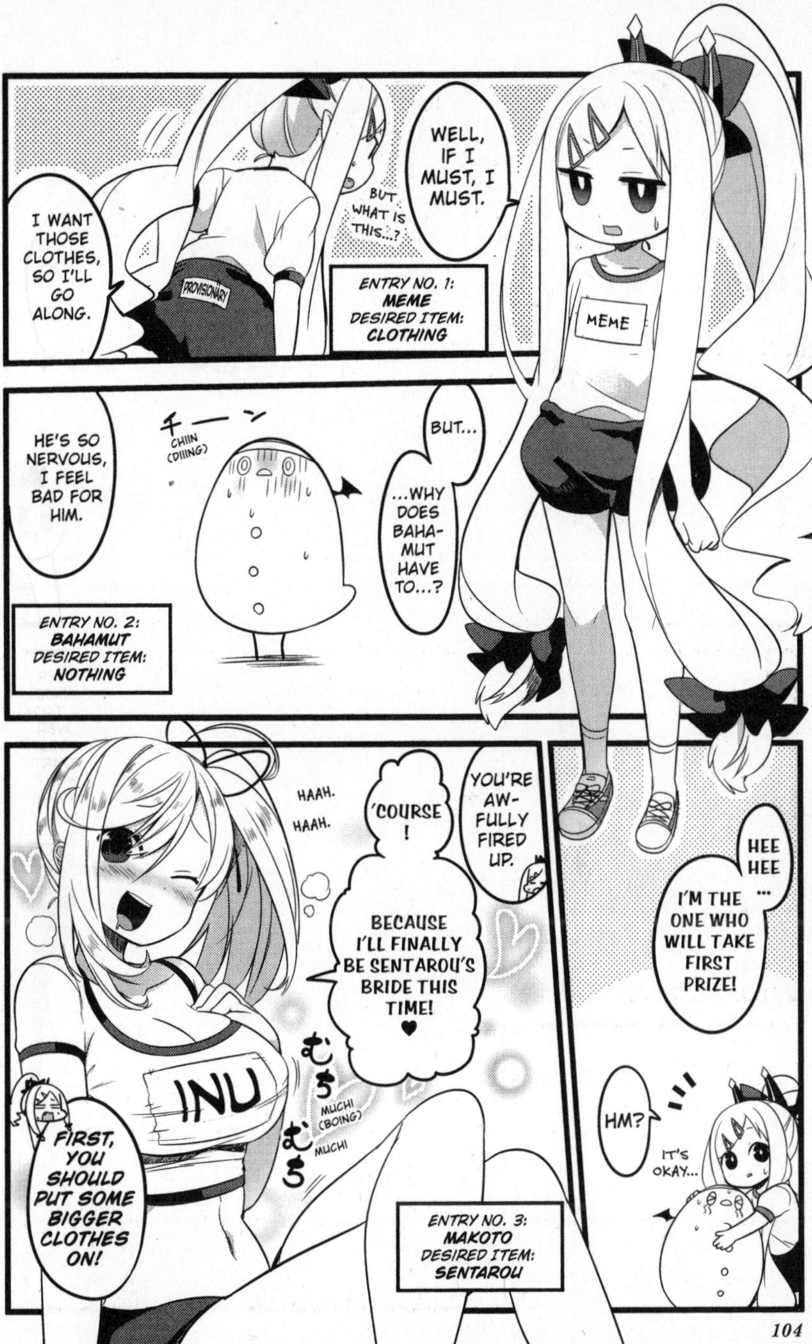
WELL, IF I MUST, I MUST.
BUT WHAT IS THIS...?
ENTRY NO. 1: MEME DESIRED ITEM: CLOTHING
I WANT THOSE CLOTHES, SO I'LL GO ALONG.
PROVISIONARY
MEME
BUT...
...WHY DOES BAHAMUT HAVE TO...?
チーン
CHIIN (DIIING)
HE'S SO NERVOUS, I FEEL BAD FOR HIM.
ENTRY NO. 2: BAHAMUT DESIRED ITEM: NOTHING
HEE HEE... I'M THE ONE WHO WILL TAKE FIRST PRIZE!
HM?
IT'S OKAY...
YOU'RE AWFULLY FIRED UP.
'COURSE!
BECAUSE I'LL FINALLY BE SENTAROU'S BRIDE THIS TIME! ♥
HAAH. HAAH.
むち MUCHI (BOING)
むち MUCHI
INU
FIRST, YOU SHOULD PUT SOME BIGGER CLOTHES ON!
ENTRY NO. 3: MAKOTO DESIRED ITEM: SENTAROU

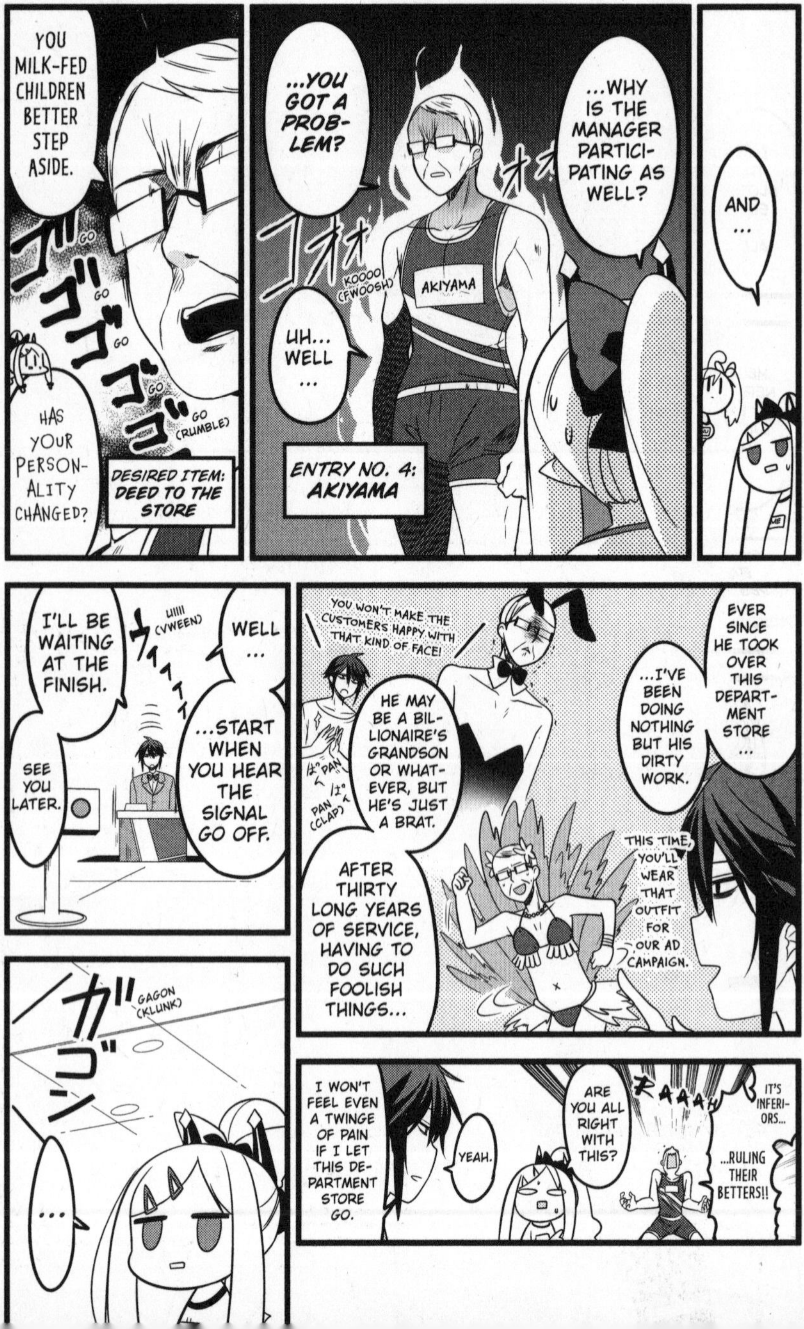
AND ...
...WHY IS THE MANAGER PARTICIPATING AS WELL?
...YOU GOT A PROBLEM?
KOOOO (FWOOSH)
AKIYAMA
UH... WELL ...
ENTRY NO. 4: AKIYAMA
YOU MILK-FED CHILDREN BETTER STEP ASIDE.
GO GO GO GO GO (RUMBLE)
HAS YOUR PERSONALITY CHANGED?
DESIRED ITEM: DEED TO THE STORE
EVER SINCE HE TOOK OVER THIS DEPARTMENT STORE ...
...I'VE BEEN DOING NOTHING BUT HIS DIRTY WORK.
YOU WON'T MAKE THE CUSTOMERS HAPPY WITH THAT KIND OF FACE!
HE MAY BE A BILLIONAIRE'S GRANDSON OR WHATEVER, BUT HE'S JUST A BRAT.
PAN PAN (CLAP)
THIS TIME, YOU'LL WEAR THAT OUTFIT FOR OUR AD CAMPAIGN.
AFTER THIRTY LONG YEARS OF SERVICE, HAVING TO DO SUCH FOOLISH THINGS...
WELL ...
...START WHEN YOU HEAR THE SIGNAL GO OFF.
UIIII (VWEEN)
I'LL BE WAITING AT THE FINISH.
SEE YOU LATER.
IT'S INFERIORS...
...RULING THEIR BETTERS!!
RAAAH
ARE YOU ALL RIGHT WITH THIS?
YEAH.
I WON'T FEEL EVEN A TWINGE OF PAIN IF I LET THIS DEPARTMENT STORE GO.
GAGON (KLUNK)
...

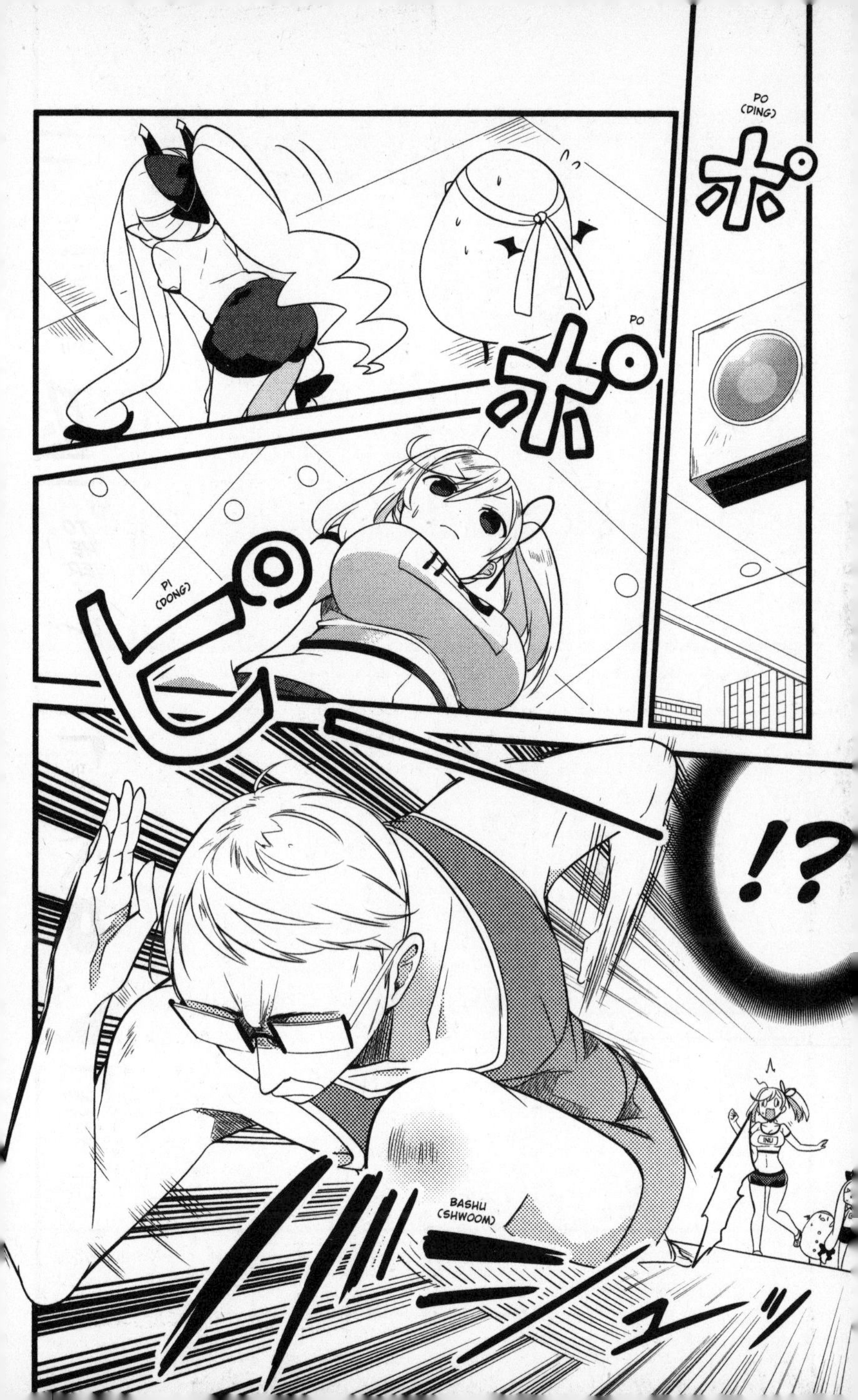
PO
(DING)
PO
PI
(DONG)
!?
BASHU
(SHWOOM)
INU

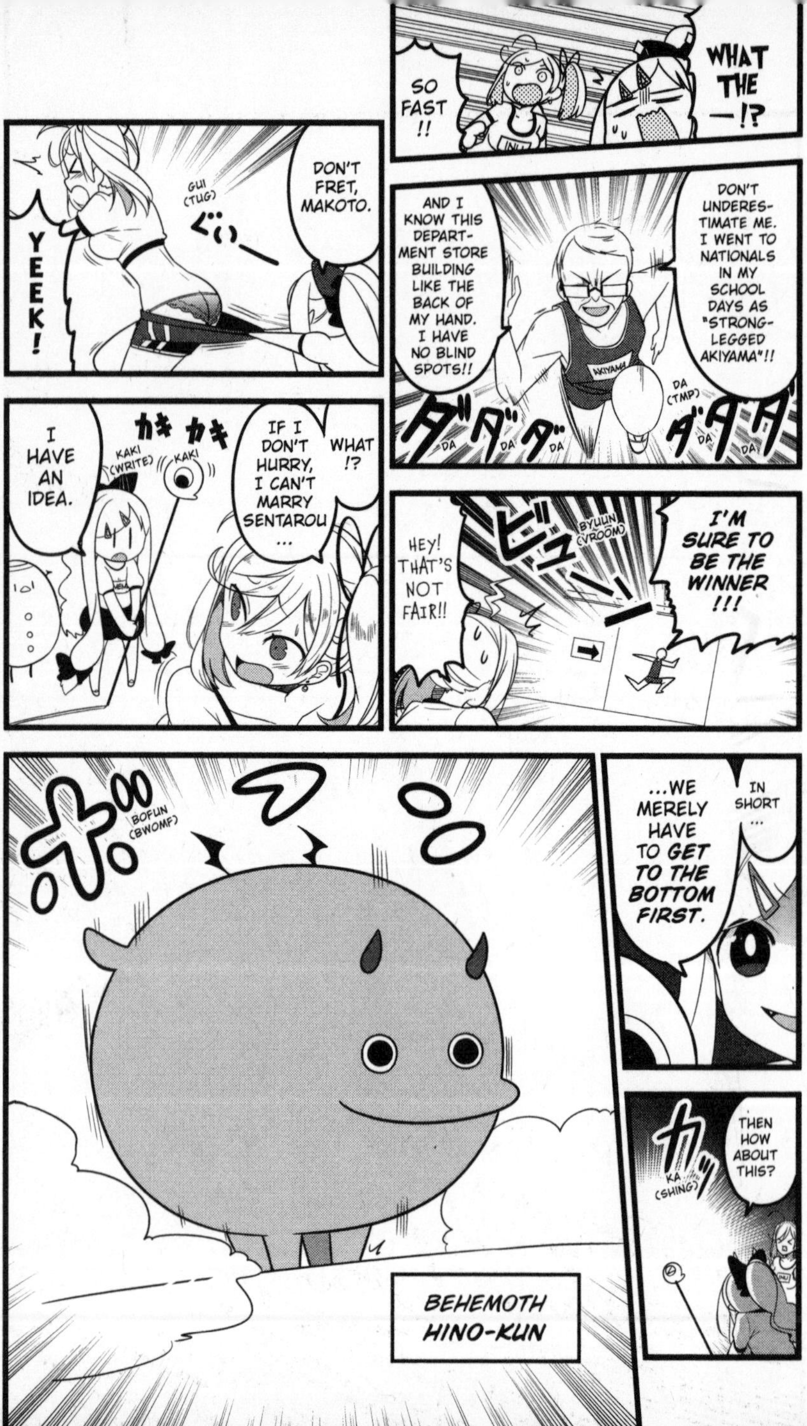
WHAT THE —!?
SO FAST!!
DON'T UNDERESTIMATE ME. I WENT TO NATIONALS IN MY SCHOOL DAYS AS "STRONG-LEGGED AKIYAMA"!!
AND I KNOW THIS DEPARTMENT STORE BUILDING LIKE THE BACK OF MY HAND. I HAVE NO BLIND SPOTS!!
DA (TMP)
DON'T FRET, MAKOTO.
GUI (TUG)
YEEK!
I'M SURE TO BE THE WINNER!!!
BYUUN (VROOM)
HEY! THAT'S NOT FAIR!!
WHAT!?
IF I DON'T HURRY, I CAN'T MARRY SENTAROU...
KAKI (WRITE) KAKI
I HAVE AN IDEA.
IN SHORT...
...WE MERELY HAVE TO GET TO THE BOTTOM FIRST.
THEN HOW ABOUT THIS?
KA (SHING)
BOFUN (BWOMF)
BEHEMOTH HINO-KUN

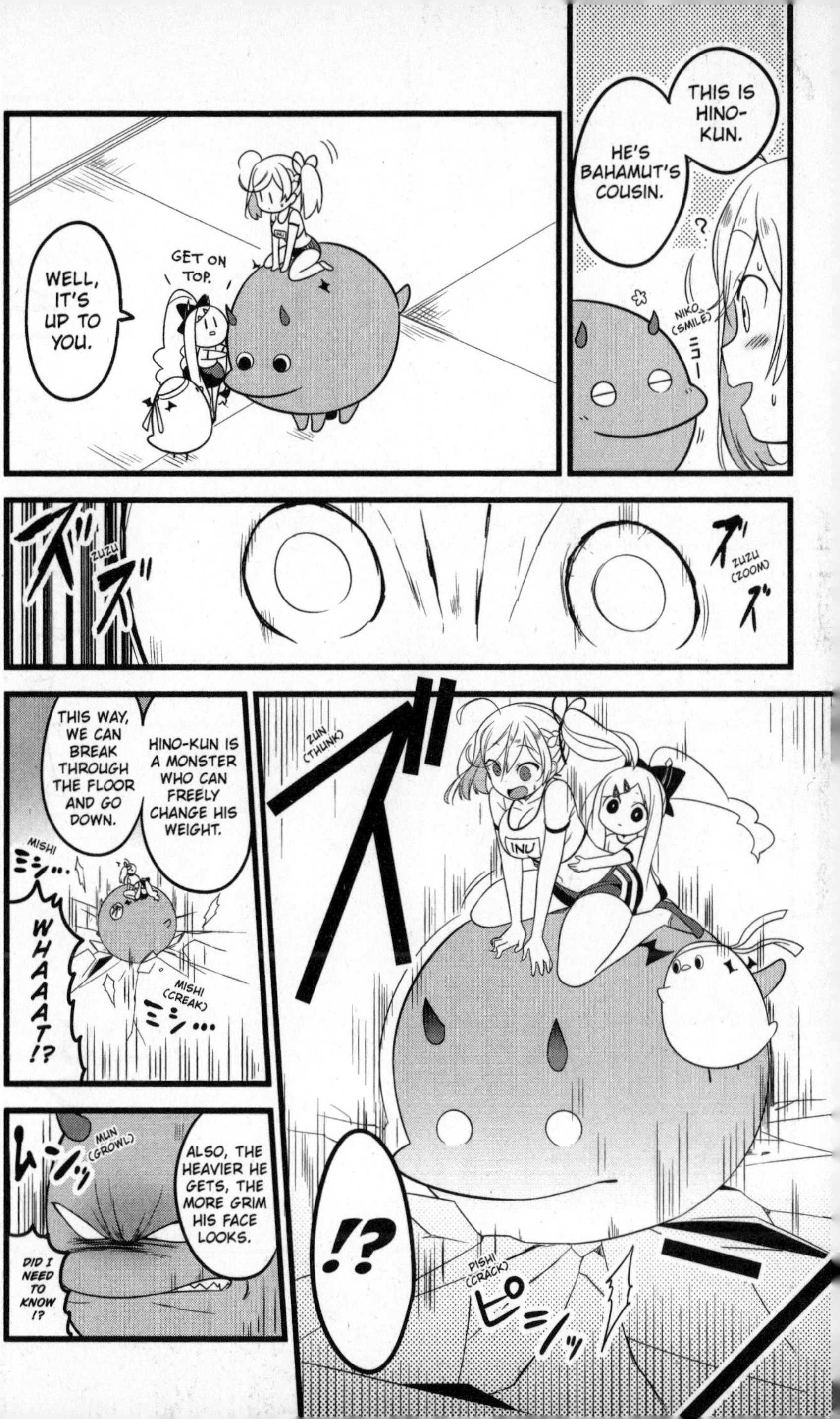
THIS IS HINO-KUN.
HE'S BAHAMUT'S COUSIN.
?
NIKO (SMILE)
ニコー
GET ON TOP.
WELL, IT'S UP TO YOU.
ズズ
ZUZU (ZOOM)
ズズ
ZUZU
ズ
ZUN (THUNK)
!?
PISHI (CRACK)
ピシッ
HINO-KUN IS A MONSTER WHO CAN FREELY CHANGE HIS WEIGHT.
THIS WAY, WE CAN BREAK THROUGH THE FLOOR AND GO DOWN.
MISHI
ミシ…
MISHI (CREAK)
ミシ…
WHAAAAT!?
ALSO, THE HEAVIER HE GETS, THE MORE GRIM HIS FACE LOOKS.
MUN (GROWL)
ムンッ
DID I NEED TO KNOW!?

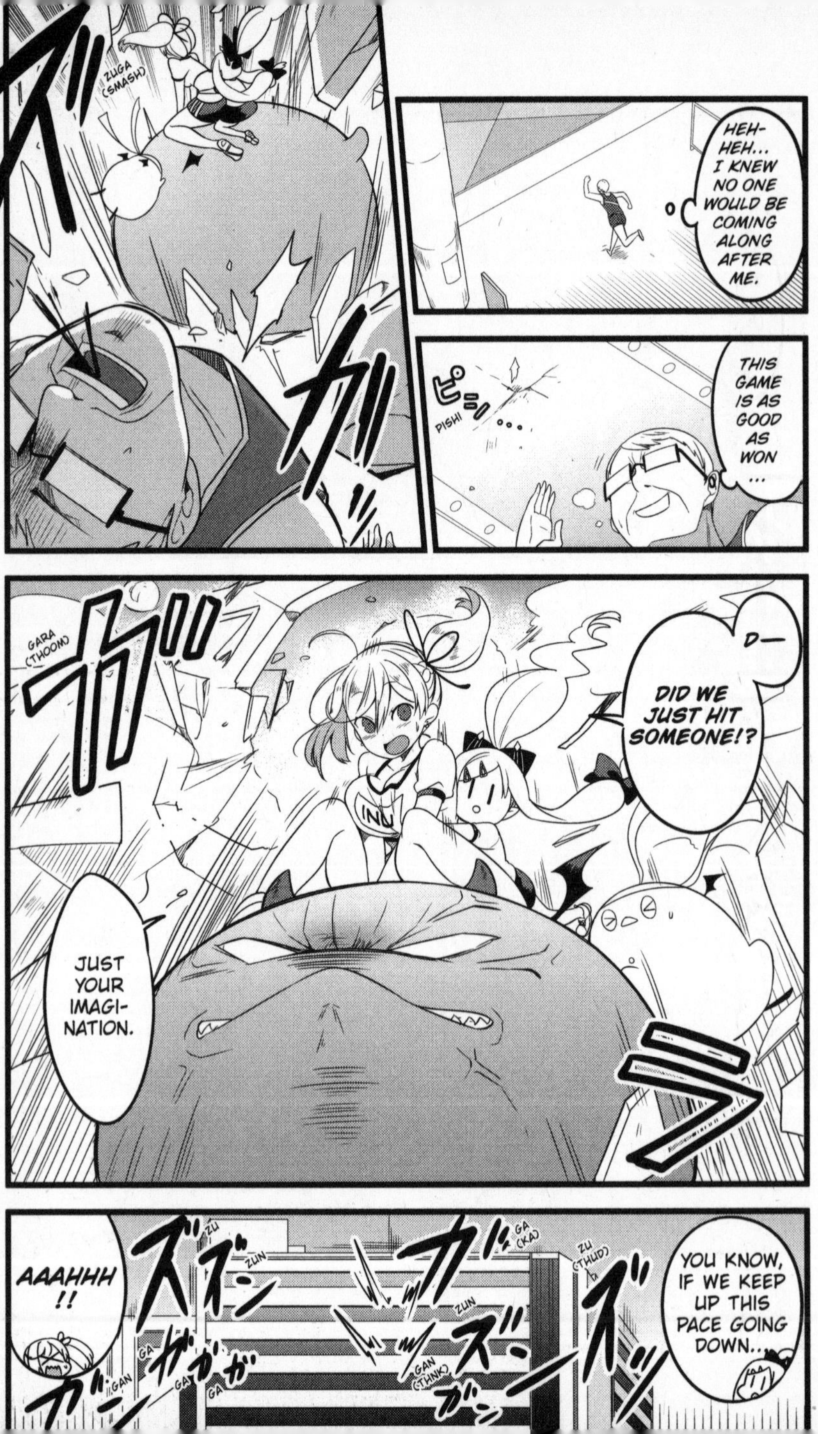
HEH-HEH... I KNEW NO ONE WOULD BE COMING ALONG AFTER ME.
PISHI
THIS GAME IS AS GOOD AS WON...
ZUGA (SMASH)
GARA (THOOM)
D—
DID WE JUST HIT SOMEONE!?
JUST YOUR IMAGINATION.
YOU KNOW, IF WE KEEP UP THIS PACE GOING DOWN...
ZU (THUD)
ZUN
GAN (THNK)
GA (KA)
ZUN
ZU
GA
GA
GA
GA
GAN
AAAHHH!!

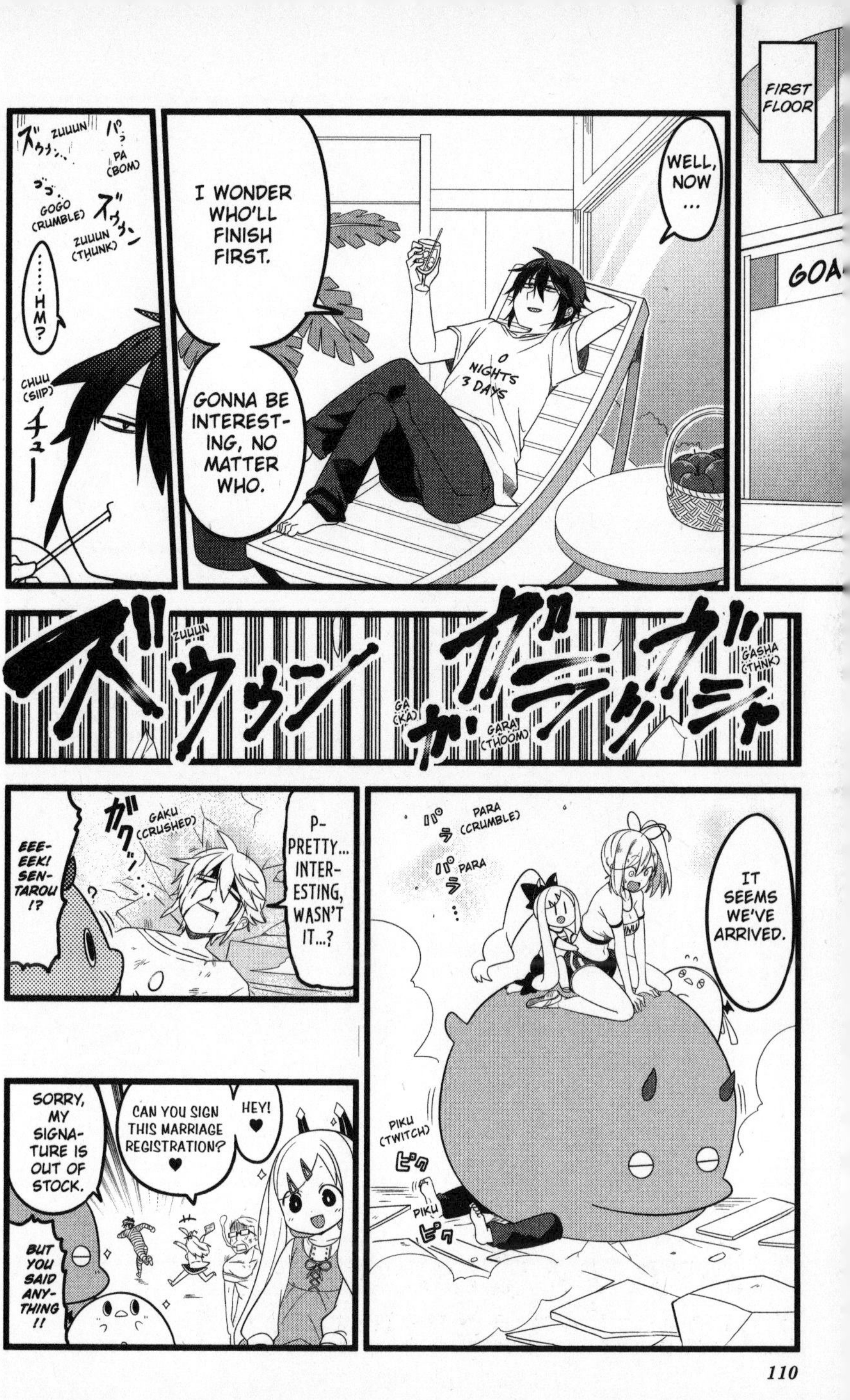
FIRST FLOOR
GOA
WELL, NOW...
I WONDER WHO'LL FINISH FIRST.
GONNA BE INTERESTING, NO MATTER WHO.
PA (BOM)
ZUUUN
GOGO (RUMBLE)
ZUUUN (THUNK)
......HM?
CHUU (SIIP)
ZUUUN
GA (KA)
GARA (THOOM)
GASHA (THNK)
PARA (CRUMBLE)
PARA
IT SEEMS WE'VE ARRIVED.
PIKU (TWITCH)
PIKU
P-PRETTY... INTERESTING, WASN'T IT...?
GAKU (CRUSHED)
EEEEEK! SENTAROU!?
HEY! ♥
CAN YOU SIGN THIS MARRIAGE REGISTRATION? ♥
SORRY, MY SIGNATURE IS OUT OF STOCK.
BUT YOU SAID ANYTHING!!

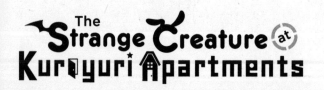

The Strange Creature at Kuroyuri Apartments

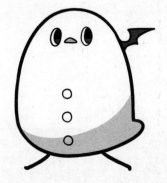

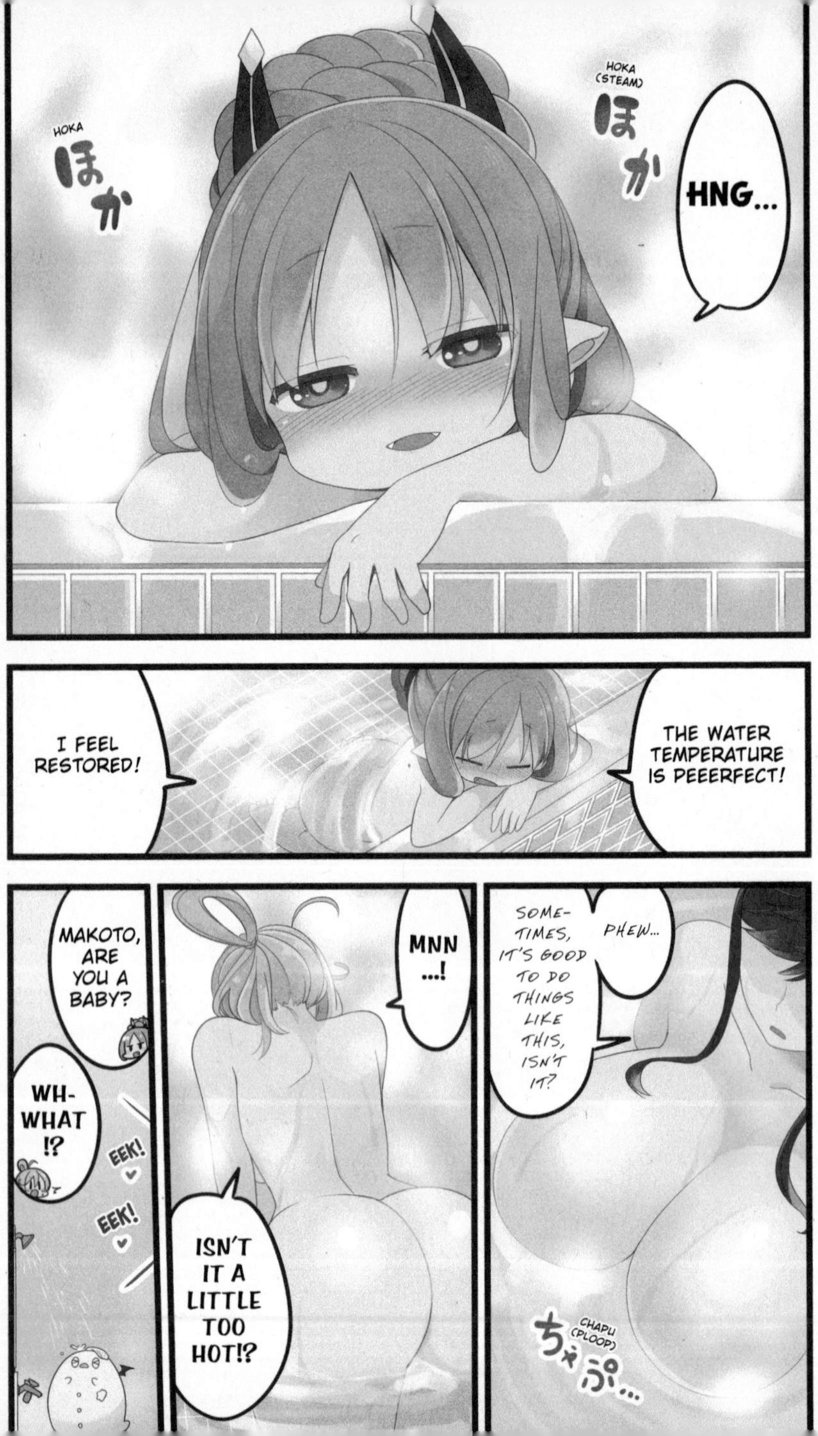
HNG...
HOKA (STEAM)
ほか
HOKA
ほか
THE WATER TEMPERATURE IS PEEERFECT!
I FEEL RESTORED!
PHEW...
SOMETIMES, IT'S GOOD TO DO THINGS LIKE THIS, ISN'T IT?
CHAPU (PLOOP)
ちゃぷ...
MNN ...!
ISN'T IT A LITTLE TOO HOT!?
MAKOTO, ARE YOU A BABY?
WH-WHAT!?
EEK!
EEK!

CREATURE 8: STEAM PARADISE

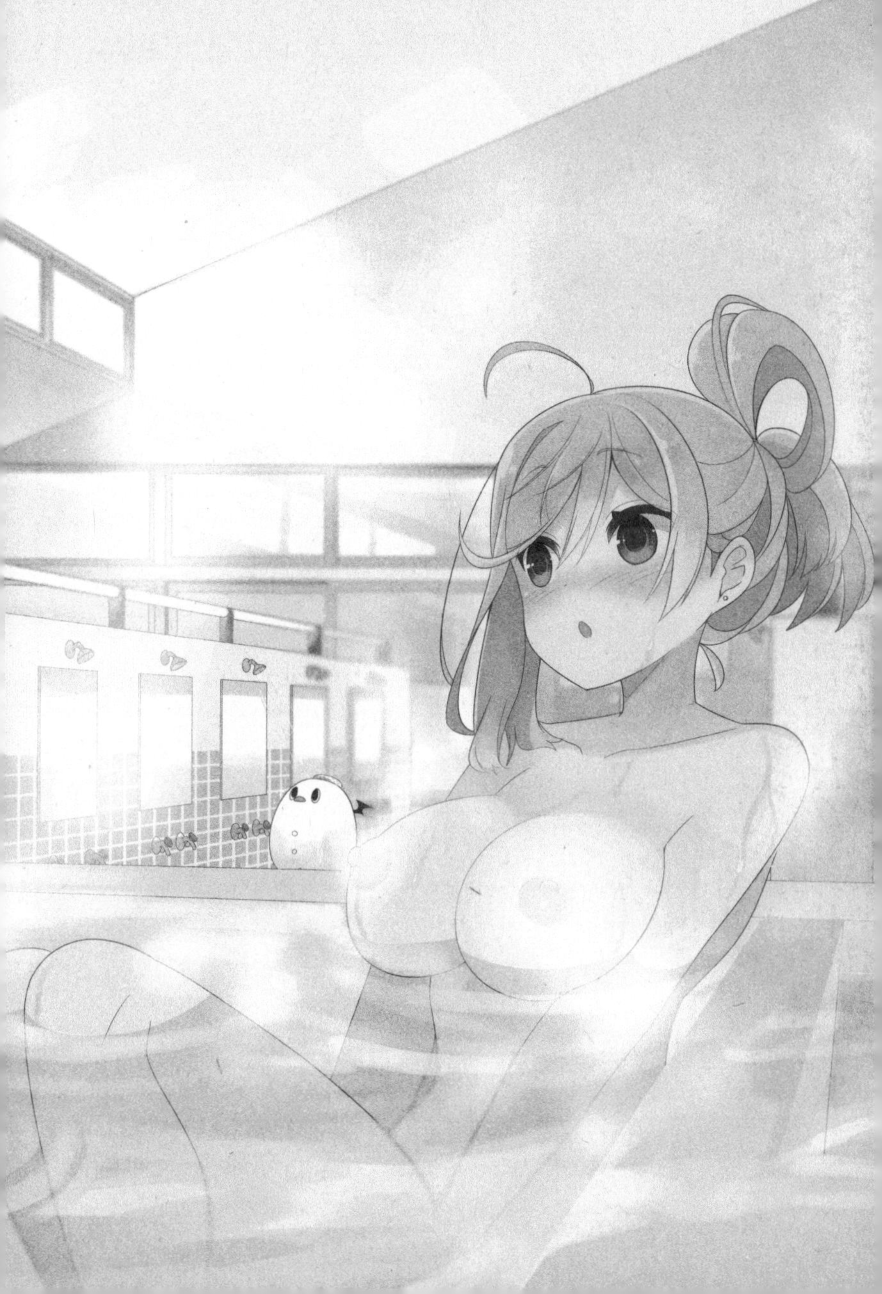

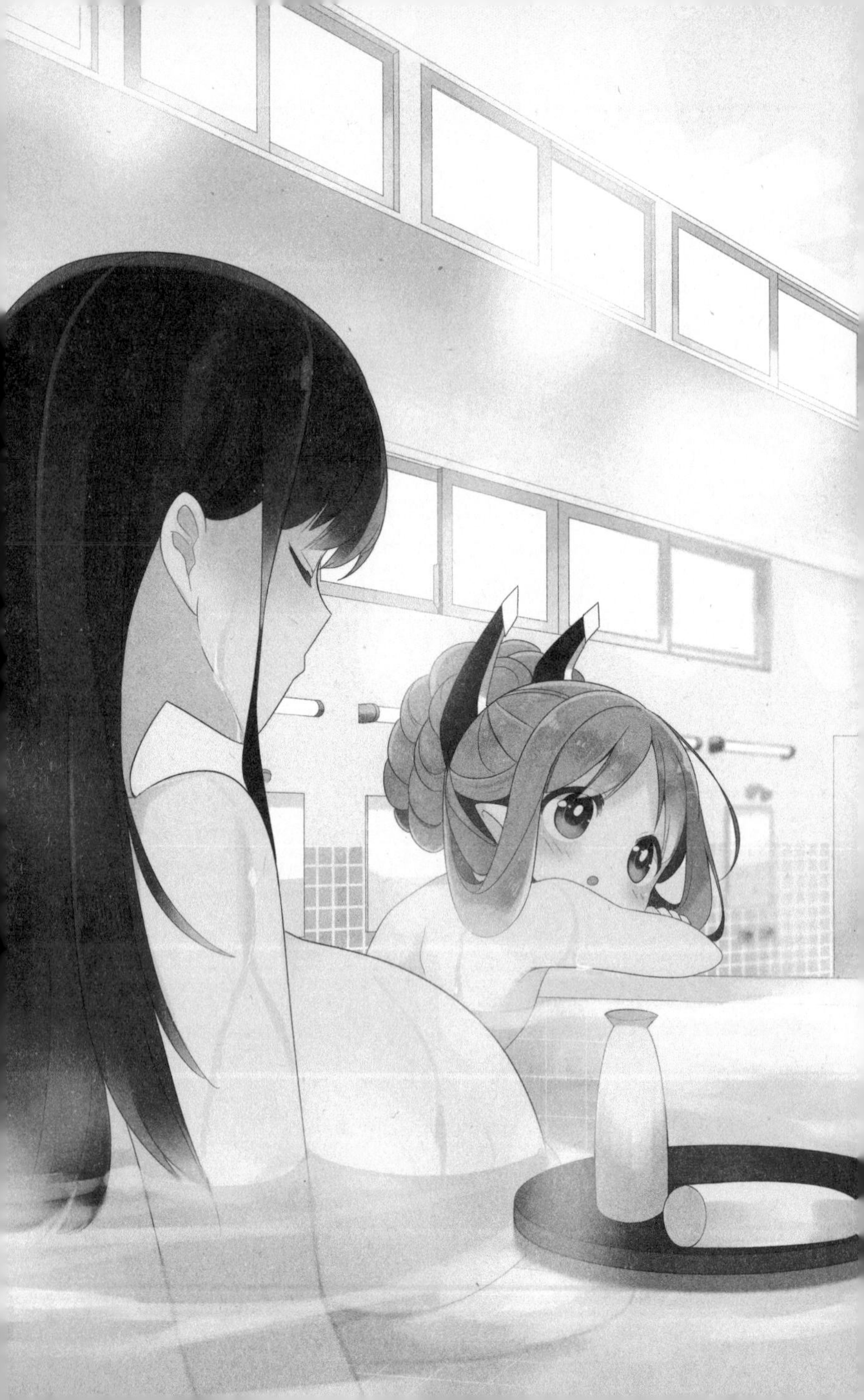

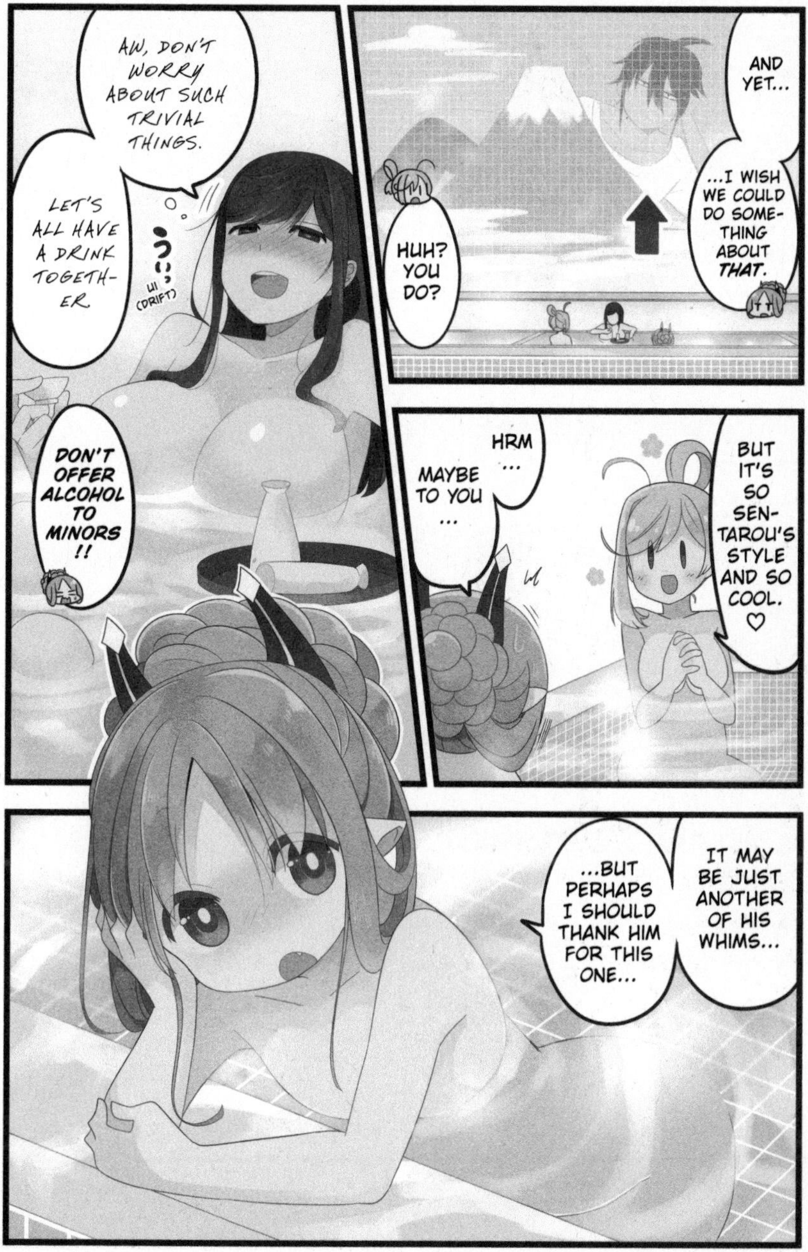
AND YET...
...I WISH WE COULD DO SOME-THING ABOUT THAT.
HUH? YOU DO?
BUT IT'S SO SEN-TAROU'S STYLE AND SO COOL. ♡
HRM...
MAYBE TO YOU...
AW, DON'T WORRY ABOUT SUCH TRIVIAL THINGS.
LET'S ALL HAVE A DRINK TOGETH-ER.
うぃっ
UI (DRIFT)
DON'T OFFER ALCOHOL TO MINORS!!
IT MAY BE JUST ANOTHER OF HIS WHIMS...
...BUT PERHAPS I SHOULD THANK HIM FOR THIS ONE...

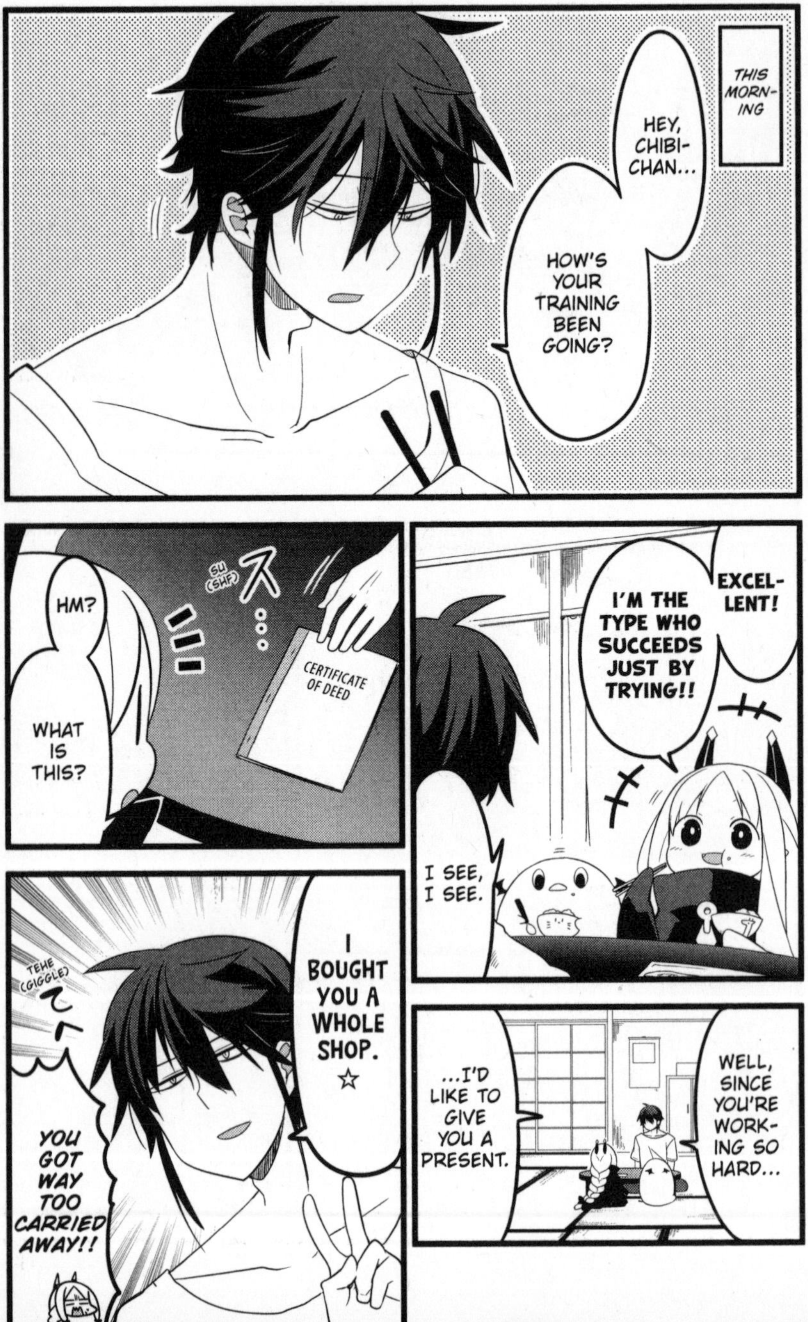
THIS MORNING
HEY, CHIBI-CHAN...
HOW'S YOUR TRAINING BEEN GOING?
EXCEL-LENT!
I'M THE TYPE WHO SUCCEEDS JUST BY TRYING!!
I SEE, I SEE.
WELL, SINCE YOU'RE WORKING SO HARD...
...I'D LIKE TO GIVE YOU A PRESENT.
SU (SHF)
HM?
CERTIFICATE OF DEED
WHAT IS THIS?
I BOUGHT YOU A WHOLE SHOP. ☆
TEHE (GIGGLE)
YOU GOT WAY TOO CARRIED AWAY!!

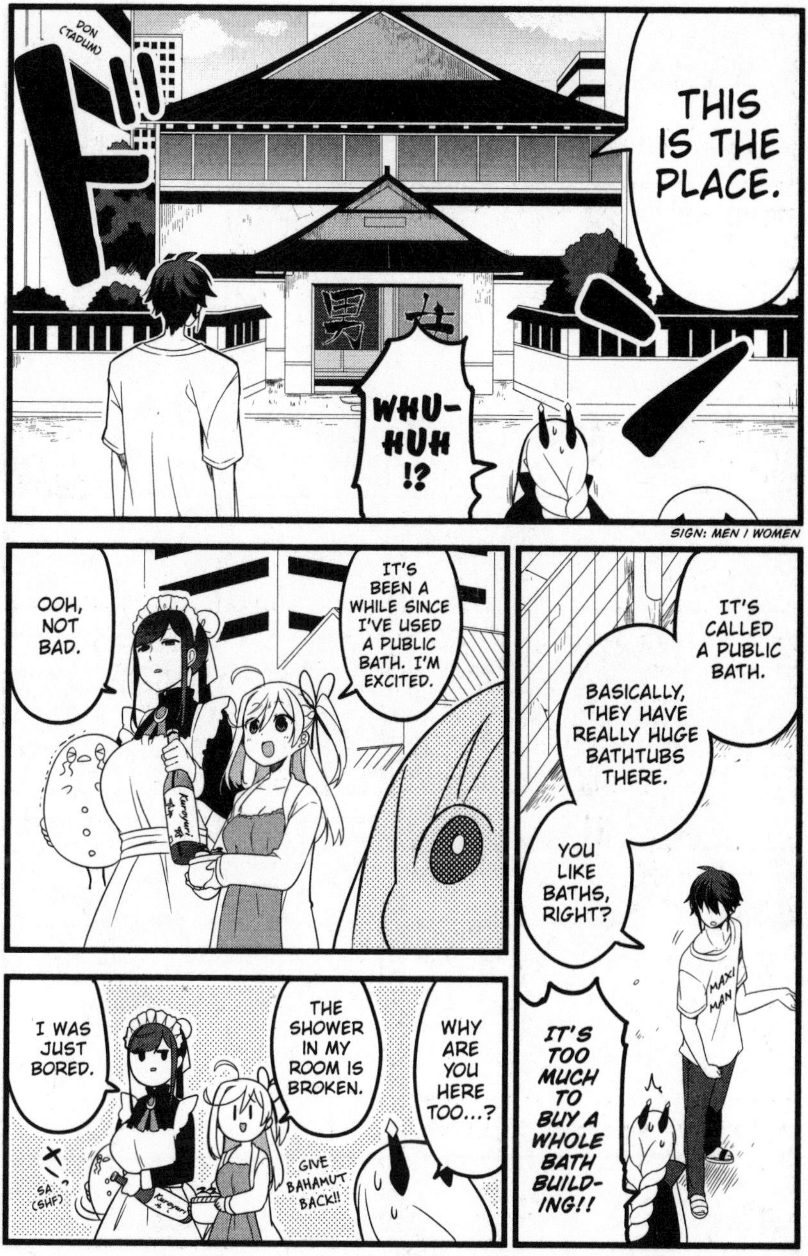
THIS IS THE PLACE.
DON (TADUM)
WHU-HUH!?
SIGN: MEN / WOMEN
IT'S CALLED A PUBLIC BATH.
BASICALLY, THEY HAVE REALLY HUGE BATHTUBS THERE.
YOU LIKE BATHS, RIGHT?
IT'S TOO MUCH TO BUY A WHOLE BATH BUILDING!!
MAXI MAN
IT'S BEEN A WHILE SINCE I'VE USED A PUBLIC BATH. I'M EXCITED.
OOH, NOT BAD.
WHY ARE YOU HERE TOO...?
THE SHOWER IN MY ROOM IS BROKEN.
I WAS JUST BORED.
GIVE BAHAMUT BACK!!
SA (SHF)

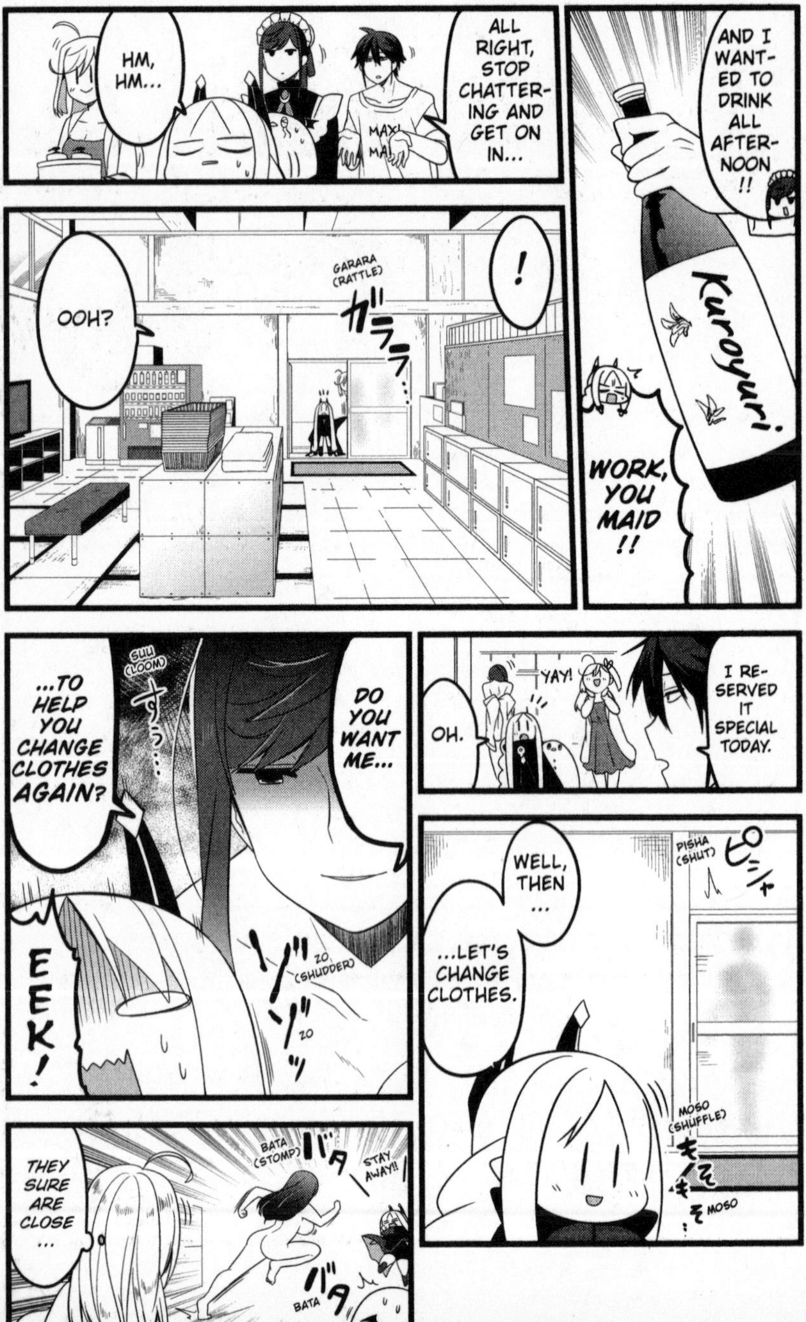
AND I WANTED TO DRINK ALL AFTERNOON!!
Kuroyuri
WORK, YOU MAID!!
ALL RIGHT, STOP CHATTERING AND GET ON IN...
MAX! MAX!
HM, HM...
!
GARARA (RATTLE)
OOH?
I RESERVED IT SPECIAL TODAY.
YAY!
OH.
PISHA (SHUT)
WELL, THEN...
...LET'S CHANGE CLOTHES.
MOSO (SHUFFLE)
MOSO
DO YOU WANT ME...
SUU (LOOM)
...TO HELP YOU CHANGE CLOTHES AGAIN?
ZO (SHUDDER)
ZO
EEK!
STAY AWAY!!
BATA (STOMP)
THEY SURE ARE CLOSE...
BATA

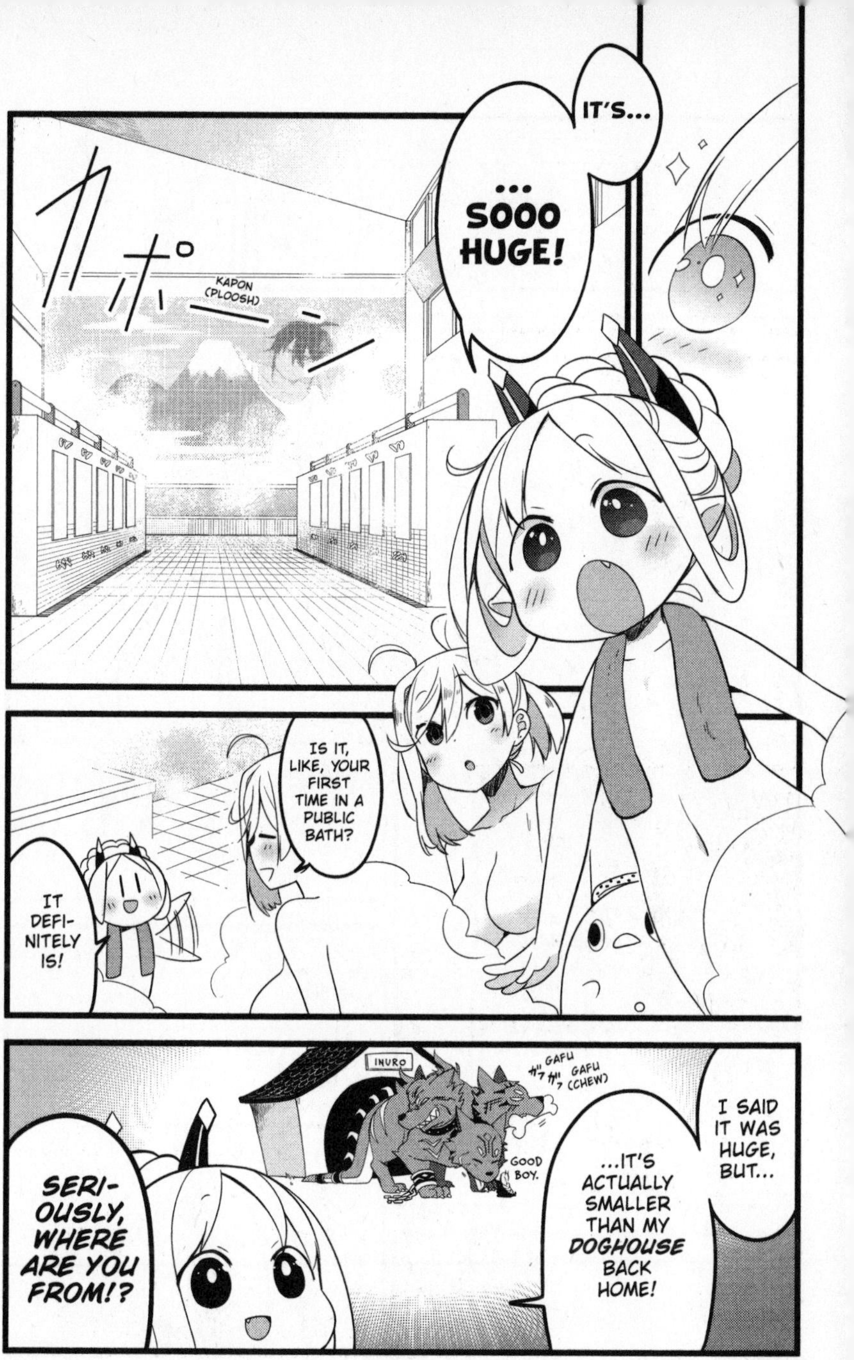
IT'S...
...SOOO HUGE!
KAPON (PLOOSH)
IS IT, LIKE, YOUR FIRST TIME IN A PUBLIC BATH?
IT DEFI-NITELY IS!
I SAID IT WAS HUGE, BUT...
...IT'S ACTUALLY SMALLER THAN MY DOGHOUSE BACK HOME!
GAFU GAFU (CHEW)
INURO
GOOD BOY.
SERI-OUSLY, WHERE ARE YOU FROM!?

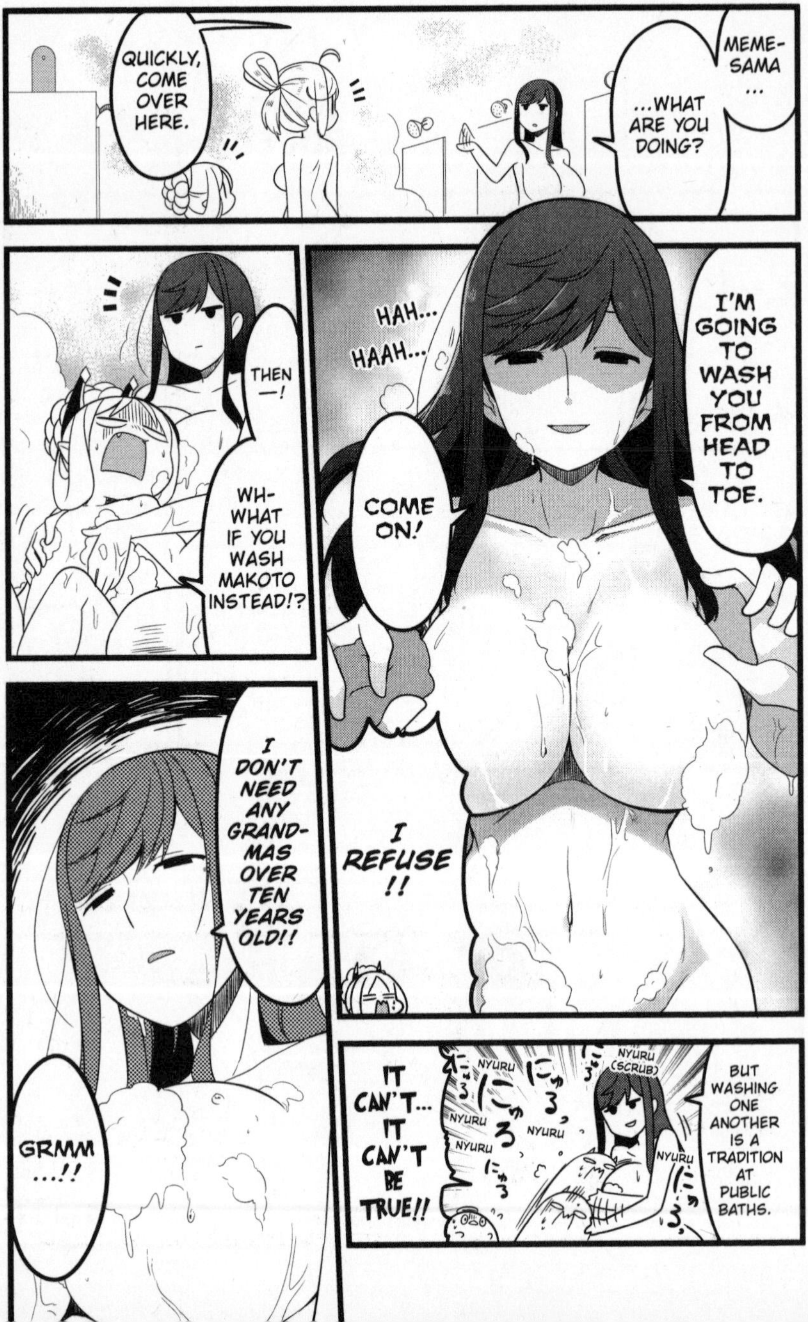
MEME-SAMA ...
...WHAT ARE YOU DOING?
QUICKLY, COME OVER HERE.
I'M GOING TO WASH YOU FROM HEAD TO TOE.
HAH... HAAH...
COME ON!
I REFUSE!!
THEN—!
WH-WHAT IF YOU WASH MAKOTO INSTEAD!?
I DON'T NEED ANY GRANDMAS OVER TEN YEARS OLD!!
GRMM ...!!
BUT WASHING ONE ANOTHER IS A TRADITION AT PUBLIC BATHS.
NYURU (SCRUB)
NYURU
NYURU
NYURU
NYURU
IT CAN'T... IT CAN'T BE TRUE!!

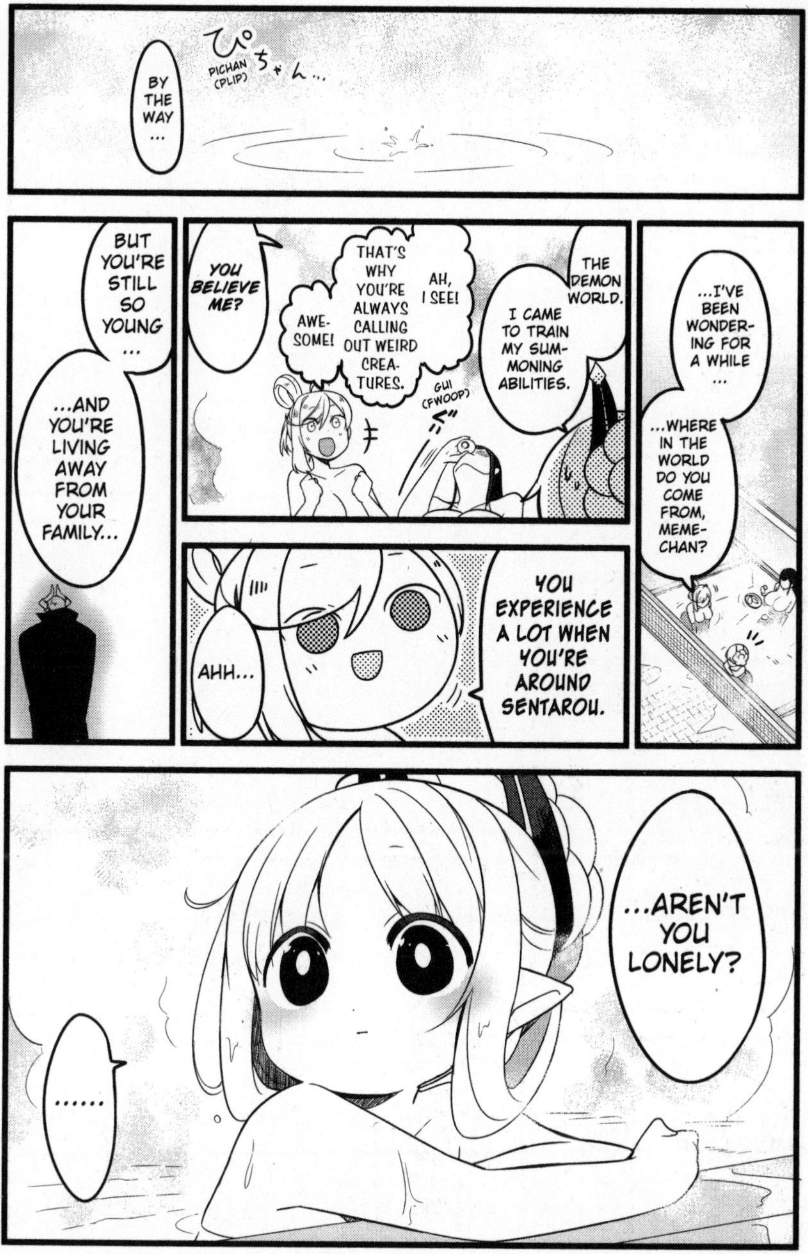
ぴちゃん…
PICHAN (PLIP)
BY THE WAY...
...I'VE BEEN WONDERING FOR A WHILE...
...WHERE IN THE WORLD DO YOU COME FROM, MEME-CHAN?
THE DEMON WORLD.
I CAME TO TRAIN MY SUMMONING ABILITIES.
AH, I SEE!
THAT'S WHY YOU'RE ALWAYS CALLING OUT WEIRD CREATURES.
AWESOME!
GUI (FWOOP)
YOU BELIEVE ME?
YOU EXPERIENCE A LOT WHEN YOU'RE AROUND SENTAROU.
AHH...
BUT YOU'RE STILL SO YOUNG...
...AND YOU'RE LIVING AWAY FROM YOUR FAMILY...
...AREN'T YOU LONELY?
......

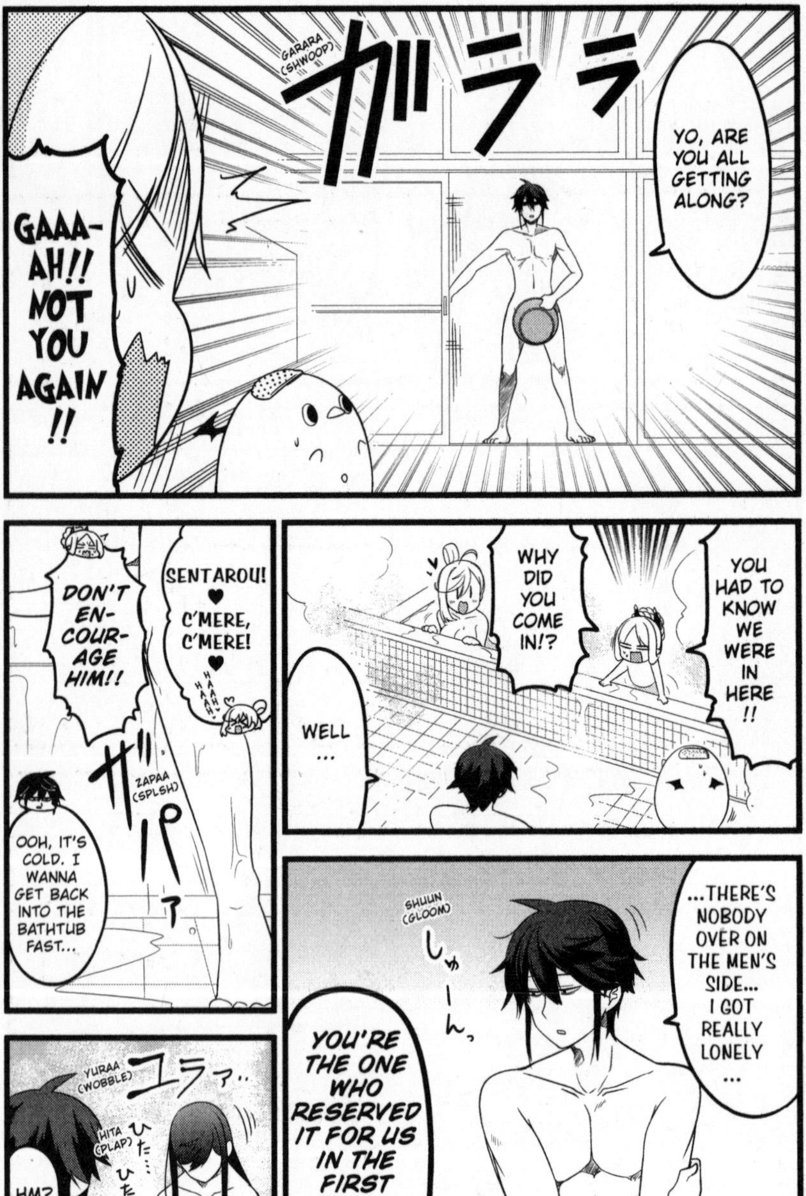
GARARA (SHWOOP)
ガララ
YO, ARE YOU ALL GETTING ALONG?
GAAAH!! NOT YOU AGAIN!!
YOU HAD TO KNOW WE WERE IN HERE!!
WHY DID YOU COME IN!?
WELL...
SENTAROU! ♥ C'MERE, C'MERE! ♥
HAAH HAAH
DON'T ENCOURAGE HIM!!
ZAPAA (SPLSH)
ザパァ
OOH, IT'S COLD. I WANNA GET BACK INTO THE BATHTUB FAST...
...THERE'S NOBODY OVER ON THE MEN'S SIDE... I GOT REALLY LONELY...
SHUUN (GLOOM)
しゅーん
YOU'RE THE ONE WHO RESERVED IT FOR US IN THE FIRST PLACE!
YURAA (WOBBLE)
ユラァ...
HITA (PLAP)
ひた... ひた...
HITA
HM?

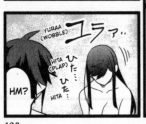

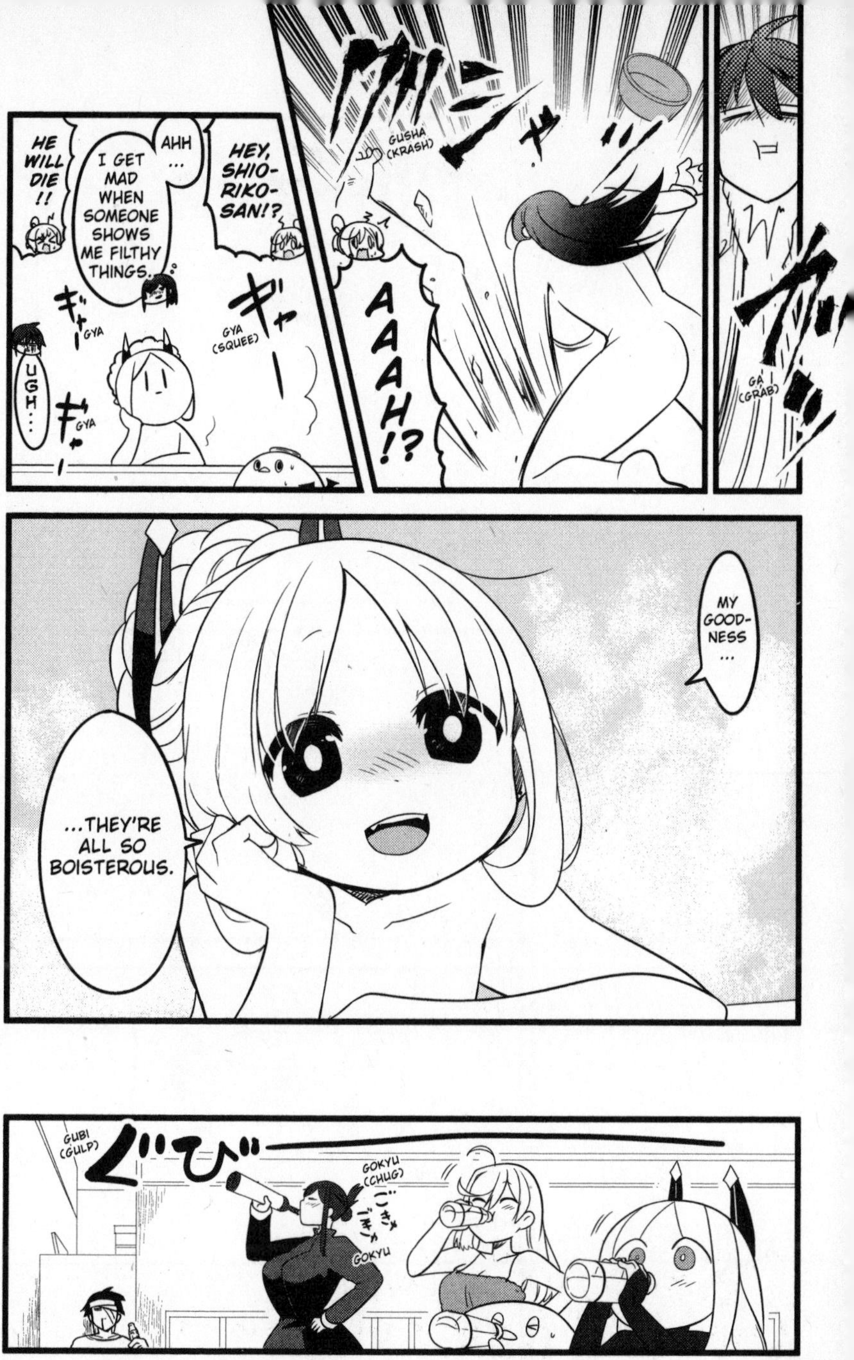
GA (GRAB)
GUSHA (KRASH)
AAAAH!?
HEY, SHIORIKO-SAN!?
AHH...
I GET MAD WHEN SOMEONE SHOWS ME FILTHY THINGS.
HE WILL DIE!!
GYA (SQUEE)
GYA
UGH...
GYA
MY GOODNESS...
...THEY'RE ALL SO BOISTEROUS.
GUBI (GULP)
GOKYU (CHUG)
GOKYU

The Strange Creature at Kuroyuri Apartments

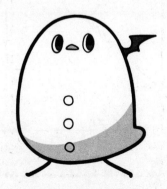

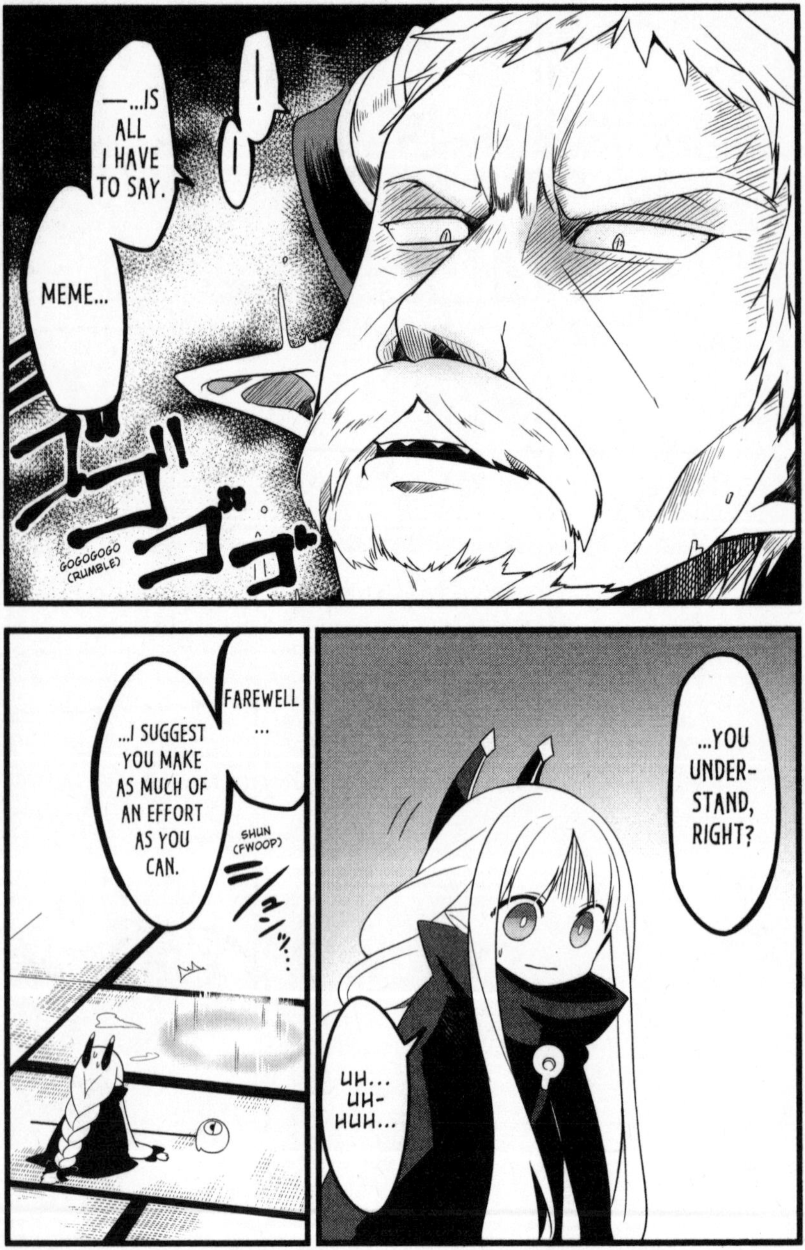
!
—...IS ALL I HAVE TO SAY.
MEME...
GOGOGOGO (RUMBLE)
...YOU UNDER-STAND, RIGHT?
UH... UH-HUH...
FAREWELL...
...I SUGGEST YOU MAKE AS MUCH OF AN EFFORT AS YOU CAN.
SHUN (FWOOP)

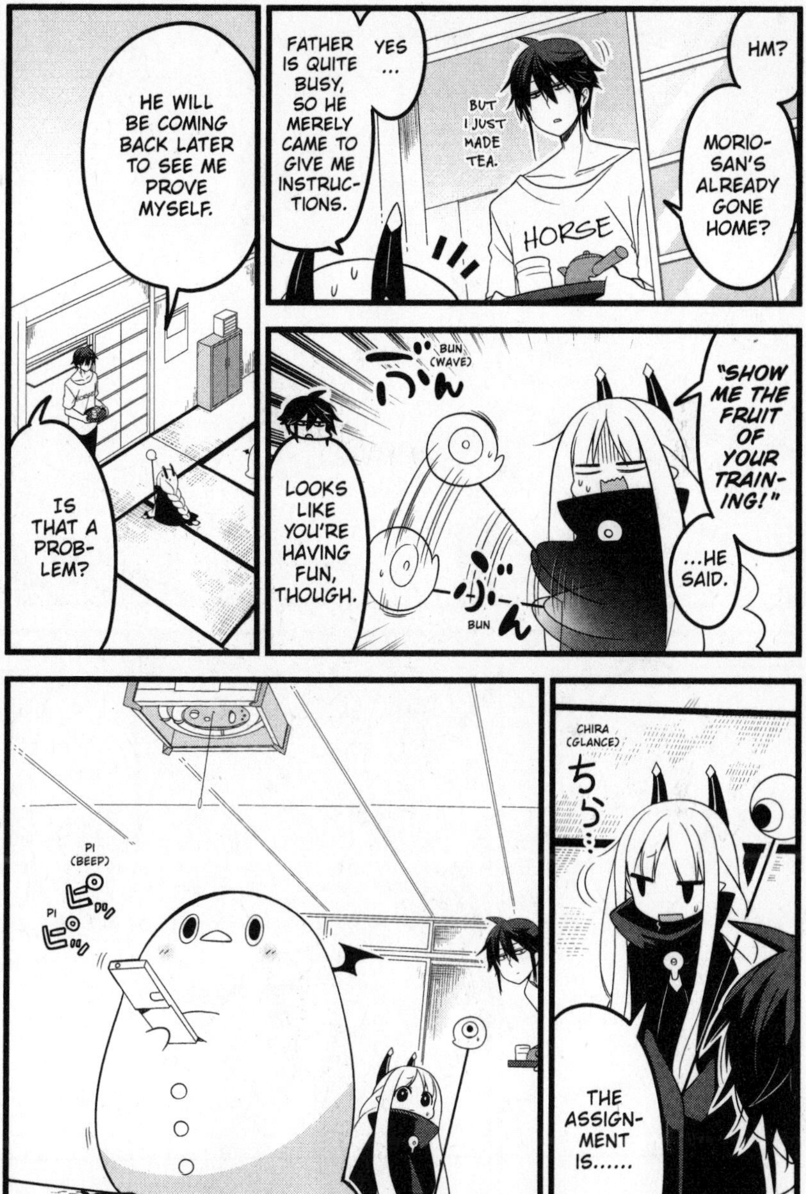
HM?
MORIO-SAN'S ALREADY GONE HOME?
BUT I JUST MADE TEA.
YES...
FATHER IS QUITE BUSY, SO HE MERELY CAME TO GIVE ME INSTRUCTIONS.
"SHOW ME THE FRUIT OF YOUR TRAINING!"
...HE SAID.
BUN (WAVE)
ぶん
LOOKS LIKE YOU'RE HAVING FUN, THOUGH.
ぶん
BUN
HE WILL BE COMING BACK LATER TO SEE ME PROVE MYSELF.
IS THAT A PROBLEM?
CHIRA (GLANCE)
ちら…
THE ASSIGNMENT IS......
PI (BEEP)
ピッ
PI
ピッ

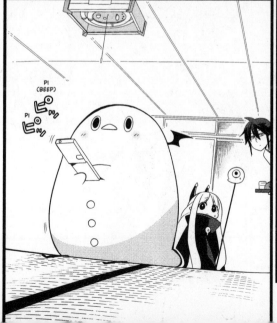

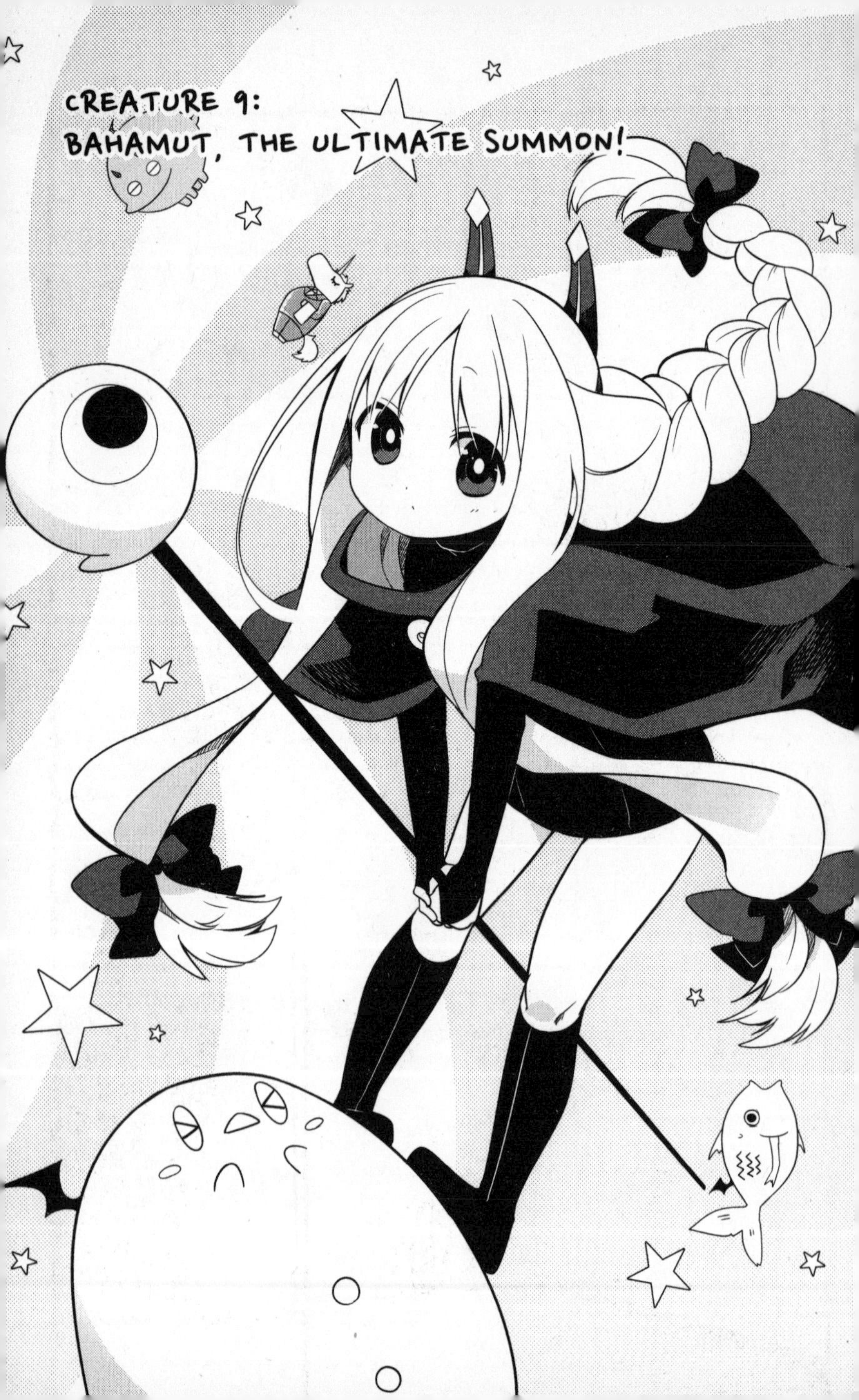
CREATURE 9:
BAHAMUT, THE ULTIMATE SUMMON!

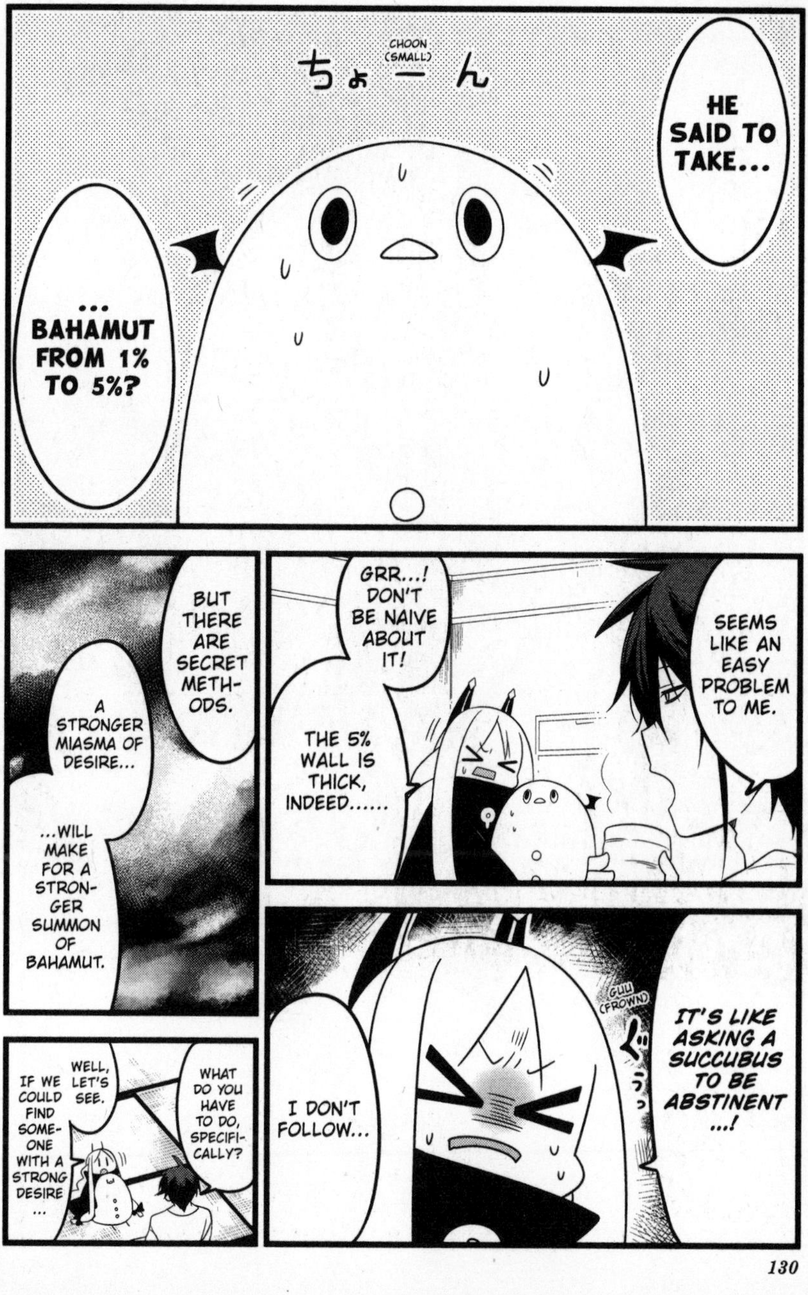
HE SAID TO TAKE...
ちょーん
CHOON (SMALL)
...BAHAMUT FROM 1% TO 5%?
SEEMS LIKE AN EASY PROBLEM TO ME.
GRR...! DON'T BE NAIVE ABOUT IT!
THE 5% WALL IS THICK, INDEED......
BUT THERE ARE SECRET METH-ODS.
A STRONGER MIASMA OF DESIRE...
...WILL MAKE FOR A STRON-GER SUMMON OF BAHAMUT.
IT'S LIKE ASKING A SUCCUBUS TO BE ABSTINENT...!
GUU (FROWN)
I DON'T FOLLOW...
WHAT DO YOU HAVE TO DO, SPECIFI-CALLY?
WELL, LET'S SEE.
IF WE COULD FIND SOME-ONE WITH A STRONG DESIRE...

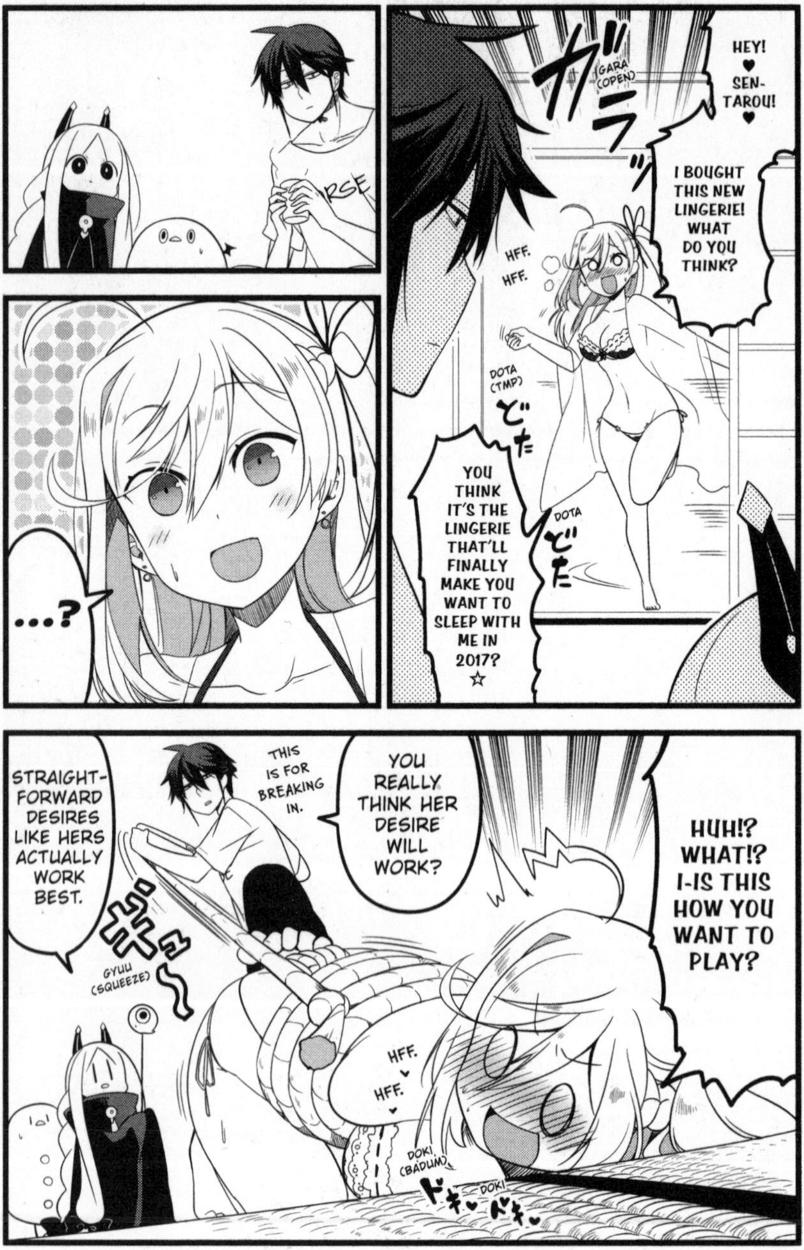
HEY! ♥ SEN-TAROU! ♥
ガラッ
GARA (OPEN)
I BOUGHT THIS NEW LINGERIE! WHAT DO YOU THINK?
HFF. HFF.
DOTA (TMP)
どた
YOU THINK IT'S THE LINGERIE THAT'LL FINALLY MAKE YOU WANT TO SLEEP WITH ME IN 2017? ☆
DOTA
どた
...?
HUH!? WHAT!? I-IS THIS HOW YOU WANT TO PLAY?
YOU REALLY THINK HER DESIRE WILL WORK?
THIS IS FOR BREAKING IN.
STRAIGHT-FORWARD DESIRES LIKE HERS ACTUALLY WORK BEST.
GYUU (SQUEEZE)
HFF. ♥ HFF. ♥
DOKI (BADUM)
DOKI

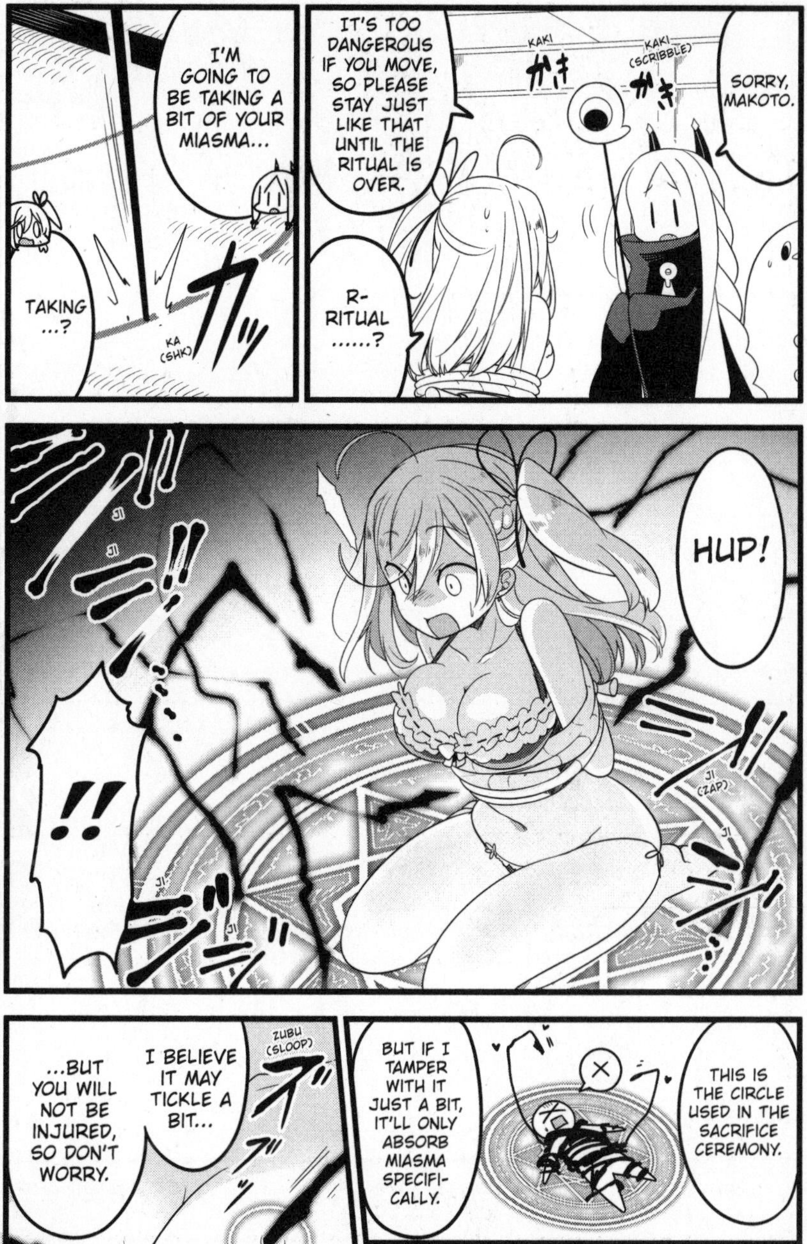
SORRY, MAKOTO.
KAKI
KAKI (SCRIBBLE)
IT'S TOO DANGEROUS IF YOU MOVE, SO PLEASE STAY JUST LIKE THAT UNTIL THE RITUAL IS OVER.
R-RITUAL ......?
I'M GOING TO BE TAKING A BIT OF YOUR MIASMA...
TAKING ...?
KA (SHK)
HUP!
JI
JI
JI (ZAP)
JI
JI
JI
!!
THIS IS THE CIRCLE USED IN THE SACRIFICE CEREMONY.
BUT IF I TAMPER WITH IT JUST A BIT, IT'LL ONLY ABSORB MIASMA SPECIFICALLY.
I BELIEVE IT MAY TICKLE A BIT...
ZUBU (SLOOP)
...BUT YOU WILL NOT BE INJURED, SO DON'T WORRY.

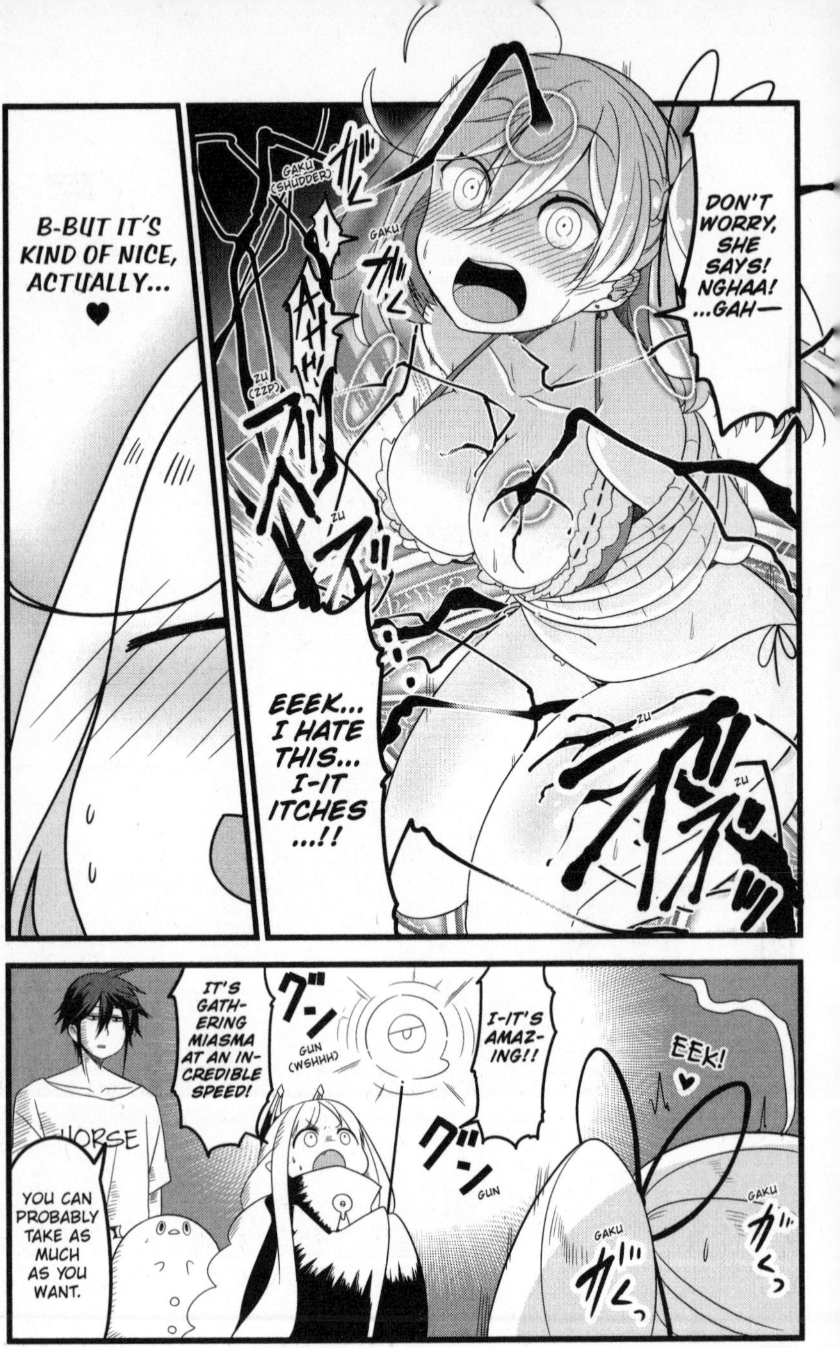
DON'T WORRY, SHE SAYS! NGHAA! ...GAH—
GAKU (SHUDDER)
GAKU
AHH!
ZU (ZZP)
ZU
EEEK... I HATE THIS... I-IT ITCHES ...!!
ZU
ZU
B-BUT IT'S KIND OF NICE, ACTUALLY... ♥
EEK! ♥
GAKU
GAKU
I-IT'S AMAZING!!
GUN (WSHHH)
IT'S GATHERING MIASMA AT AN INCREDIBLE SPEED!
GUN
HORSE
YOU CAN PROBABLY TAKE AS MUCH AS YOU WANT.

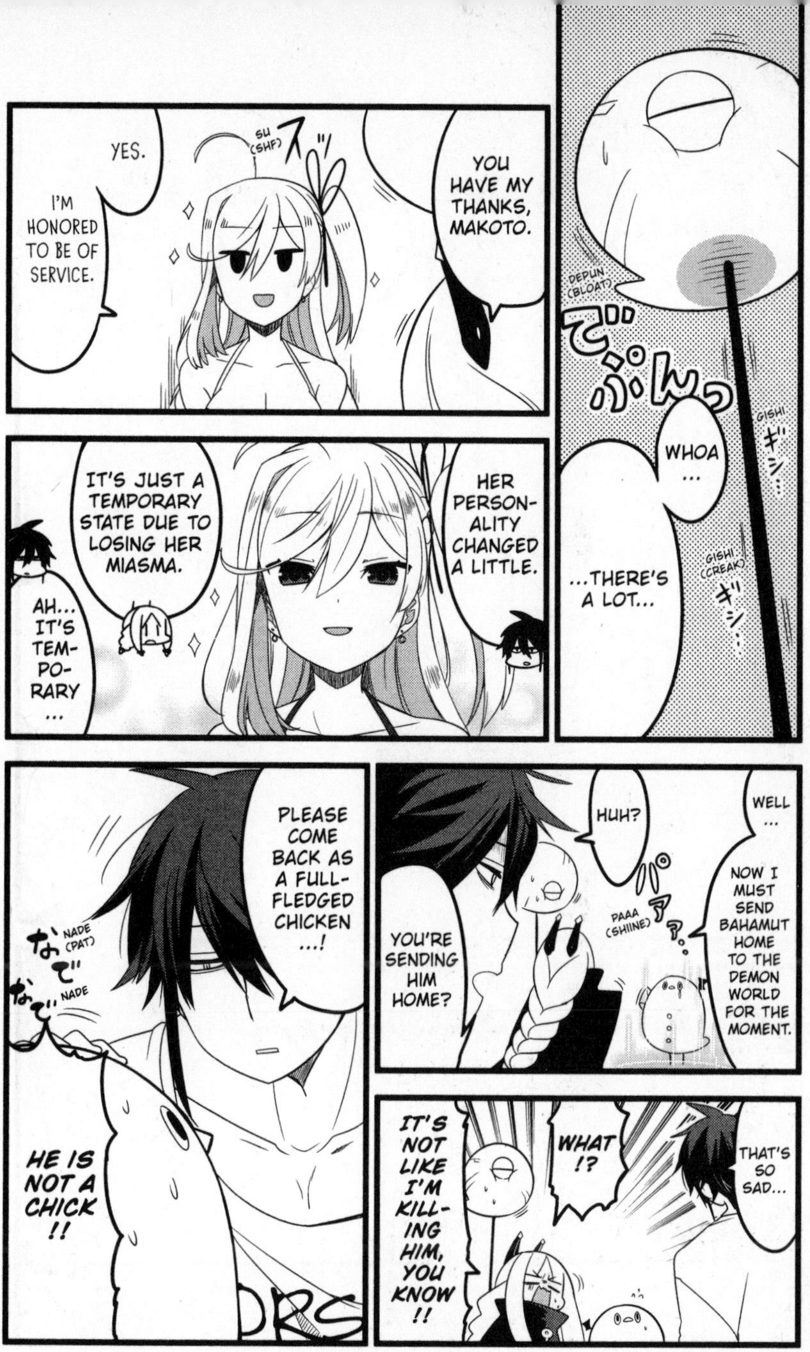
DEPUN (BLOAT)
でぷんっ
WHOA...
GISHI
ギシ...
...THERE'S A LOT...
GISHI (CREAK)
ギシ...
YOU HAVE MY THANKS, MAKOTO.
SU (SHF)
スッ
YES.
I'M HONORED TO BE OF SERVICE.
HER PERSONALITY CHANGED A LITTLE.
IT'S JUST A TEMPORARY STATE DUE TO LOSING HER MIASMA.
AH... IT'S TEMPORARY...
WELL...
NOW I MUST SEND BAHAMUT HOME TO THE DEMON WORLD FOR THE MOMENT.
HUH?
PAAA (SHIINE)
パァ
YOU'RE SENDING HIM HOME?
THAT'S SO SAD...
WHAT!?
IT'S NOT LIKE I'M KILLING HIM, YOU KNOW!!
PLEASE COME BACK AS A FULL-FLEDGED CHICKEN...!
NADE (PAT)
なで
NADE
なで
HE IS NOT A CHICK!!

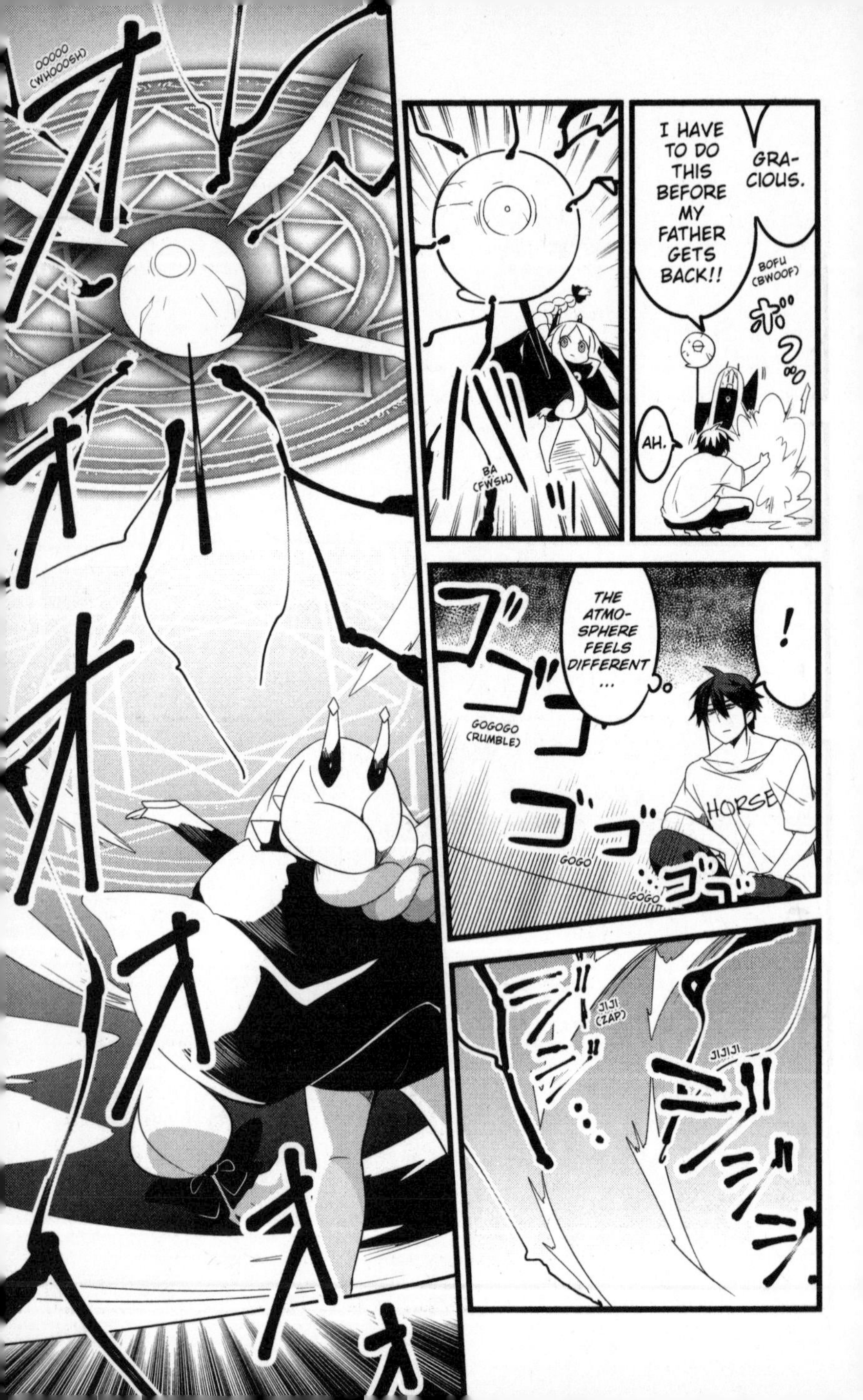
GRA-CIOUS.
I HAVE TO DO THIS BEFORE MY FATHER GETS BACK!!
BOFU (BWOOF)
AH.
BA (FWSH)
!
THE ATMO-SPHERE FEELS DIFFERENT...
GOGOGO (RUMBLE)
GOGO
GOGO
JIJIJI
JIJI (ZAP)
...
OOOOO (WHOOOSH)

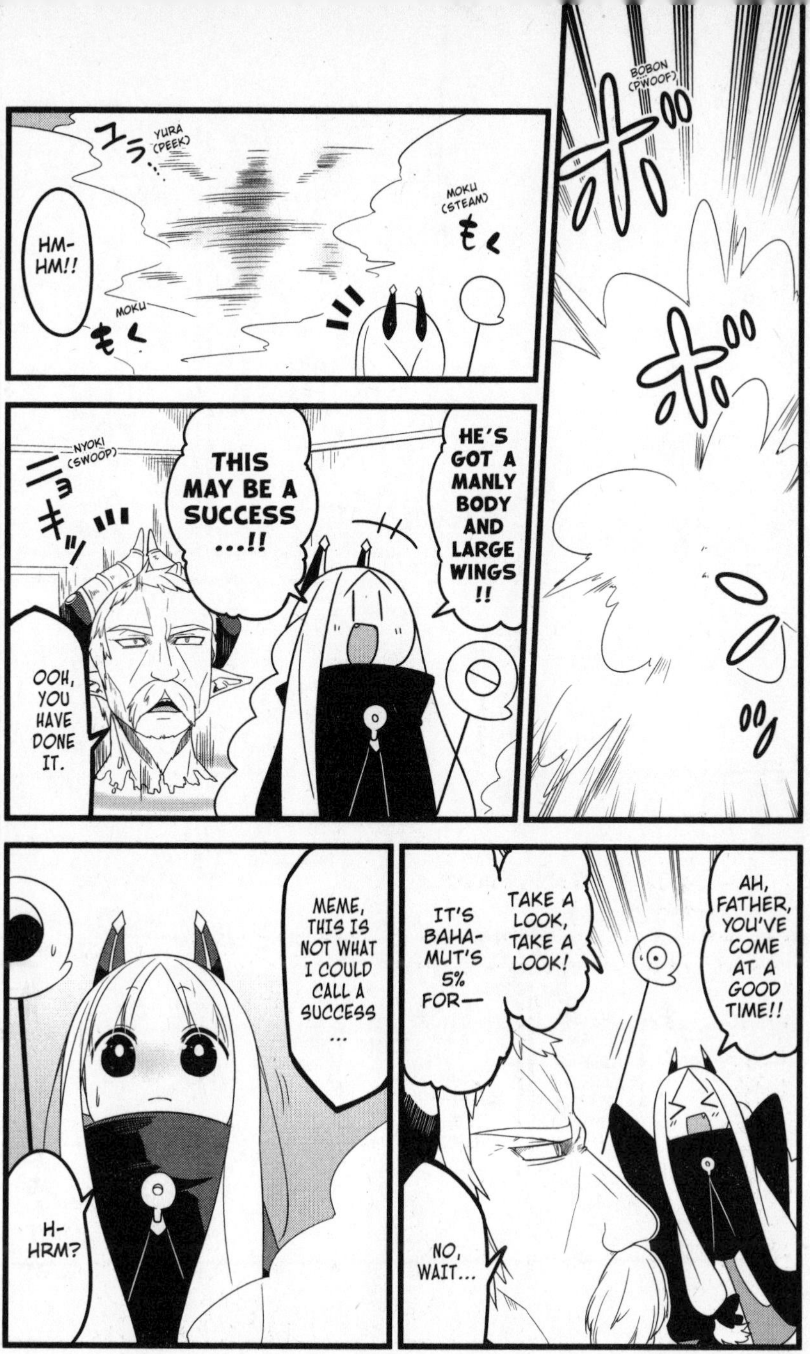
BOBON (PWOOF)
YURA (PEEK)
MOKU (STEAM)
HM-HM!!
MOKU
HE'S GOT A MANLY BODY AND LARGE WINGS!!
THIS MAY BE A SUCCESS...!!
NYOKI (SWOOP)
OOH, YOU HAVE DONE IT.
AH, FATHER, YOU'VE COME AT A GOOD TIME!!
TAKE A LOOK, TAKE A LOOK!
IT'S BAHAMUT'S 5% FOR—
NO, WAIT...
MEME, THIS IS NOT WHAT I COULD CALL A SUCCESS...
H-HRM?

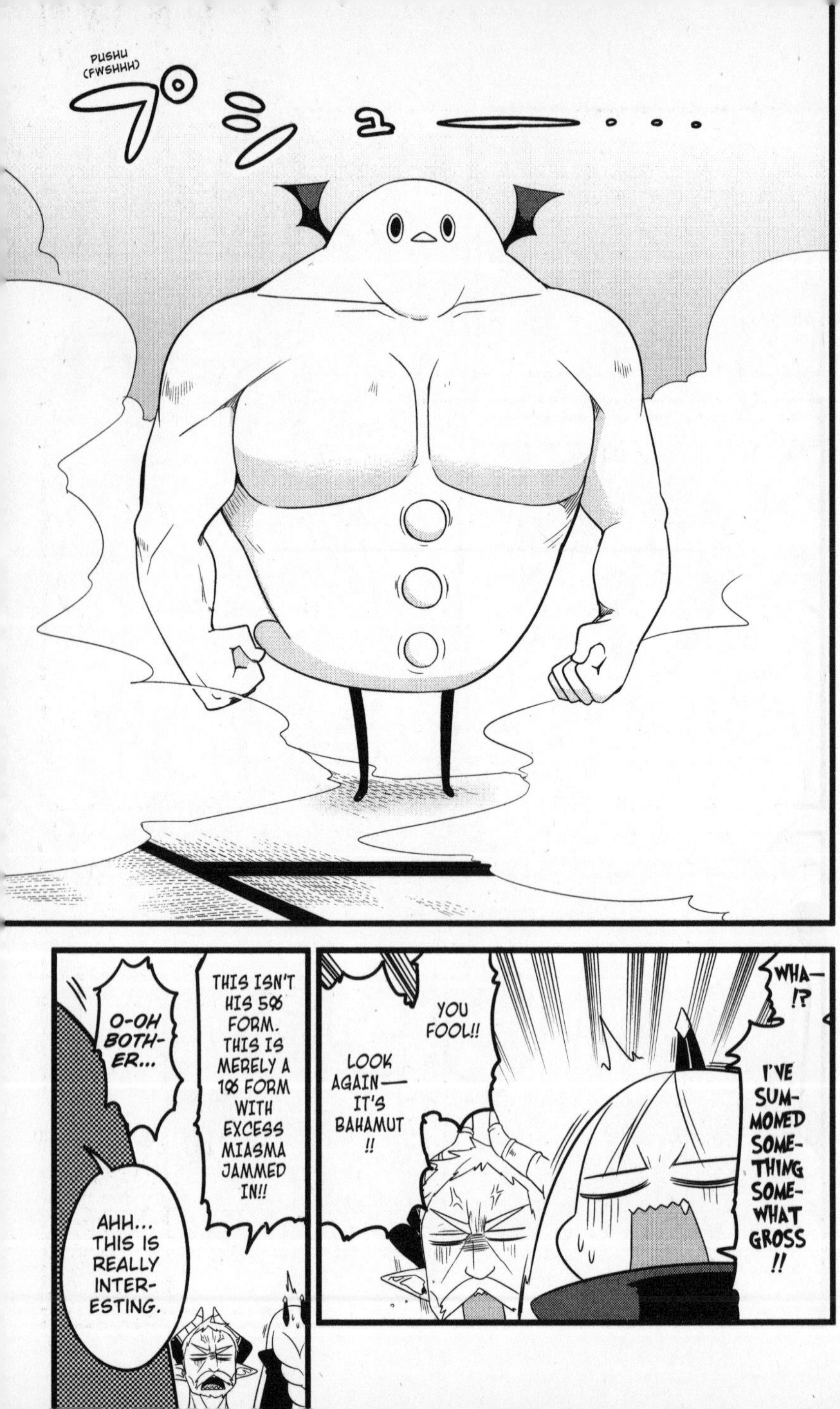
PUSHU (FWSHHH)
プシュ—…
WHA—!?
I'VE SUMMONED SOMETHING SOMEWHAT GROSS!!
YOU FOOL!!
LOOK AGAIN—IT'S BAHAMUT!!
THIS ISN'T HIS 5% FORM. THIS IS MERELY A 1% FORM WITH EXCESS MIASMA JAMMED IN!!
O-OH BOTHER...
AHH... THIS IS REALLY INTERESTING.

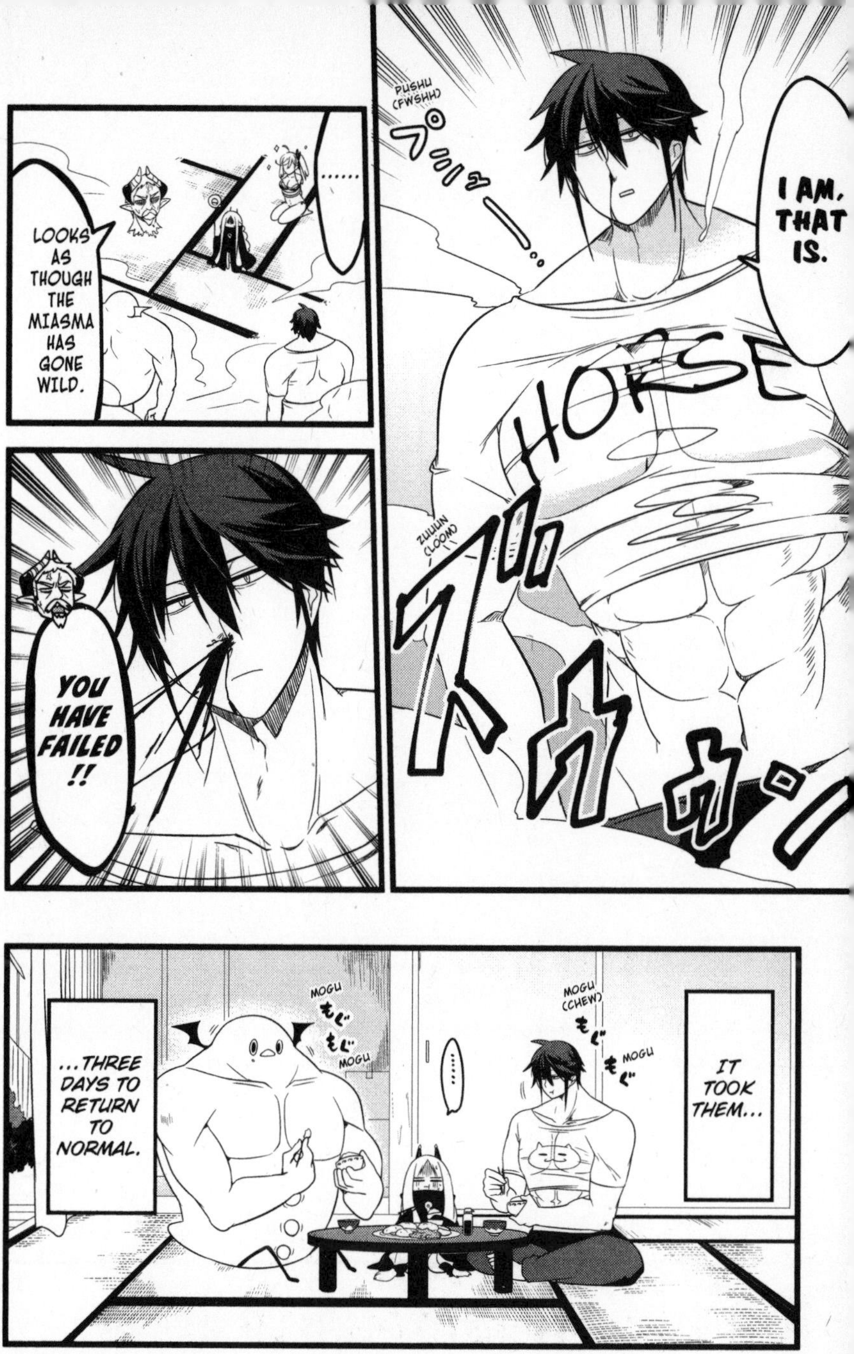
PUSHU (FWSHH)
プシュー
I AM, THAT IS.
HORSE
ZUUUN (LOOM)
......
LOOKS AS THOUGH THE MIASMA HAS GONE WILD.
YOU HAVE FAILED!!
IT TOOK THEM...
MOGU (CHEW)
もぐ もぐ
MOGU
......
MOGU
もぐ もぐ
MOGU
...THREE DAYS TO RETURN TO NORMAL.

The Strange Creature at Kuroyuri Apartments

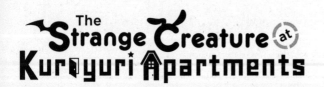

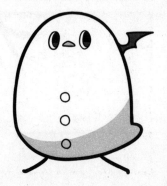

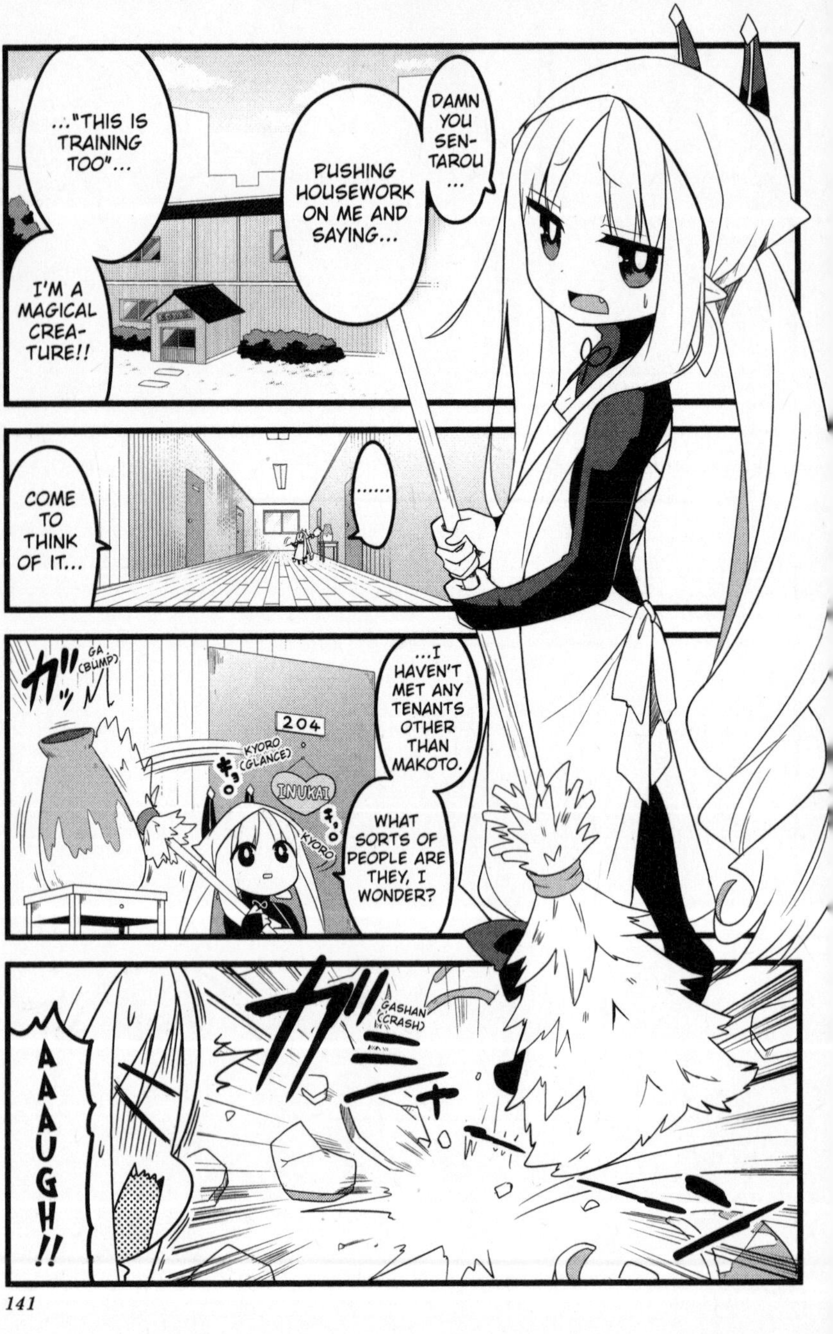
DAMN YOU SEN-TAROU ...
PUSHING HOUSEWORK ON ME AND SAYING...
..."THIS IS TRAINING TOO"...
I'M A MAGICAL CREA-TURE!!
......
COME TO THINK OF IT...
...I HAVEN'T MET ANY TENANTS OTHER THAN MAKOTO.
WHAT SORTS OF PEOPLE ARE THEY, I WONDER?
KYORO
KYORO (GLANCE)
204
INUKAI
GA (BUMP)
GASHAN (CRASH)
AAAAUGH!!

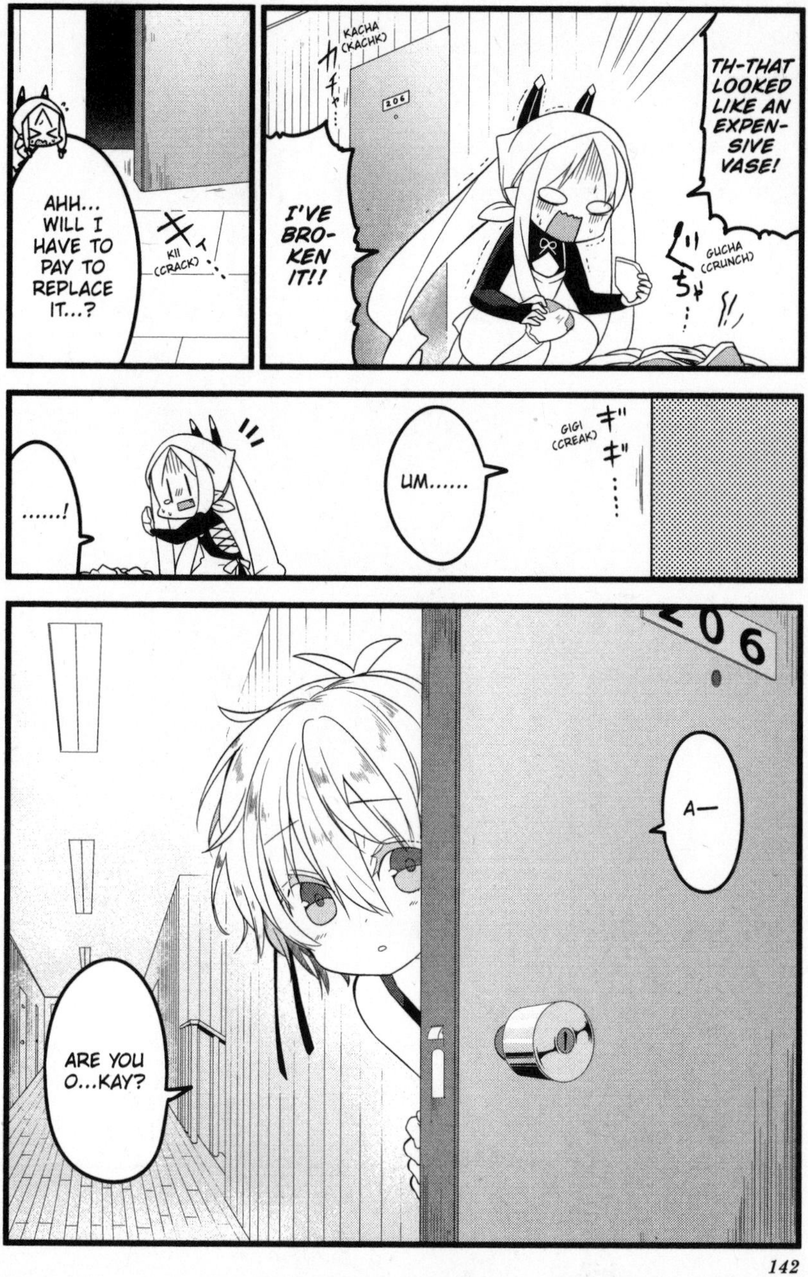
TH-THAT LOOKED LIKE AN EXPENSIVE VASE!
GUCHA (CRUNCH)
KACHA (KACHK)
I'VE BROKEN IT!!
KII (CRACK)
AHH... WILL I HAVE TO PAY TO REPLACE IT...?
GIGI (CREAK)
UM......
......!
A—
ARE YOU O...KAY?

CREATURE 10:
DO BEAUTIFUL FLOWERS HAVE POISONOUS THORNS!?

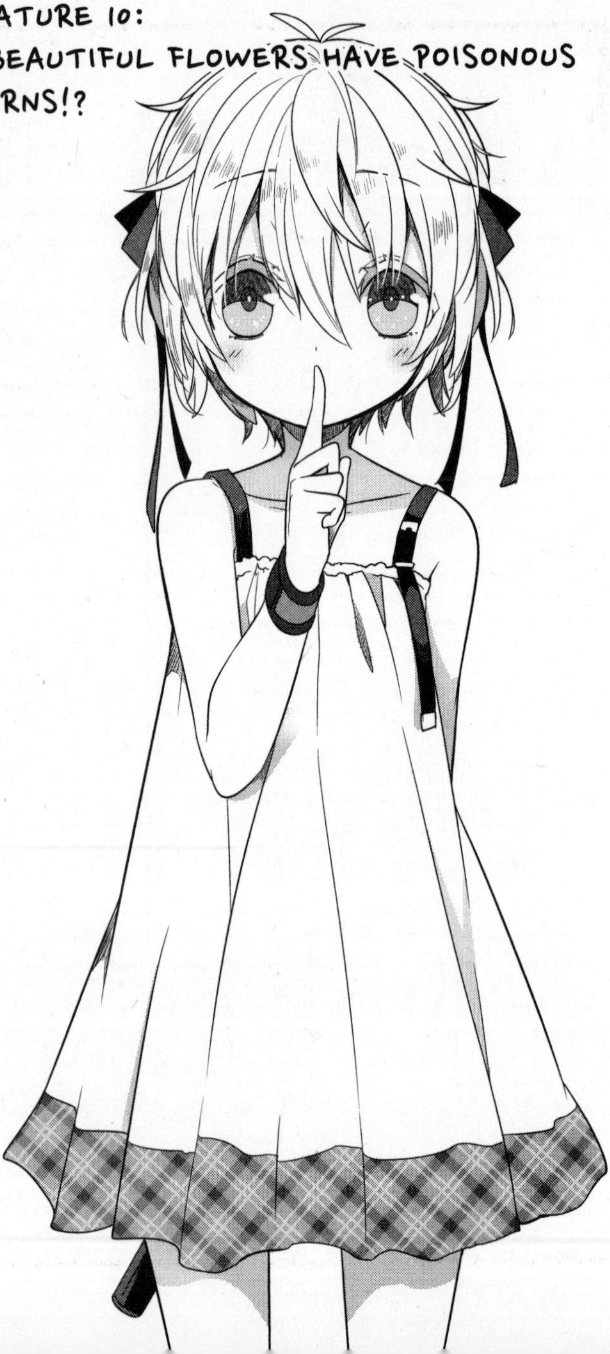

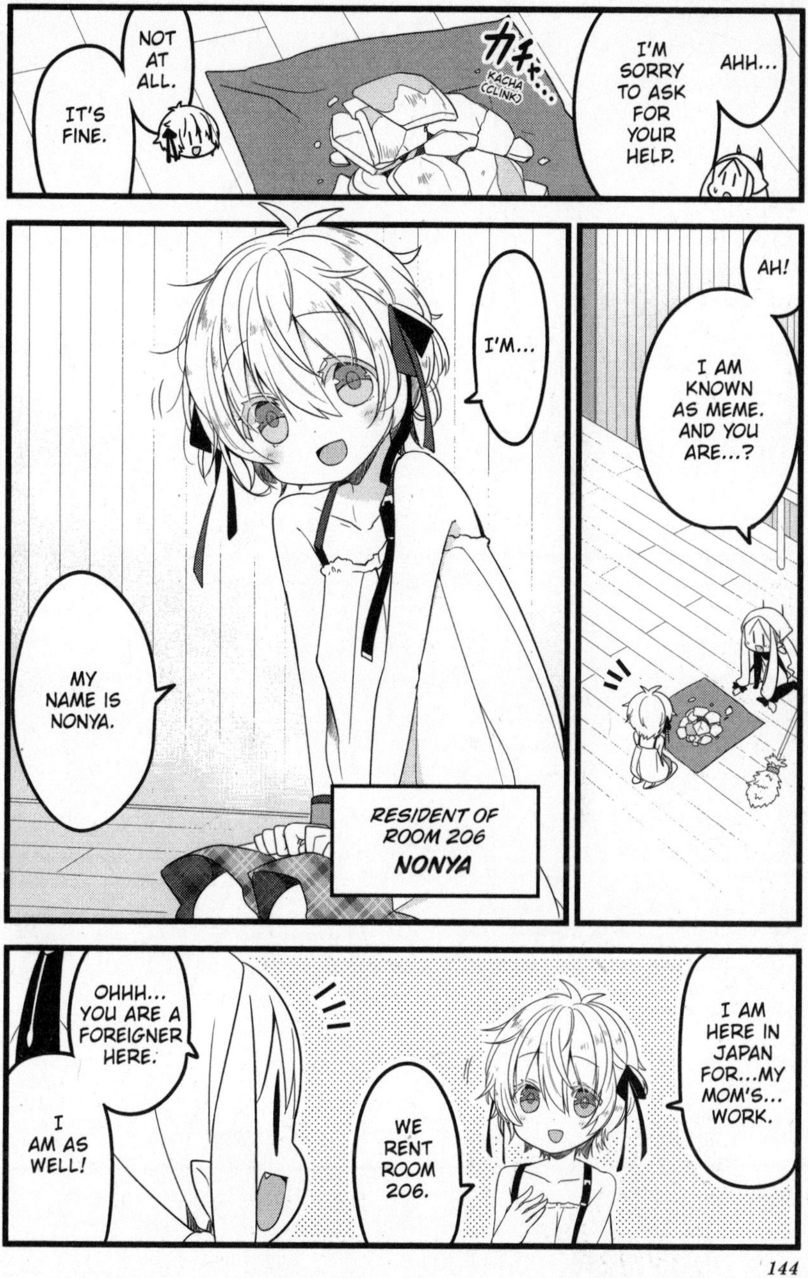
AHH...
I'M SORRY TO ASK FOR YOUR HELP.
カチャ...
KACHA (CLINK)
NOT AT ALL.
IT'S FINE.
AH!
I AM KNOWN AS MEME. AND YOU ARE...?
I'M...
MY NAME IS NONYA.
RESIDENT OF ROOM 206
NONYA
I AM HERE IN JAPAN FOR...MY MOM'S... WORK.
WE RENT ROOM 206.
OHHH... YOU ARE A FOREIGNER HERE.
I AM AS WELL!

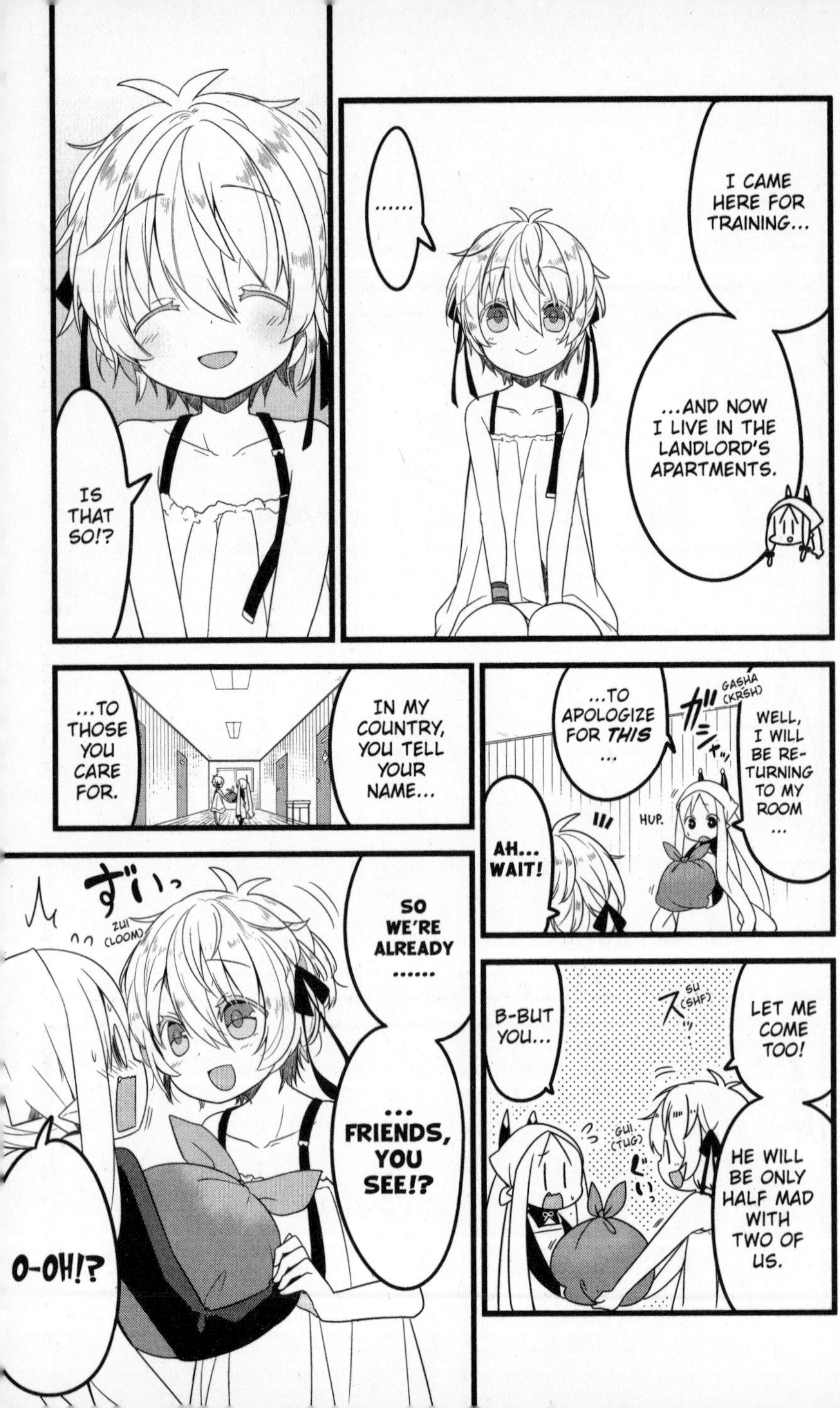
I CAME HERE FOR TRAINING...
......
...AND NOW I LIVE IN THE LANDLORD'S APARTMENTS.
IS THAT SO!?
WELL, I WILL BE RE-TURNING TO MY ROOM...
ガシャッ
GASHA (KRSH)
...TO APOLOGIZE FOR THIS...
HUP.
AH... WAIT!
IN MY COUNTRY, YOU TELL YOUR NAME...
...TO THOSE YOU CARE FOR.
LET ME COME TOO!
スッ
SU (SHF)
B-BUT YOU...
HE WILL BE ONLY HALF MAD WITH TWO OF US.
ぐいっ
GUI (TUG)
SO WE'RE ALREADY......
...FRIENDS, YOU SEE!?
ずいっ
ZUI (LOOM)
O-OH!?

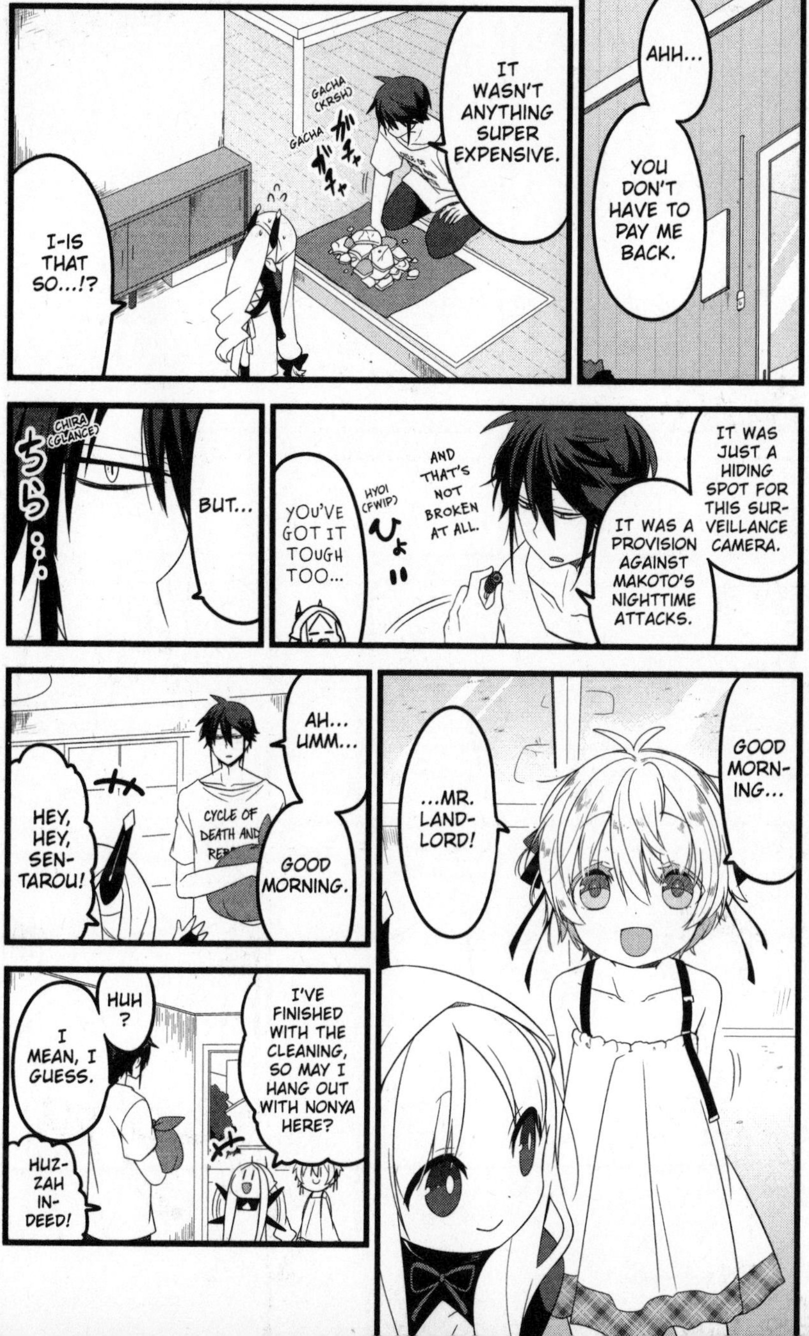
AHH...
YOU DON'T HAVE TO PAY ME BACK.
IT WASN'T ANYTHING SUPER EXPENSIVE.
GACHA (KRSH)
GACHA
I-IS THAT SO...!?
IT WAS JUST A HIDING SPOT FOR THIS SUR-VEILLANCE CAMERA.
IT WAS A PROVISION AGAINST MAKOTO'S NIGHTTIME ATTACKS.
AND THAT'S NOT BROKEN AT ALL.
HYOI (FWIP)
YOU'VE GOT IT TOUGH TOO...
CHIRA (GLANCE)
BUT...
GOOD MORNING...
...MR. LAND-LORD!
AH... UMM...
HEY, HEY, SEN-TAROU!
GOOD MORNING.
I'VE FINISHED WITH THE CLEANING, SO MAY I HANG OUT WITH NONYA HERE?
HUH?
I MEAN, I GUESS.
HUZ-ZAH IN-DEED!

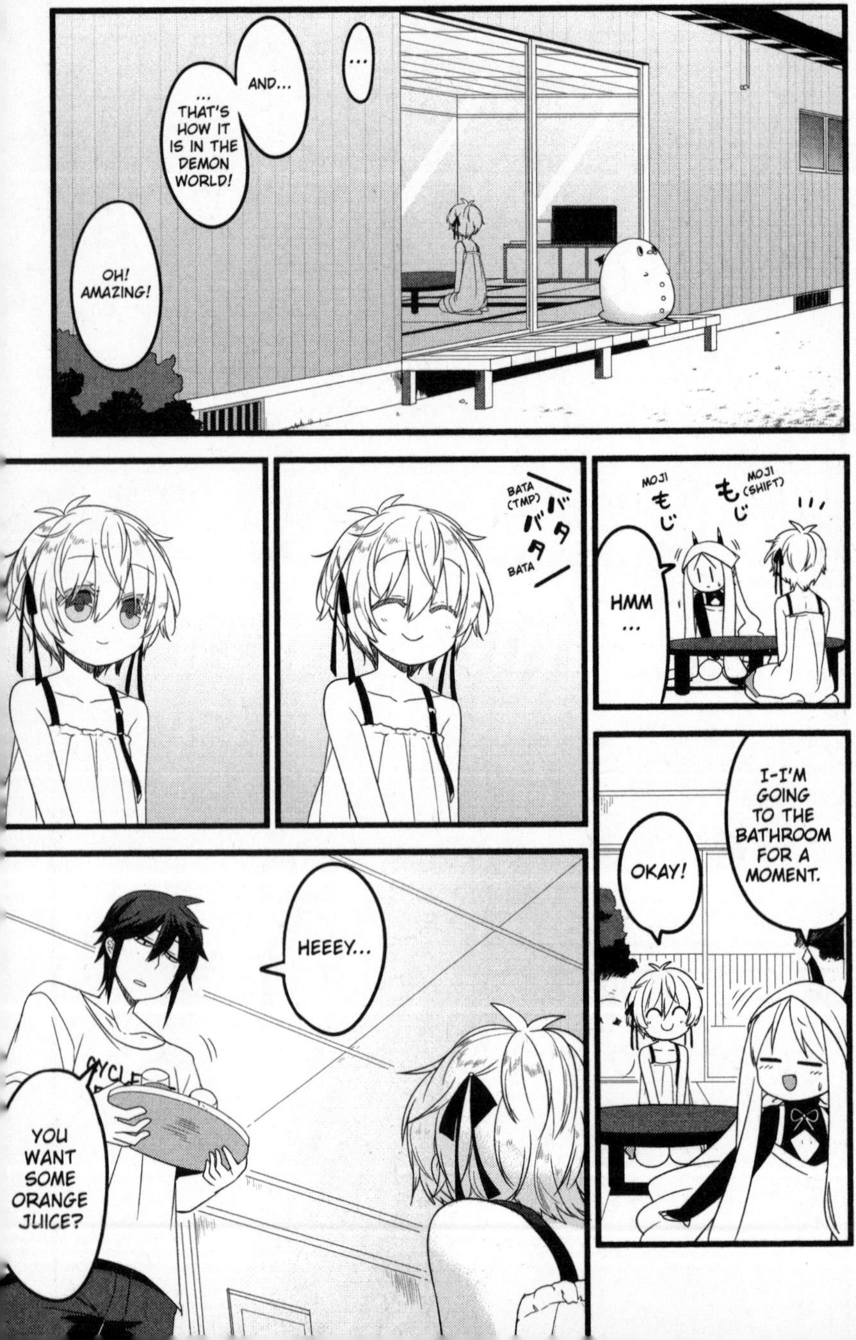
...
AND... ... THAT'S HOW IT IS IN THE DEMON WORLD!
OH! AMAZING!
MOJI もじ
MOJI (SHIFT) もじ
HMM...
BATA (TMP) バタ
バタ BATA
I-I'M GOING TO THE BATHROOM FOR A MOMENT.
OKAY!
HEEEY...
YOU WANT SOME ORANGE JUICE?

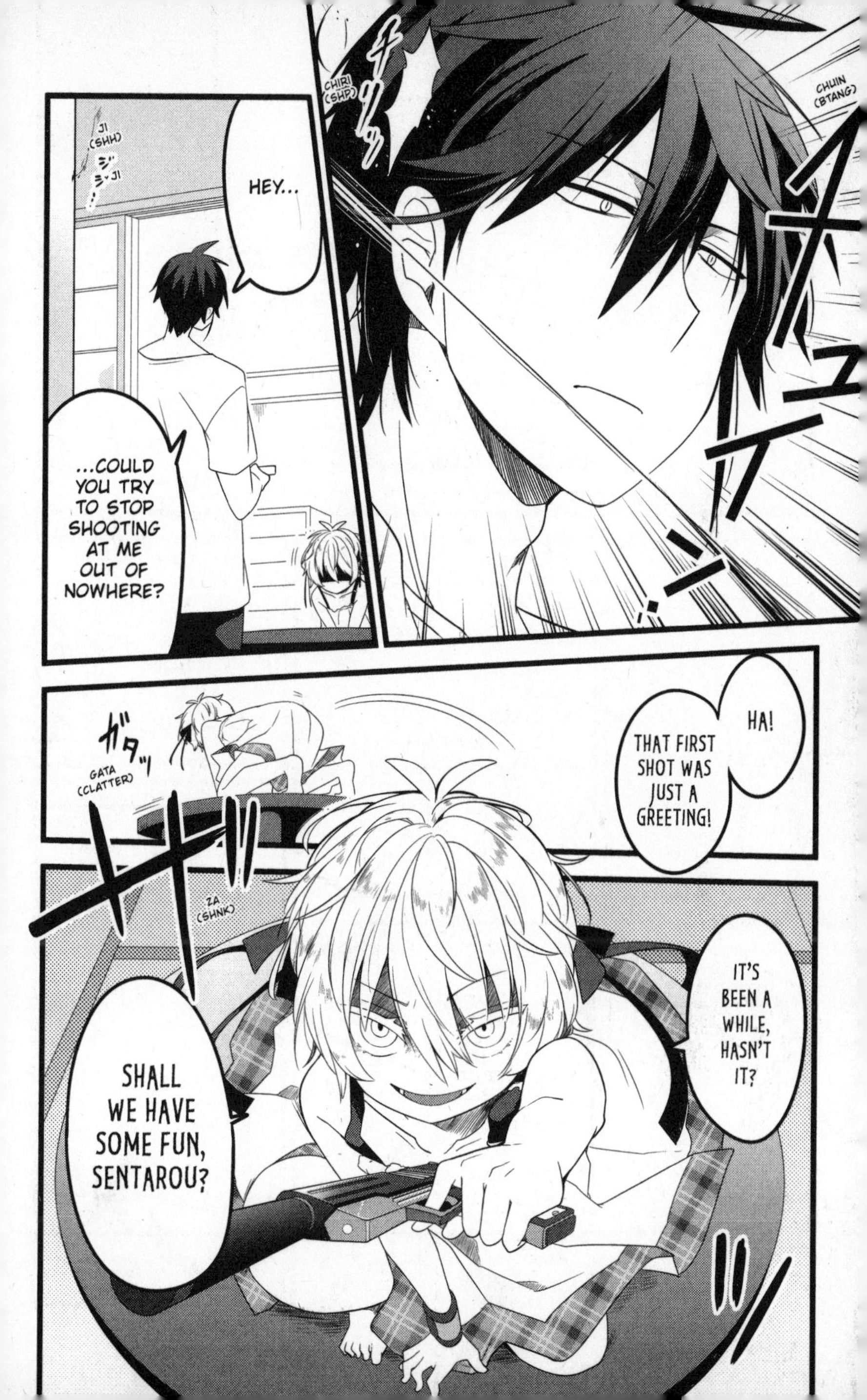
CHUIN (BTANG)
CHIRI (SHP)
JI (SHH)
HEY...
...COULD YOU TRY TO STOP SHOOTING AT ME OUT OF NOWHERE?
HA!
THAT FIRST SHOT WAS JUST A GREETING!
GATA (CLATTER)
IT'S BEEN A WHILE, HASN'T IT?
ZA (SHNK)
SHALL WE HAVE SOME FUN, SENTAROU?

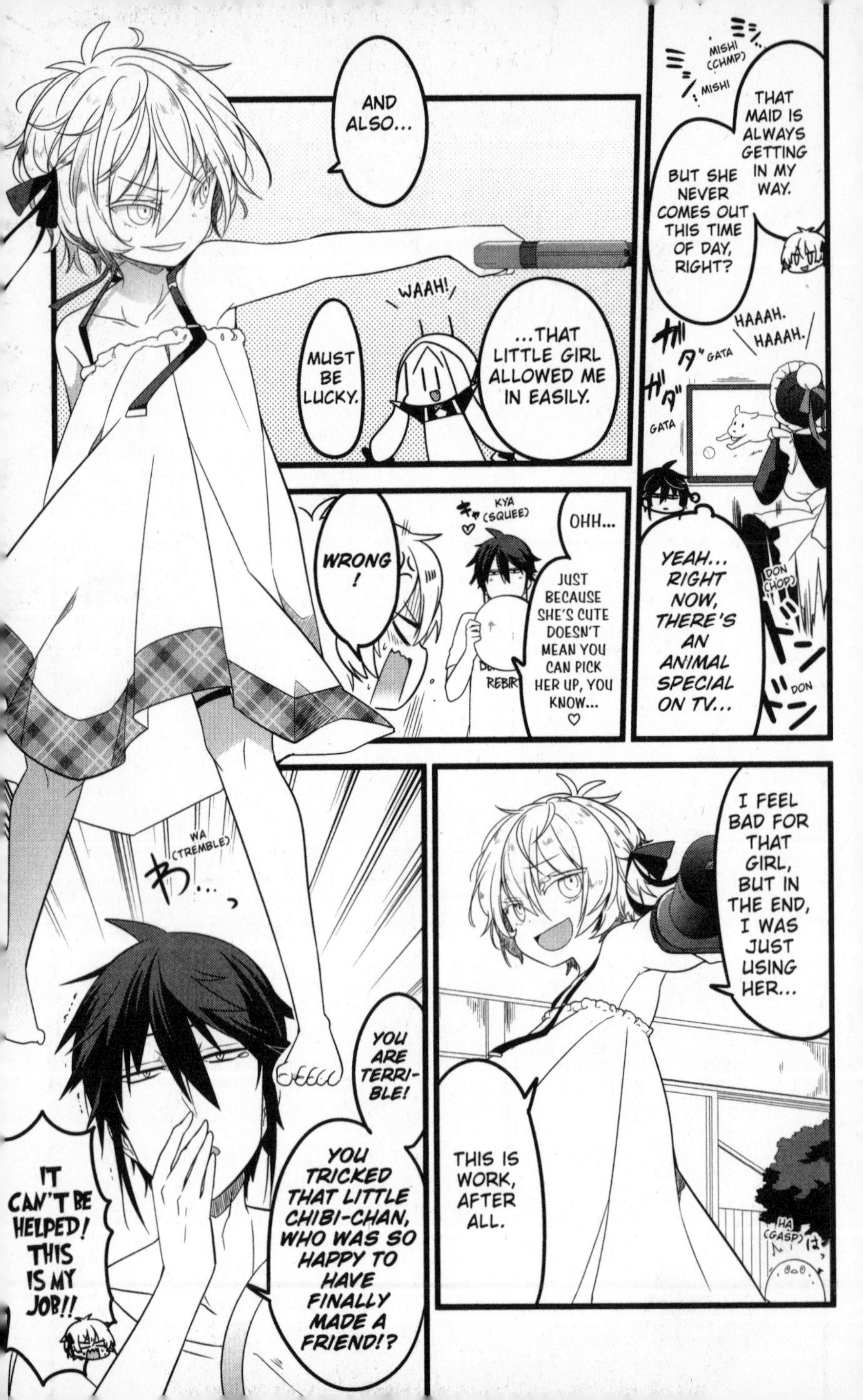
MISHI (CHMP)
MISHI
THAT MAID IS ALWAYS GETTING IN MY WAY.
BUT SHE NEVER COMES OUT THIS TIME OF DAY, RIGHT?
HAAAH. HAAAH.
GATA
GATA
YEAH... RIGHT NOW, THERE'S AN ANIMAL SPECIAL ON TV...
DON (CHOP)
DON
AND ALSO...
...THAT LITTLE GIRL ALLOWED ME IN EASILY.
WAAH!
MUST BE LUCKY.
OHH...
JUST BECAUSE SHE'S CUTE DOESN'T MEAN YOU CAN PICK HER UP, YOU KNOW... ♡
KYA (SQUEE)
WRONG!
I FEEL BAD FOR THAT GIRL, BUT IN THE END, I WAS JUST USING HER...
THIS IS WORK, AFTER ALL.
HA (GASP)
YOU ARE TERRIBLE!
YOU TRICKED THAT LITTLE CHIBI-CHAN, WHO WAS SO HAPPY TO HAVE FINALLY MADE A FRIEND!?
WA (TREMBLE)
IT CAN'T BE HELPED! THIS IS MY JOB!!

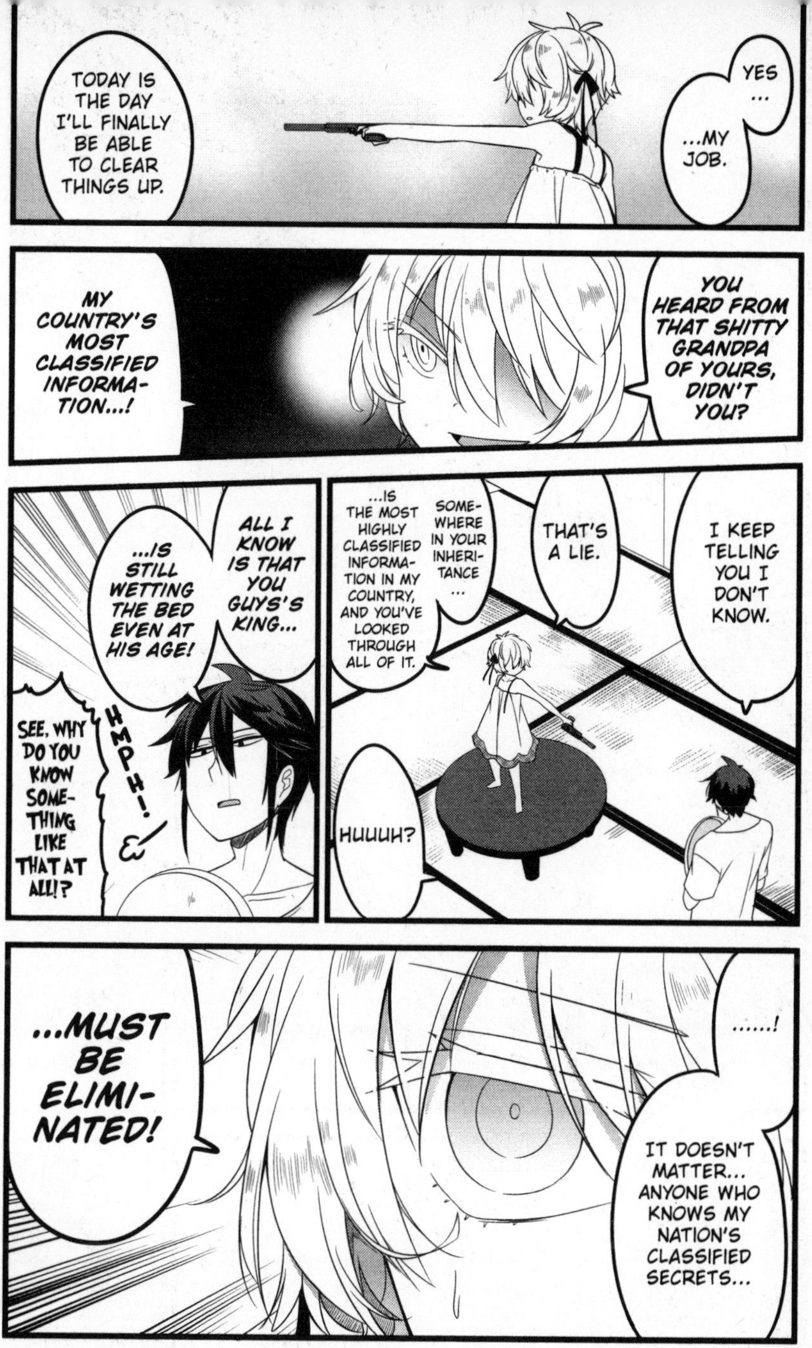
YES... ...MY JOB.
TODAY IS THE DAY I'LL FINALLY BE ABLE TO CLEAR THINGS UP.
YOU HEARD FROM THAT SHITTY GRANDPA OF YOURS, DIDN'T YOU?
MY COUNTRY'S MOST CLASSIFIED INFORMATION...!
I KEEP TELLING YOU I DON'T KNOW.
THAT'S A LIE.
SOMEWHERE IN YOUR INHERITANCE...
...IS THE MOST HIGHLY CLASSIFIED INFORMATION IN MY COUNTRY, AND YOU'VE LOOKED THROUGH ALL OF IT.
HUUUH?
ALL I KNOW IS THAT YOU GUYS'S KING...
...IS STILL WETTING THE BED EVEN AT HIS AGE!
HMPH!
SEE, WHY DO YOU KNOW SOMETHING LIKE THAT AT ALL!?
......!
IT DOESN'T MATTER... ANYONE WHO KNOWS MY NATION'S CLASSIFIED SECRETS...
...MUST BE ELIMINATED!

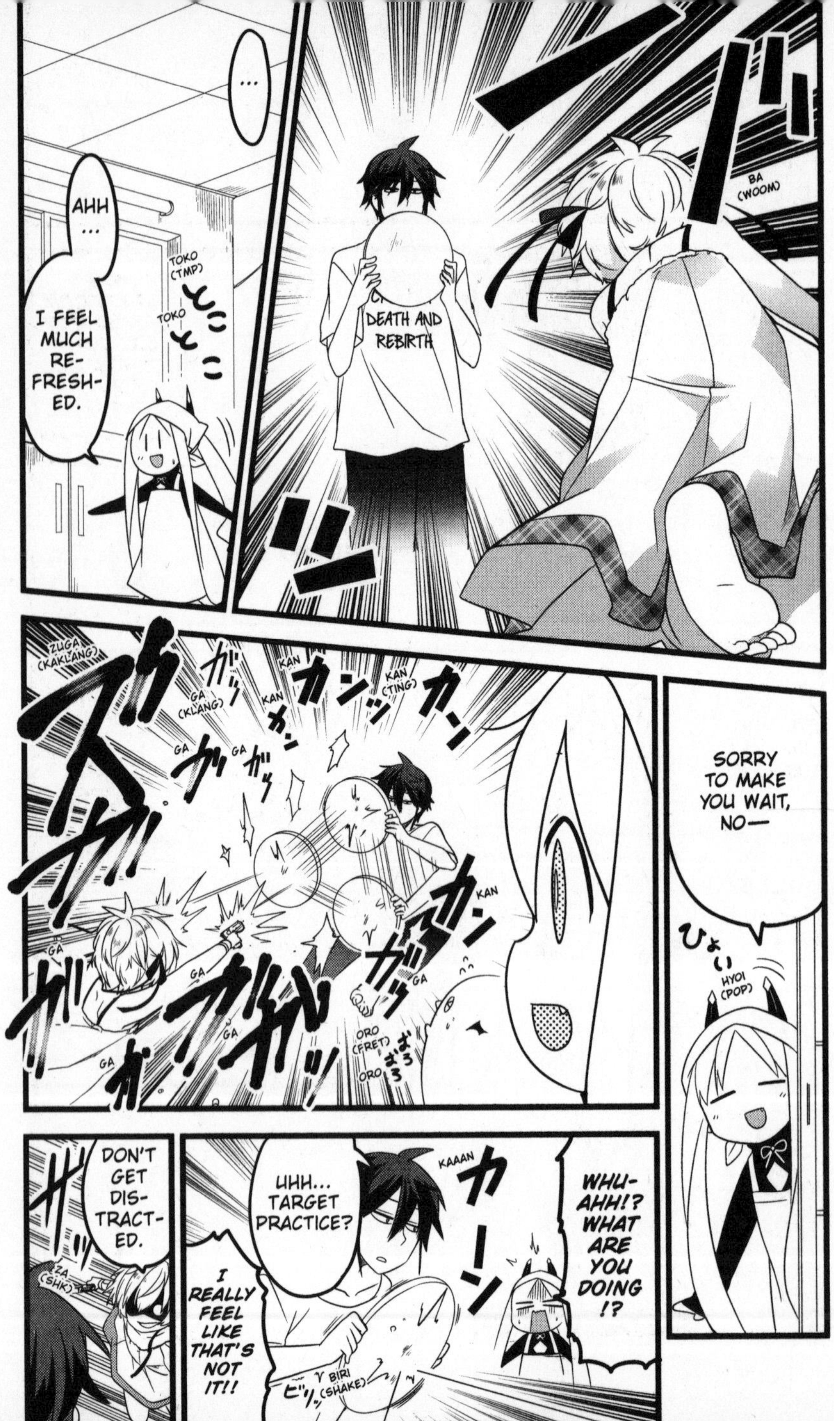
BA (WOOM)
DEATH AND REBIRTH
...
AHH... I FEEL MUCH RE-FRESH-ED.
TOKO (TMP) TOKO
SORRY TO MAKE YOU WAIT, NO—
HYOI (POP)
ZUGA (KAKLANG)
GA (KLANG)
KAN KAN (TING) KAN
GA GA
KAN
GA GA GA GA GA
ORO (FRET) ORO
WHU-AHH!? WHAT ARE YOU DOING!?
KAAAN
UHH... TARGET PRACTICE?
I REALLY FEEL LIKE THAT'S NOT IT!!
BIRI (SHAKE)
DON'T GET DIS-TRACT-ED.
ZA (SHK)

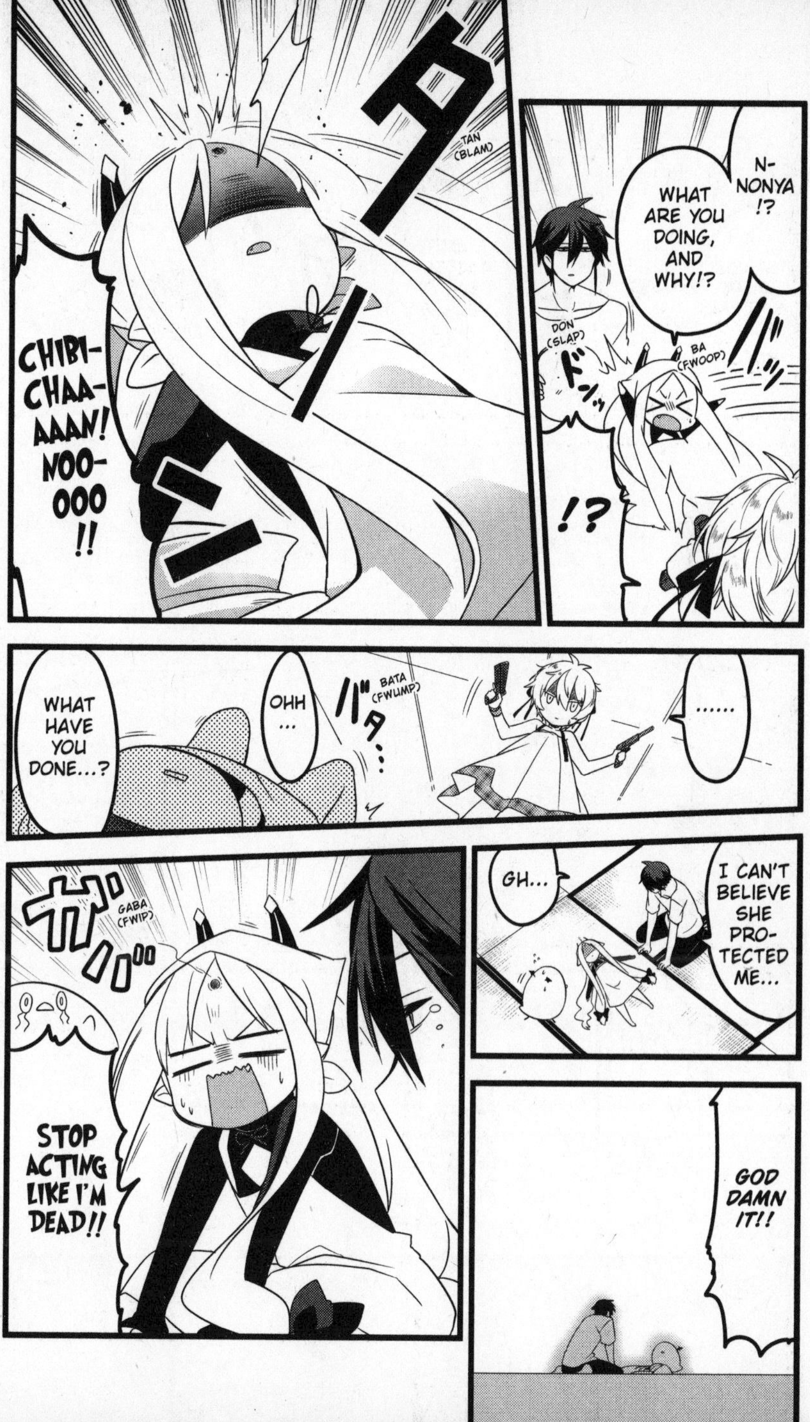
N-NONYA!?
WHAT ARE YOU DOING, AND WHY!?
DON (SLAP)
BA (FWOOP)
!?
TAN (BLAM)
CHIBI-CHAAAAAN! NOOOOO!!
......
BATA (FWUMP)
OHH...
WHAT HAVE YOU DONE...?
I CAN'T BELIEVE SHE PROTECTED ME...
GH...
GOD DAMN IT!!
GABA (FWIP)
STOP ACTING LIKE I'M DEAD!!

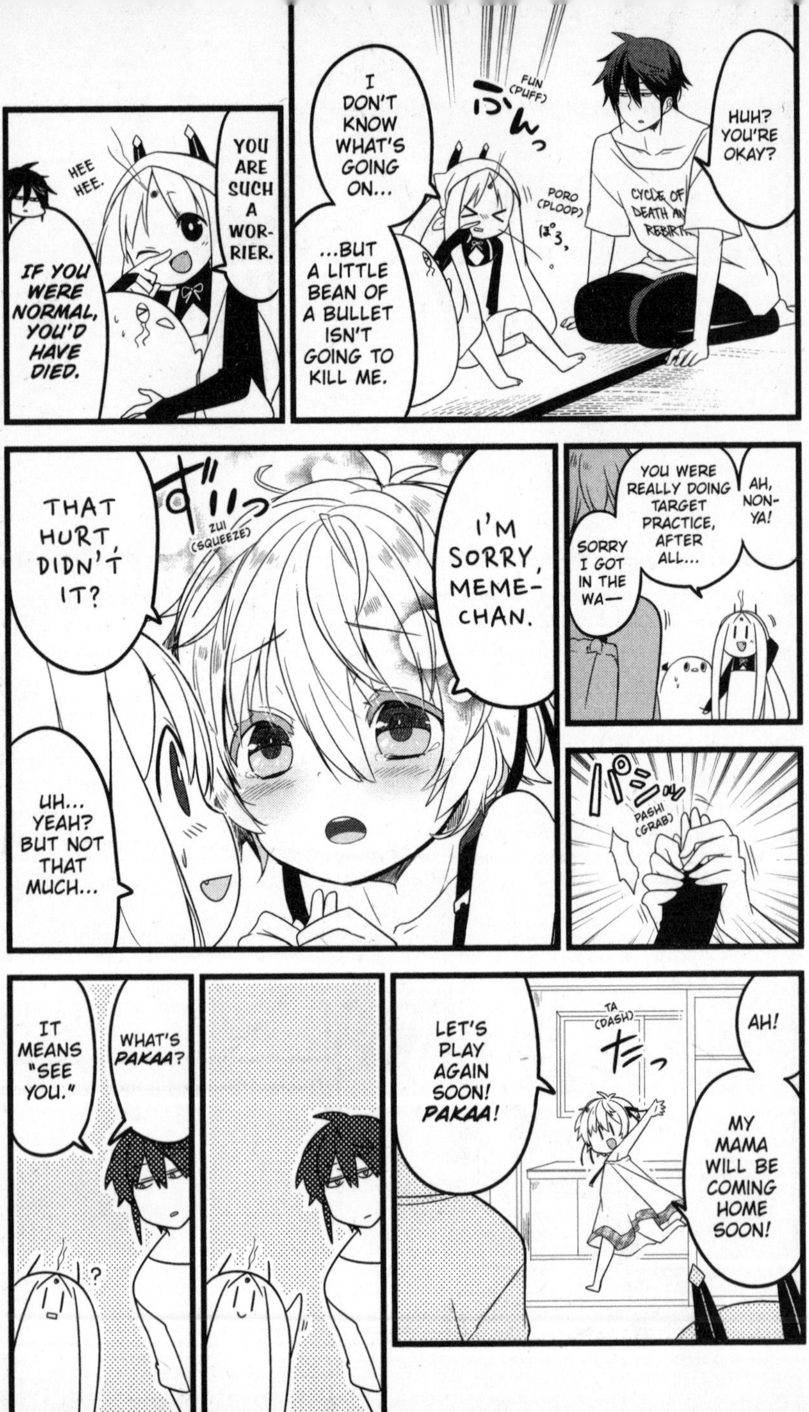
HUH? YOU'RE OKAY?
CYCLE OF DEATH AN REBIRT
PORO (PLOOP)
FUN (PUFF)
I DON'T KNOW WHAT'S GOING ON...
...BUT A LITTLE BEAN OF A BULLET ISN'T GOING TO KILL ME.
YOU ARE SUCH A WORRIER.
HEE HEE.
IF YOU WERE NORMAL, YOU'D HAVE DIED.
AH, NON-YA!
YOU WERE REALLY DOING TARGET PRACTICE, AFTER ALL...
SORRY I GOT IN THE WA—
PASHI (GRAB)
I'M SORRY, MEME-CHAN.
ZUI (SQUEEZE)
THAT HURT, DIDN'T IT?
UH... YEAH? BUT NOT THAT MUCH...
AH!
MY MAMA WILL BE COMING HOME SOON!
TA (DASH)
LET'S PLAY AGAIN SOON! PAKAA!
WHAT'S PAKAA?
IT MEANS "SEE YOU."
?

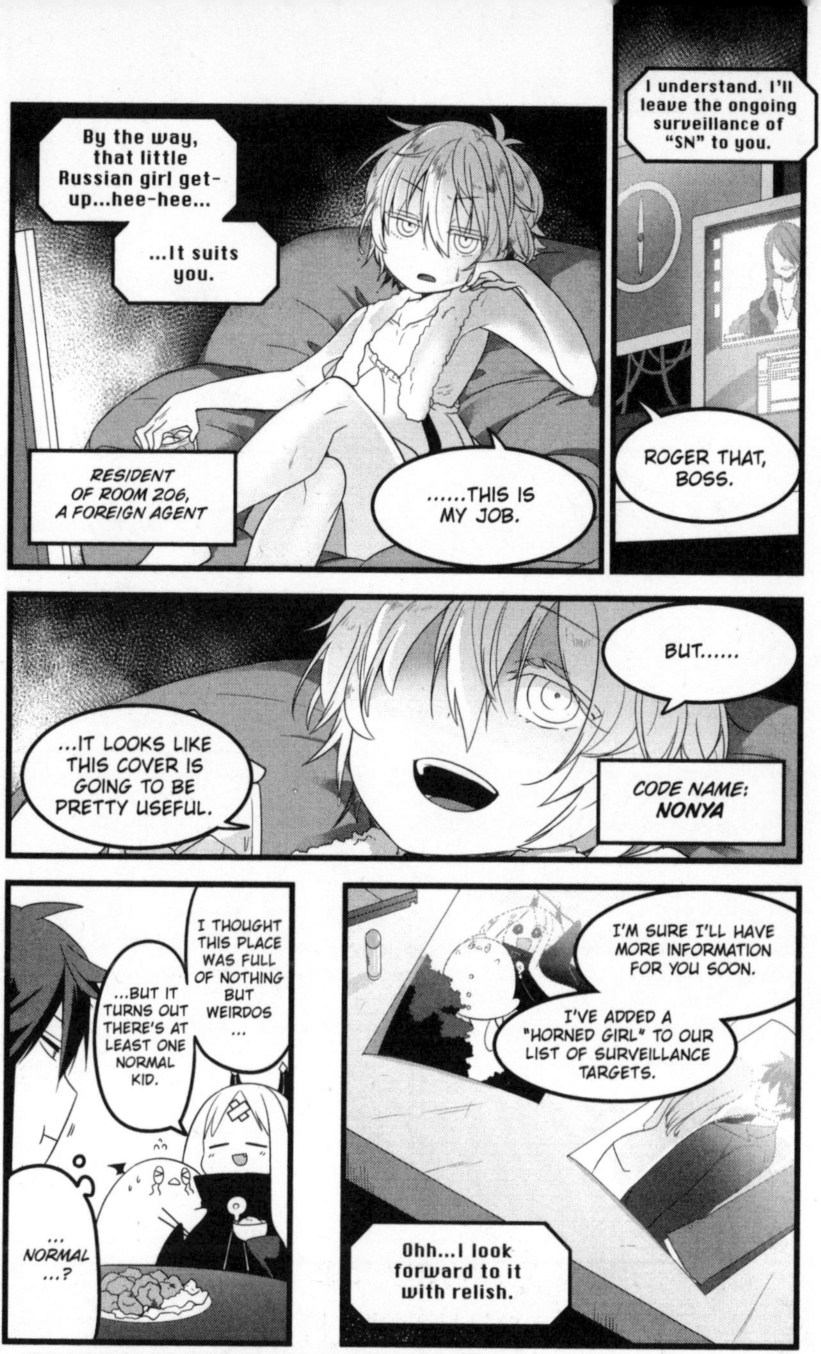
I understand. I'll leave the ongoing surveillance of "SN" to you.
ROGER THAT, BOSS.
By the way, that little Russian girl get-up...hee-hee...
...It suits you.
......THIS IS MY JOB.
RESIDENT OF ROOM 206, A FOREIGN AGENT
BUT......
CODE NAME: NONYA
...IT LOOKS LIKE THIS COVER IS GOING TO BE PRETTY USEFUL.
I'M SURE I'LL HAVE MORE INFORMATION FOR YOU SOON.
I'VE ADDED A "HORNED GIRL" TO OUR LIST OF SURVEILLANCE TARGETS.
Ohh...I look forward to it with relish.
I THOUGHT THIS PLACE WAS FULL OF NOTHING BUT WEIRDOS ...
...BUT IT TURNS OUT THERE'S AT LEAST ONE NORMAL KID.
... NORMAL ...?

The Strange Creature at Kuroyuri Apartments

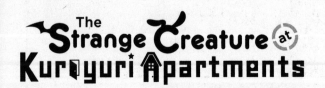

TRANSLATION NOTES

COMMON HONORIFICS
no honorific: Indicates familiarity or closeness; if used without permission or reason, addressing someone in this manner would constitute an insult.
-san: The Japanese equivalent of Mr./Mrs./Miss. If a situation calls for politeness, this is the fail-safe honorific.
-sama: Conveys great respect; may also indicate that the social status of the speaker is lower than that of the addressee.
-kun: Used most often when referring to boys, this indicates affection or familiarity. Occasionally used by older men among their peers, but it may also be used by anyone referring to a person of lower standing.
-chan: An affectionate honorific indicating familiarity used mostly in reference to girls; also used in reference to cute persons or animals of either gender.

GENERAL NOTES
One hundred yen is roughly equivalent to one US dollar.

PAGE 14
Chibi refers to a style of caricature where a character is drawn at one-third or half their normal height. It can also be used as a nickname, implying cuteness and short stature. Sentarou calling Meme **"Chibi-chan"** is much like calling her "Shorty" or "Kiddo."

PAGE 77
What Meme originally accusingly calls Shioriko is **"NEET."** NEET is a British term that has been adopted by Japan, and stands for "not in education, employment, or training." It is usually used pejoratively, to look down on people who are seen as lazy or as freeloaders who won't get a job.

PAGE 124
It is considered a tradition to drink a cold glass of milk after soaking in the tub, especially after having been to a public bathhouse.

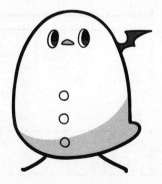

NEXT TO KUROYURI APARTMENTS

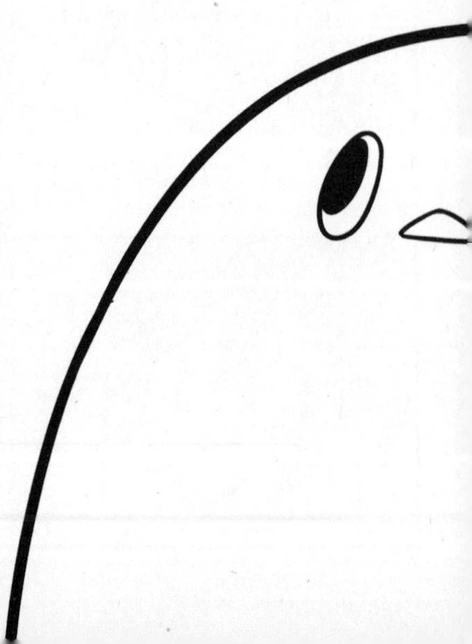

VOICE-OVER

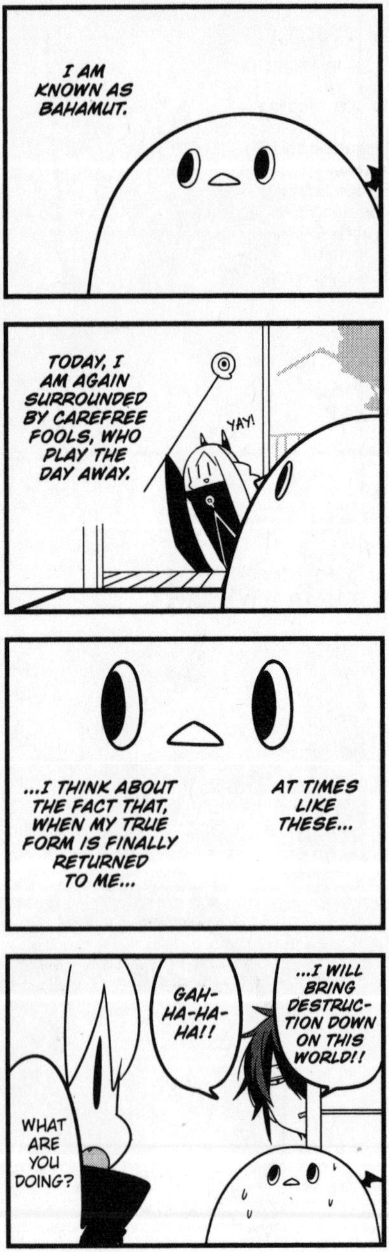
I AM KNOWN AS BAHAMUT.
YAY!
TODAY, I AM AGAIN SURROUNDED BY CAREFREE FOOLS, WHO PLAY THE DAY AWAY.
AT TIMES LIKE THESE...
...I THINK ABOUT THE FACT THAT, WHEN MY TRUE FORM IS FINALLY RETURNED TO ME...
...I WILL BRING DESTRUCTION DOWN ON THIS WORLD!!
GAH-HA-HA-HA!!
WHAT ARE YOU DOING?

THE 0.5TH CREATURE

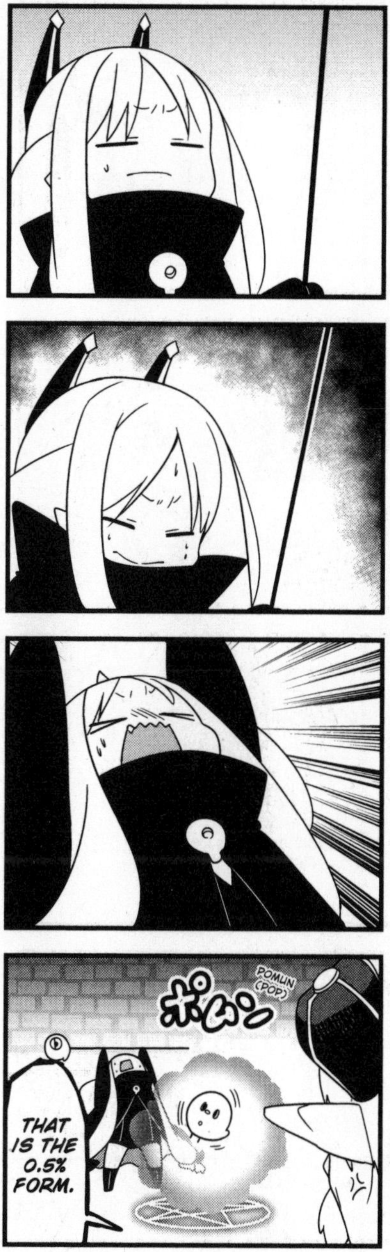
POMUN (POP)
ポムン
THAT IS THE 0.5% FORM.

GOING SHOPPING

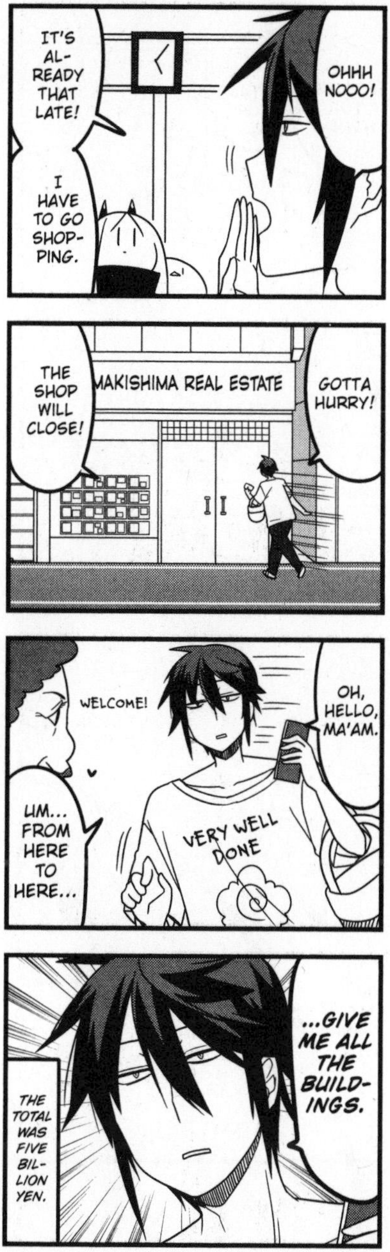
OHHH NOOO!
IT'S ALREADY THAT LATE!
I HAVE TO GO SHOPPING.
GOTTA HURRY!
MAKISHIMA REAL ESTATE
THE SHOP WILL CLOSE!
OH, HELLO, MA'AM.
WELCOME!
VERY WELL DONE
UM... FROM HERE TO HERE...
...GIVE ME ALL THE BUILDINGS.
THE TOTAL WAS FIVE BILLION YEN.

DESPOILED

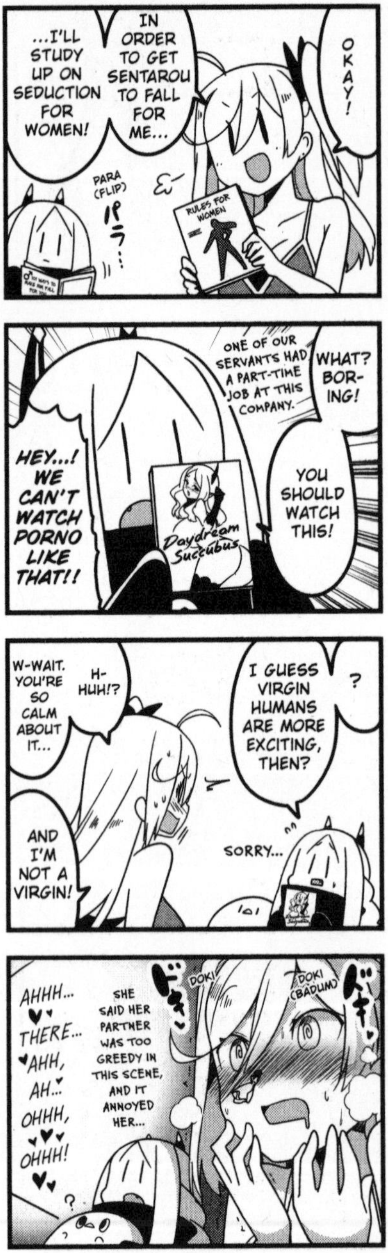
OKAY!
IN ORDER TO GET SENTAROU TO FALL FOR ME...
...I'LL STUDY UP ON SEDUCTION FOR WOMEN!
PARA (FLIP)
パラ…
RULES FOR WOMEN
WHAT? BOR-ING!
ONE OF OUR SERVANTS HAD A PART-TIME JOB AT THIS COMPANY.
YOU SHOULD WATCH THIS!
Daydream Succubus
HEY...! WE CAN'T WATCH PORNO LIKE THAT!!
?
I GUESS VIRGIN HUMANS ARE MORE EXCITING, THEN?
H-HUH!?
W-WAIT. YOU'RE SO CALM ABOUT IT...
SORRY...
AND I'M NOT A VIRGIN!
ドキ
DOKI (BADUMP)
DOKI
ドキ
SHE SAID HER PARTNER WAS TOO GREEDY IN THIS SCENE, AND IT ANNOYED HER...
AHHH... ♥ THERE... ♥AHH, AH...♥ OHHH, ♥♥ OHHH! ♥♥
?

THE LAST VESTIGE OF SELF-CONTROL

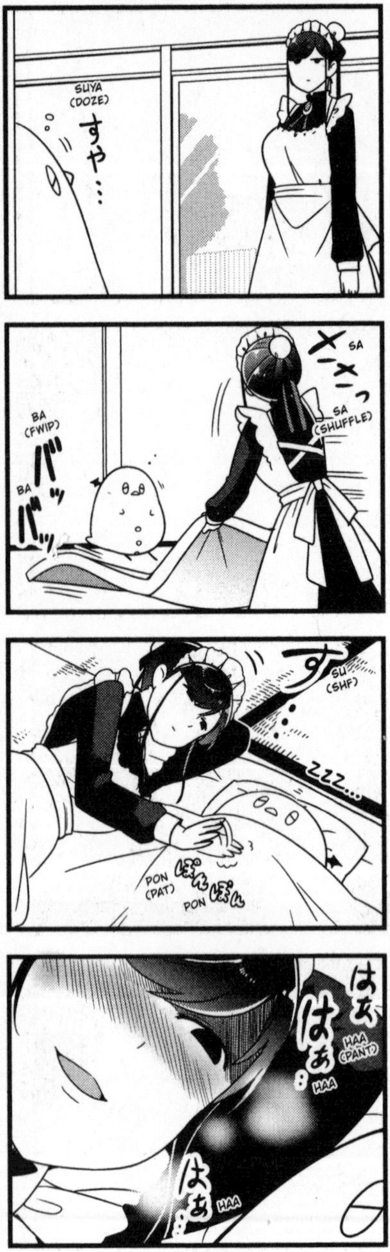
SUYA (DOZE)
すや…
SA
SA (SHUFFLE)
BA (FWIP)
バッ
BA
バッ
す
SU (SHF)
ZZZ...
PON (PAT)
ぽん
ぽん
PON
はぁ
はぁ…
HAA (PANT)
HAA
はぁ…
HAA

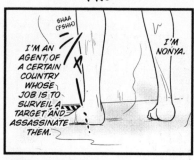

PRO

I'M NONYA.
SHAA (FSHH)
I'M AN AGENT OF A CERTAIN COUNTRY WHOSE JOB IS TO SURVEIL A TARGET AND ASSASSINATE THEM.
IN ORDER TO KEEP THE TARGET FROM BEING ALERTED, I DISGUISE MYSELF AS A GIRL TO GET CLOSE TO THEM, WHICH MEANS I CAN'T BE NEGLIGENT WITH DAILY EFFORTS.
AND I CAN'T POSSIBLY IGNORE ANY MEANS...
...TO MAKE MYSELF LOOK AS GIRLISH AS POSSIBLE.
PETA (PAP)
PETA
You're certainly devoted. Your skin was already so youthful even before all that.
SHA (SHINE)
Oh, I'm going to be coming to Japan soon, so will you do that to me too? Hee-hee.
SHA
BOSS...I'M NOT DOING THIS FOR FUN...

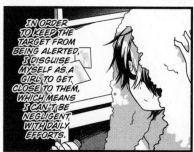

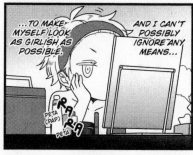

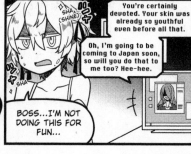

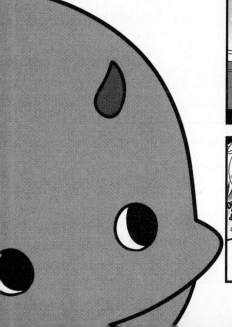

Afterword

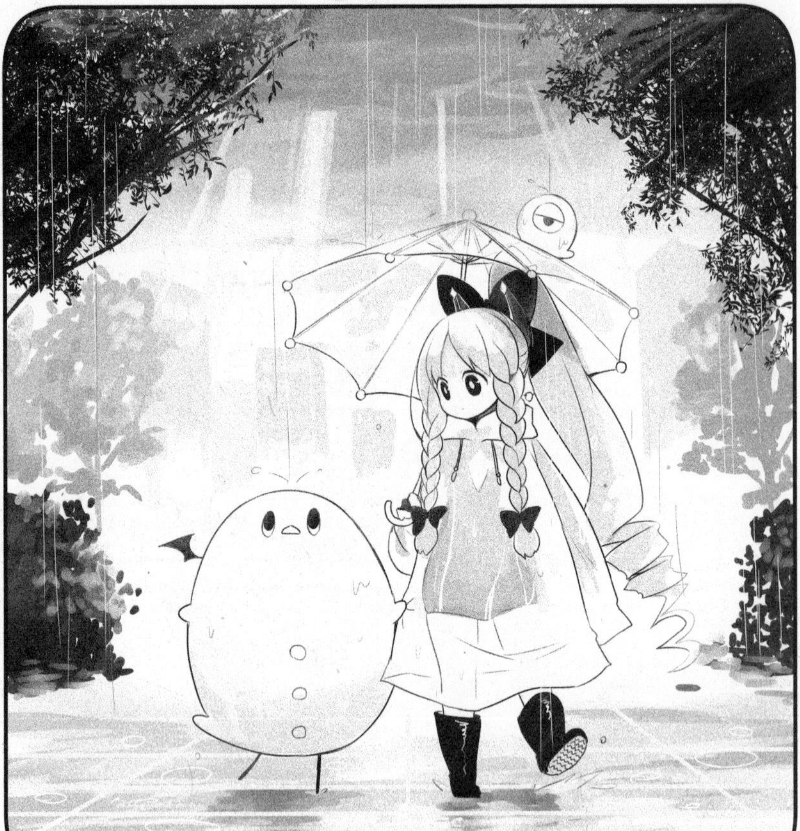

Thanks for picking up a copy of The Strange Creature at Kuroyuri Apartments, volume 1! It's been a super long time since I made an original work, so I ran into a lot of problems. But let's keep going forward together, all right?

by GAO YUZUKI

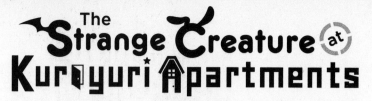

The Strange Creature at Kuroyuri Apartments

Gao Yuzuki

Translation: Abby Lehrke
Lettering: Rochelle Gancio

KUROYURI-SO NO HEN NA IKIMONO vol. 1
©2017 Gao Yuzuki/SQUARE ENIX CO., LTD.
First published in Japan in 2017 by SQUARE ENIX CO., LTD. English translation rights arranged with SQUARE ENIX CO., LTD. and Yen Press, LLC through Tuttle-Mori Agency, Inc.

English translation © 2018 by SQUARE ENIX CO., LTD.

Yen Press
1290 Avenue of the Americas
New York, NY 10104

Visit us at yenpress.com

facebook.com/yenpress
twitter.com/yenpress

yenpress.tumblr.com
instagram.com/yenpress

First Yen Press Edition: June 2018

Yen Press is an imprint of Yen Press, LLC.
The Yen Press name and logo are trademarks of Yen Press, LLC.

The publisher is not responsible for websites (or their content) that are not owned by the publisher.

Library of Congress Control Number: 2018935619

ISBNs: 978-1-9753-2756-9 (paperback)
978-1-9753-2801-6 (ebook)

10 9 8 7 6 5 4 3 2 1

WOR

Printed in the United States of America